To Fields Near and Far

A History of the Adrian Dominican Sisters 1933-1961

Nadine Foley, OP
and
Arlene Bachanov

Adrian Dominican Congregation

To Fields Near and Far
Copyright © 2015 by the Adrian Dominican Congregation

All rights reserved. No part of this publication may be reproduced, stored in a retrieval system, or transmitted in any form or by any means without written permission from the publisher, except by a reviewer who wishes to quote brief passages in connection with a review written for inclusion in a broadcast, magazine, newspaper or other media.

Adrian Dominican Sisters
1257 East Siena Heights Drive
Adrian, Michigan 49221
517-266-3400
www.adriandominicans.org

Cover art by Janet Wright, OP
Cover and graphic design by Melinda P. Ziegler
Printed by McNaughton & Gunn, Saline, Michigan

ISBN #978-0-9967140-0-6

Reflecting the ecological concerns of the Adrian Dominican Sisters, this book is printed with soy inks on 100% post-consumer recycled paper, processed chlorine-free, and made with renewable energy.

Dedication

Dedicated gratefully to all those sisters
who in these years of expansion and growth
went near and far in response to the enlightened leadership
of Mother Mary Gerald Barry, OP.

Table of Contents

Acknowledgments	*vii*
Foreword	*ix*
Introduction	1
Chapter One: "A Truly Valiant Woman"	5
Chapter Two: Mother Gerald's First Term: 1933-1939	37
Chapter Three: Mother Gerald's Second Term: 1939-1945	73
Chapter Four: Mother Gerald's Third Term: 1945-1951	117
Chapter Five: Mother Gerald's Fourth Term: 1951-1957	147
Chapter Six: Mother Gerald's Fifth Term: 1957-1961	203
Afterword	235
Appendix One: Mother Gerald and Priests	239
Appendix Two: A Circle of Devoted Support	283
Index	315

Acknowledgments

The publication of a book requires many insights, talents, proficiencies, and resources to bring it to completion. As writers, we have been blessed with the proverbial "abundance of riches" in those who have given us time and assistance as we have searched near and far and come to this end point. Sister Attracta Kelly, OP, Prioress of the Adrian Dominican Congregation, has given us authorization, support, and encouragement, as well as personal reflections on her Irish heritage. Sister Rose Celeste O'Connell, OP, Secretary of the Congregation and Director of Information, has supported the process throughout. We are grateful.

Melinda P. Ziegler, graphic designer in our Office of Communications, has devoted hours and days in developing the book's print and electronic layout, artistry, and in conferring with Sister Janet Wright, OP, artist, whose painting is incorporated into the cover. Sister Elise D. García, OP, our Director of Communications, supervised the final production and Sister Barbara Kelley, OP, of the same department, proofread the text.

We are in debt to those who read the manuscript at various stages of development and gave us valuable responses: Sister Maria Riley, OP, Sister Patricia Walter, OP, Sister Sharon Weber, OP, and Mary Weeber, Administrative Assistant to Sister Attracta Kelly, OP.

For searching through our archives to reply to our many requests we thank Sister Beverly Bobola, OP, Congregation Archivist, and her predecessor Sister Marilyn Francoeur, OP. Other archivists who provided documents and photographs were: Ximena Valdivia, Manager of the Barry University Archives and Special Collections; Sister Mary Beaubien, OP, Siena Heights University Archivist; Sister Rose Marie Martin, OP, Archivist of the Grand Rapids Dominican Sisters; Steve Wejroch, Assistant Archivist, Archdiocese of Detroit; and Father Carl Faria, Archivist for the Diocese of Monterey, California.

Others who responded to our requests were: Doug Goodnough, Director of Integrated University Marketing, Siena Heights University; Father Liam Kelly, St. Paul Church, Jacksonville Beach, Florida (now retired); Mike Lee, Communications and Marketing Department, Dignity Health Dominican Hospital, Santa Cruz, California; Kim Haley, External Communications Specialist, Dignity Health St. Rose Dominican Hospital, Las Vegas, Nevada; Sister Joan Mumaw, IHM; and countless Adrian Dominican Sisters, without whose recollections and support this book would not have been possible.

Foreword

This book, *To Fields Near and Far*, portrays the history of the Adrian Dominican Sisters from 1933 to 1961 as one of growth—in institutions, in the education of the sisters, and in the increasing awareness of the role of women religious in the Church and the world. The history of the Congregation during those years is inextricably tied to the legendary Mother General, Mother Mary Gerald Barry. In this third volume of history, Sister Nadine Foley and Arlene Bachanov have succeeded not only in thoroughly presenting Mother Gerald's many accomplishments in her twenty-eight years as leader of the Congregation, but also in capturing the wonderful testimony to the Dominican way of life, as well as the courage and daring, creativity and faith of so many unsung heroines. They were years of incredible growth and vitality.

This span of less than thirty years was a hinge between two eras. In 1933 the Congregation was firmly tied to the almost semi-cloistered traditions of religious life, but as the years progressed the Congregation began in many ways to feel and adapt to the winds of change in the Church and in society. Without realizing what was ahead, the Congregation was nonetheless changing in ways that prepared the sisters for tumultuous times to come: the closing of parochial schools; a movement to new ministries in fields related to a closer reading of the Gospels; and Vatican II, which challenged religious orders to live not by rules and routines, but rather through the founder's charism.

When Mother Gerald sent sisters out to open hospitals, schools, colleges, and more, the sisters probably questioned—but only to themselves—how prepared they were to carry out their assigned missions. But knowing that Mother Gerald saw them as talented women capable of the challenge no doubt gave them the courage and strength to do what was needed. And they did. As I read this book, it was easy to follow the physical growth of the Congregation with many sisters entering, new institutions being built, and new ministries being explored; the changes taking place in the sisters individually and as a Congregation were not as obvious, but were equally important.

The authors beautifully capture this era in the Congregation's history and the complex woman and leader who prepared the Congregation in so many ways for a changing world and Church. Mother Gerald's Irish immigrant background perhaps instilled in her a great independence of character and a strong belief in the ability of women to respond fully to God's call. This confidence and trust became part of the sisters during these years as they went wherever they were sent with courage and daring to take on the mission.

                                        Attracta Kelly, OP
                                        Prioress of the Congregation
                                        2010-2016

Introduction

What was the character of the Catholic Church in America in 1933—the year in which Sister Mary Gerald Barry assumed the office of Mother General for the Adrian Dominican Sisters? And what was the position that the Catholic sisterhoods were playing in the Church and in the country at that time?

In a word one might say that the Catholic Church was in its "ascendancy." Some of the early suspicions and antipathies about the Church, composed largely of hordes of European immigrants having come to this "land of promise" in the nineteenth century, were being dissipated. The sisterhoods, long appreciated for their nursing during the Civil War and assistance during natural disasters, were also growing in numbers and providing the Church with an able and willing workforce, especially in building the Catholic educational and health care systems throughout the country.

Among the congregations of sisters there were many of Irish heritage. In general, the Irish settled in major cities like Boston, New York, Chicago, and San Francisco. Initially, many young Irish women had come unattended to the United States to become factory workers, maids, and nannies. They became an important factor in the growth of the Church in America. It is said that the iconic St. Patrick Cathedral in New York City was constructed with generous contributions from the meager earnings of young Irish working women, among others. The youthful Catherine Barry, however, did not come for this kind of work.

She came to assist other family members, particularly her brother Gerald and his family, in Chicago. As lawyers, Gerald and another brother, Frank, were members of the growing class of professionals among the Irish immigrants.

Because she had two brothers in the legal profession, Catherine became something of a paralegal, as she would be called today. She assisted Gerald in his law office in Chicago first and then joined Frank in Nogales, Arizona. She made the latter move because she felt that Frank had the greater need and fewer resources. Her decision to go to Nogales, however, was life changing for her and, as it turned out, for many. She became acquainted with the Adrian Dominicans in the short-lived mission of the Congregation located there. It is interesting that she did not meet the Congregation while in Chicago, where the presence of Adrian Dominicans was everywhere, but rather in this small area near the Mexican border.

Catherine Barry at age eighteen. PHOTO CREDIT: BARRY UNIVERSITY ARCHIVES AND SPECIAL COLLECTIONS

Introduction

Not only was the mission in Nogales far removed from other Adrian Dominican outposts, but it was also close to the ongoing skirmishes along the border that made the area unsafe. The dangers of the situation led the Adrian Dominicans to abandon their mission there in 1917. One of the fruits of their efforts in Nogales, however, was Catherine Barry who, after getting to know the sisters, decided to enter the Congregation and did so in February 1912 at the age of thirty-one. From a tiny little border town came a woman who would lead the Adrian Dominican Sisters to become an important influence on the growth of the Catholic Church in the United States.

Catherine brought with her considerable skills honed through her service with her lawyer brothers. They were immediately recognized by Mother Camilla Madden and her successor, Mother Augustine Walsh. Sister Mary Gerald, as she was now called, became a valued assistant to both women. She served as Novice Mistress, a position that enabled her to influence the growing number of young women who were entering the Congregation. At the General Chapter of 1924 she was elected to the General Council, and when Mother Augustine was re-elected Mother General of the

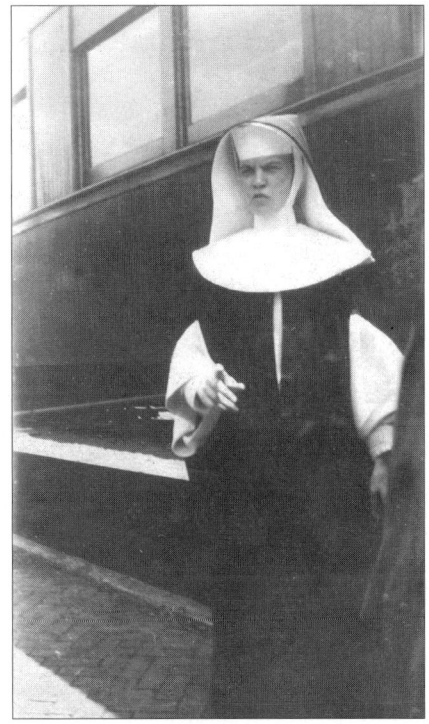

Sister Mary Gerald in 1923.

Congregation in 1930, Sister Gerald was elected Vicaress General.

Upon Mother Augustine's death in 1933, Sister Gerald was an obvious choice to be elected Mother General of the Congregation. With the canonical process of postulation[1] she was to serve in that capacity until her death in 1961.

The country in 1933 was mired in the Great Depression. It was also still in recovery from World War I, the "War to End All Wars," while looking warily abroad at ominous stirrings of yet another war to come. Mother Gerald's focus, however, was on the Church and its mission of "saving souls." Her zeal for that mission could not be derailed. Yet, as the Second World War came to Europe and eventually involved her newly adopted country, she was conscious of the toll it was taking on her sisters and their families, as well as of the suffering of people in Europe and elsewhere. She urged her sisters to prayer and forms of self denial. She also sent regular monetary donations to the Pope through his representative in the United States.

Mother Gerald was a woman of strong personality and indomitable will. She assumed her position as head of a young religious congregation with a determination to serve the Church through its resources of talent and potential. She put great trust in her youthful sisters. When she sent them out to begin new missions, she did not tell them what to do. She simply expected them to succeed. The years ahead offered great possibilities and she was ready to take advantage of them.

---

[1] See pp. 117-118 for an explanation of "postulation."

Chapter One
"A Truly Valiant Woman"

When she was elected Mother General of the Adrian Dominican Sisters for the first time in 1933, Sister Gerald Barry found herself at the helm of a congregation of approximately 825 members operating some seventy-five schools. Twenty-eight years later, the Very Reverend Vincent R. Hughes, OP,[1] was able to say in the homily delivered at her funeral, held November 25, 1961,

> *"Fruit both serviceable and astonishing in the vineyard of the Lord." Such is the record of the Adrian Dominican Community today, with more than 2,200 Sisters, working in 38 dioceses and archdioceses in the United States; 215 convents of Sisters, stretching from New York to California, and from Lake Superior to the Caribbean Sea. These institutions include three colleges, 45 high schools and academies, three hospitals, a home for the aged, and a residence for business women. As Mother General, Mother Gerald was also responsible for the Catholic education of over 100,000 students in Catholic schools, and the catechetical instruction of 40,000 young people attending public schools.*

Mother Gerald was first elected Mother General[2] of the Congregation on June 24, 1933, at the General Chapter held after the death of Mother Augustine Walsh on January 8 of that year. But in many ways, she had already been in charge of key Congregation matters for a long time.

Named Mistress of Novices in 1921, after having made first profession only seven years earlier, she was elected a member of the General Council in 1924 and again in 1930, at which election she was chosen to serve as Vicaress General.[3] She went on to conduct much of the Congregation's business during Mother Augustine's nine-year tenure. Mother Augustine was greatly afflicted by severe respiratory problems, requiring her to spend much of each summer at the convent in Munising, Michigan, well away from the southern Michigan pollen. She counted heavily on Sister Gerald to carry on the business of the Congregation in her absence.

After Mother Augustine's death it fell to Sister Gerald, as Vicaress General, to lead the Congregation until a General Chapter could be held. When the Chapter convened, some six months later, she was elected as Mother Augustine's successor. For the next three decades, she steered the Adrian Dominican Sisters through a period of tremendous growth—in numbers, in the education and health care work they undertook, and in influence on Catholics across the country and internationally. The words spoken by Father Hughes at her funeral ring as true today as they did that late November day in 1961.

> *Here was a truly valiant woman the Catholic Church can be proud of, one who caught and passed on the enthusiasm of the first Christian centuries, when the Faith was young. We shall not soon see her likeness.*

Rooted in Ireland

To understand Mother Gerald, at least as much as such a task is possible, it is necessary first to look back briefly at her family life and at the setting in which she grew up, late nineteenth-century Ireland.

Father (later Bishop) Patrick Barry, Catherine Barry, and Joseph Barry in Ireland.

Born Bridget Catherine Barry on March 11, 1881, in Inagh, County Clare, she was the thirteenth of the eighteen children of Michael and Catherine (Dixon) Barry. Five of the children did not live to maturity, including two Catherines who died in infancy. Michael Barry wanted a Catherine in the family in honor of their mother and therefore called Bridget by her middle name, while her mother often called her "Bridgie." She herself used "Catherine" as her first name.[4]

Michael Barry *Catherine (Dixon) Barry*

In an autobiography written during her first year in office, Mother Gerald had this to say about her parents,

*My mother taught me everything I know. My father was strict,
kind, generous and religious. He was neither wealthy nor good
looking, but neither am I. My mother was not good looking, but
she was considered the most beautiful woman by me. I could
not do anything without the goodness of my mother.*

Gerald, one of Catherine's older brothers, served as her godfather. Some time after he emigrated to the United States she followed in his footsteps, coming to live with him and his wife, Bidsy, in Chicago around 1899. In her autobiography, Mother Gerald said of her older brother, "He was my guardian; he was everything." Her deep affection for him is evident in the fact that when she entered the Congregation she took her religious name in his honor.

Catherine Barry c. 1910

Eventually, most of the Barry children ended up in the United States. Besides Catherine and Gerald, both older sisters and seven of the brothers settled in this country. Patrick, one of her older brothers, and the two youngest Barry men, William and Joseph, were ordained to the priesthood. Patrick ultimately became the fifth bishop of St. Augustine, Florida, at a time when the diocese encompassed the entire state except for the western part of the Panhandle. William, who ministered at St. Patrick Church in Miami Beach, Florida, eventually was named a Protonotary Apostolic, the highest level of monsignor. Joseph remained in Ireland.

In coming to the United States, Catherine and her siblings were but a few among the many thousands of Irish émigrés to the New World during the nineteenth century. Some were fleeing the Great Famine of the 1840s, while others left for political reasons, or because there were so few ways of making a living in Ireland, or simply because they were seeking a new adventure. About half of the new immigrants were women and, like Catherine, many were quite young.[5]

It goes without saying that Catholicism ran deeply in Irish culture. But how did Catherine's Celtic roots shape her personal faith and the way she, as Novice Mistress and Mother General, trained her young novices and professed sisters?

"I have this sense that [in the Celtic tradition] they had a much better understanding of the God of creation. Everything was holy; everything was part of the divine," said Sister Attracta Kelly, an Irish immigrant herself, from County Roscommon, who became Prioress of the Congregation in 2010.

For Irish Catholics of Mother Gerald's time and into Sister Attracta's, God was part of everything. The sense was always, said Sister Attracta, that "every place and everywhere, we are in God's presence." And their faith, along with a fair amount of superstition, a remnant of the old beliefs, shaped everything in their lives. Upon entering another person's home, a visitor always said "God save all here," a tradition that came into use for the Adrian Dominican Sisters, who used the phrase when entering the room during recreation. Similarly, in Ireland, when people greeted each other, it was always with something like "God be with you." When they passed a field in which a farmer was working, they always said "God bless the work." And, said Sister Attracta, "you never passed a cemetery without praying for those buried there."

Indeed, Mother Gerald was nothing if not imbued with this sense of God's abiding presence and how it gave her and the sisters under her charge the means to work for God's kingdom. One of the many examples of how she reminded her sisters that God is always near is found in a general letter to the Congregation on September 6, 1940, in which she wrote: "God is at hand and He only wants to be asked so that He might lend His aid. Without Him you cannot do the things He has given you to do. Make visits to Him and tell Him of your joys and your difficulties. Thank Him for allowing you to be His co-workers."

"Prayer was of the essence in Mother's life," wrote Sister Corinne O'Connor in a reminiscence written after Mother Gerald's death. "Always in her place in the early morning, she demanded promptness in her sisters, and her example was the lodestone that drew many to arrive in chapel long before the time appointed. Daily she walked the Way of the Cross[6] and encouraged the other sisters to follow Jesus' walk to His death and resurrection."

Mother Gerald's faith seems to have been practiced with humility. It was a self-deprecation which also seems to be quintessentially Irish. ". . . I want you always to know that you are all in my prayers and in all my works, and I hope they are not too disappointing to the Lord," she wrote in a general letter to the Congregation on November 18, 1953.

More than once in her letters, she referred to offering up "my poor prayers." And her general letter of March 14, 1937, contains a reflection that seems startlingly personal for a Prioress of the Congregation to share: "As I read and re-read the Gospel of the day, I chided myself with the many times I was unfaithful to the Christ who had to hide Himself in the temple from the stones that were picked up to hurl at Him. Perhaps some of these stones had my sins clinging to them."

A Proud American

Although her love for her native land ran deep indeed, and she returned to visit Ireland several times throughout her life, Mother Gerald became an American citizen on September 29, 1926, and never forgot the blessings of being an American. Her sentiments were probably shaped at least in part by the experience of being an immigrant from a country where British oppression had continued for centuries, involving everything from property rights, to the native language, to one's very faith.

She also encouraged the sisters, as teachers, to instill a love of country in their students. A December 8, 1936, letter written upon her return from Europe included this passage:

> *We learned much that was of benefit to us but nothing more important than the fact that there is no land like "America the Beautiful" and that we ought to thank God every day for the privilege of living in this glorious land of freedom. Sisters, I beg*

> *of you to try to teach the children love of country as well as love of God, and train them to pray for our president and other civil officers that they may be guided in their work.*

In the beginning of July 1939, about two weeks after being elected to her second term of office, she set sail for a visit to Ireland, returning in August not long before the outbreak of World War II in Europe on September 1. In a general letter dated September 15, she included these words:

> *I think I had the best vacation rest I ever had in my life while in Ireland this summer. It was only when I arrived in London and saw the trenches being dug for protection from air raids that I began to grow nervous and to wonder. You all know the reports from Europe but not one of us can realize the sufferings of the poor people in those war-torn countries. I wish you would all, in common at the morning prayer, appeal to Our Lady Queen of Peace with a Memorare for peace for the world and the continuance of peace for America. The poor people who are forced to go to war do not want to be at war. They want peace and God alone can grant it to them through our prayers.*
>
> *Again I ask you to grow in appreciation of your country and teach the children an appreciation of the gifts bestowed on them in a natural and supernatural way. Teach them to thank God and to ask Him to protect the little ones that are torn from their homes and mothers in other lands. You know how to do*

> all this. Teach the things that are true without any show of
> animosity for any nation.

"Thank God you are in America; consider how the nuns in Warsaw, Berlin, even London, feel today," she wrote later in that same September 15 letter. She also frequently urged the sisters to remember often their blessings as Americans and to pray for those affected by war.

Her Christmas letter of 1941, coming as it did on December 14, right after the United States entered the war, stands as her first exhortation to the sisters to do their part for the war effort. Not surprisingly, for her this included making a deeper commitment to one's spirituality—even though she did not use that word.

> We are all called upon these days to make a contribution to the defense of our Country. The call has more significance now that we have been attacked. We see the cream of the Country's youth carrying knapsacks and being led to camps or ships or troop trains and, unless someone very close to us is in this particular war picture, we take it as daily routine. . . .
>
> Could we not, for His sake and for the assistance that would come to our Country through the strength of the grace that would be ours, make and keep resolutions to be more fervent and attentive and regular in our prayers and religious exercises? . . . Could the Country have a better investment than valiant women? Could we not deny ourselves after the manner of the invitation of Christ? I think it would be a real religious

> *and patriotic act if each of us decided not to get new shoes or a new habit this Christmas . . . and set aside for defense the cost of such outfits. This can be done by each of us and it will be done by me personally, and our savings could be offered toward the program of defense in some way through the Mother House.*

Such sentiments are far from the only times her writings reflected a love of her adopted country. "I have always been mindful that there is no place in the world equal to the United States of America," she wrote on April 8, 1952, in one of many similar passages on the topic over her years in office. She also regularly reminded the sisters that voting was a privilege they had as Americans. "Next Monday, April 1, is election day and I am writing to remind you that you should exercise the precious right of voting guaranteed to us in this glorious land of ours," she wrote in a March 26, 1957, letter.

Warmhearted, Witty . . . But With a Temper

By all accounts, Mother Gerald cut an imposing and dignified figure. She was not a tall woman, but "she always had great bearing," recalled Sister Rosemary Ferguson, who described herself as a kindred spirit with Mother Gerald. "I don't know how my soul connected with hers, but it did from the very outset," she said.

In the way Mother Gerald carried herself, "she had a kind of a stride. You always knew she was a woman of import. . . . She was such a strong woman, of heart and mind and temperament."

Those who knew Mother Gerald first-hand remember her as a woman of a quick and often dry wit who was extraordinarily formidable when aroused but who could also show great kindness to the sisters in her charge. The Congregation's archives contain the fond reminiscences of numerous sisters. In 1999, Sister Marie Bentz who, as a novice assigned to take care of the guest dining room and Mother Gerald's living quarters, had "many opportunities to share precious moments with her," wrote,

> *Perhaps not realized by some, here was an extremely intelligent, witty, very human, deeply spiritual servant of God. The clergy and business men, who advised and sought advice, marveled at this sharp, astute, skillful business woman. With her knowledge, grace and wisdom, she charmed and challenged them.*
>
> *Later, while at various missions, I probably shared the anxiety and trepidation brought by news of Mother's arrival for visitation. However, in actual experience, I found only a warm smile and gentle kindness. She left each group of sisters inspired, energized, encouraged and challenged. I thank her still. How could anyone help loving our Mother Gerald, a truly valiant, courageous, and saintly woman!*

Indeed, the sisters of Mother Gerald's era can tell story after story of her great kindness to them and even to their families. "Her generosity was unbounded," said Sister Rosemary, noting that when she herself became the Congregation's Prioress in 1968, it turned out that Mother

Gerald had seen to it that funds were provided for the care of sisters' aging parents. "She was very, very generous in that regard," Sister Rosemary said.

This story was written by Sister Joseph Therese Kruse:

> When I was a postulant[7] she saw me after evening prayer and said "Now how are things coming?" And I started to cry, and she talked to me for a bit and said, "This is only natural. Don't think for one minute that because you feel this way that you don't have a vocation. You'll make the grade, don't worry." She was always very nice to me. . . . She was rough sometimes, and said what she thought, but I could never say that she was unjust. When Mother Gerald reprimanded anyone during the day, I noticed that she would ask that novice to do some favor for her or bestow some little favor on her to show that it wasn't a case of holding in hard feelings, that she was really giving her a reprimand for her own good.

Mother Gerald herself, in a letter to the Congregation written on October 30, 1940, recounts her recent experience with visiting a dying Sister Mary Celeste Graham. Her account reveals great tenderness on her part.

> I had a lovely visit with her the day before she met her Lord and Judge. She was so sweet and I left her with these words: "Don't worry about long prayers. Tell the Lord you love Him and He will, like any fond Father, pick you up and take you in His arms." She said I gave her a lovely thought and then I told her

to go to sleep and rest while I drew the shades in her room and shook the pillows. She expressed her gentle gratitude and it was the last she spoke with me for she was not conscious when I got word to go to her bedside.

The general letters Mother Gerald wrote throughout her tenure are replete with instances of her very obvious and very deep affection for her sisters. Most of the letters also contain at least some words of instruction or correction, but as her Christmas 1941 letter reads in part, "I need not tell you that, while I point out defects, I see many glorious signs of the goodness of you all and I hear many compliments from various sources."

One particular letter, that of October 6, 1941, can stand as an example of her pride in what the Adrian Dominicans could accomplish. She wrote it after visiting Santa Cruz, California, for the dedication of the hospital there that the Adrian Dominicans had taken over.

On my arrival there I felt that a great transformation had taken place since I viewed the remains of lay management last February when we promised to take it over. 'Tis a great thing to have the living Community at hand. . . .

I need not tell you that the Sisters are most enthusiastic and I am sure, between the nursing and serving of meals and attending switchboard and typewriter and all the other odds and ends, they have little time for dreaming, but they have made reality of what seemed impossibility. God bless them one and all.

To Fields Near and Far

Indeed, said Sister Rosemary Ferguson, Mother Gerald "always trusted the nuns[8] to do it, whatever 'it' was. . . . She loved the nuns, and she thought her sisters could do anything."

Many of the sisters' reminiscences also recall how, no matter what her title was, Mother Gerald pitched in to do the same manual work expected of her novices and professed sisters. Sister Corinne O'Connor wrote that while she was a St. Joseph Academy student under Sister Gerald's tutelage, "No work was beneath Sr. Gerald; she entered whole-heartedly into the most menial tasks of an understaffed institution: cleaning, scrubbing, painting."

She continued that type of service to the community even as Mother General. Sisters who were sent to start new missions often found her arriving to help get their buildings ready. Sister Frances Eugene (Mary Therese) Golden discussed in her autobiography the fact that when she and other members of the Congregation were assigned to Sacred Heart Parish in Pensacola, Florida, Mother Gerald went with them. Sister Frances Eugene was actually part of the second group of sister-teachers to staff the school. The original contingent had been withdrawn almost instantly by Mother Gerald because the conditions in the building were so poor. So, when the next group of sisters went, Mother Gerald wanted to see for herself if things had improved. Even if they had, ". . . I don't believe a speck of paint had touched the walls since it was built! We certainly had our work cut out for us!" Sister Frances Eugene said. "And Mother Gerald worked right along with the rest of us!"

Individual sisters also found themselves on the receiving end of her assistance. Sister Elizabeth Condon remembers that one day, as a novice assigned to serve in the priests' dining room, she was putting linen coverings over the chairs when Mother Gerald came in and began assisting her with the task. "I was impressed that she'd come in and help a novice," said Sister Elizabeth.

When it was required, Mother Gerald also demonstrated an even deeper humility than that which led her to help with manual chores. Sister Laurine Neville wrote about an experience with her.

> *Those who only heard the bark, and did not know the pressures behind it nor her whole self, were often in mistaken judgment of her. In her high, lonely position, she might have been thought proud. I found her to be humble, and I could quote several examples as proof of this. I will cite but one. On one occasion she had made a false judgment concerning me. Knowing the source, I decided to remain completely silent, until in God's own way, the truth was revealed. When this happened, I was sent for and in the presence of two councillors as witnesses, she knelt at my feet asking my pardon. Remembering this, which in her position she was under no obligation to do, and witnessing daily the depth of her charity, I consider her the most remarkable religious woman leader of her time, holy, humble and wise.*

Mother Gerald also made sure that the sisters knew they could come to her with their issues. "Sometimes, I understand, the sisters are told they need not bother Mother with matters, that the superior herself will take them to her," she wrote to the Congregation in November 1951. "You are all privileged to take up direct [sic] any matters that you feel you should. Do not be afraid to give your confidence direct; that is your privilege and you may use it." Early in 1953, when informing the sisters that she would be away for a few weeks' rest and that Sister Benedicta Marie Ledwidge, the Vicaress General, would be in charge, she added, "I know that you will be considerate of her and that you will not bother her unless it is absolutely necessary, although, remember, neither she nor I ever consider a letter or a request from you a bother."

But the woman whose kindness was so often seen, by sisters and by others as well, also clearly had a side to her temperament that can only be described as stern. Any number of sisters who remember her can tell stories of being called to task. Often, penances of various types, such as making the venia,[9] were prescribed for even minor transgressions such as mispronouncing a word while reading in the refectory. Sister Rosemary, who called Mother Gerald "a stickler for clean habits and shined shoes," recalled how as a novice she misread the word "misled," pronouncing it "misseld," and immediately heard Mother Gerald's ring rapping on the table. Sister Jean Irene McAllister remembered Mother Gerald saying to her, "You went through the Academy"—meaning St. Joseph Academy—"and you sing like THAT?"

And then there is this story from Sister Winifred Lynch: One day, she and some other sisters were in Holy Rosary Chapel praying after Mass when the door to the sacristy opened and out came two sisters and the chaplain, Father Cyril Burke, who was wearing a cope and carrying the Blessed Sacrament. "The prayers tapered off," Sister

Winifred said, because the sisters were watching as the three came through the gate of the altar rail and went down the aisle. There was a brief silence, then "thundering down the side aisle" came Mother Gerald. She stood before the assembled sisters and declared hotly, "Not ONE of you opened the gate when Christ came through the rail!"

"You wouldn't forget after that to open the rail," said Sister Winifred.

Still, many sisters remember her rather dry wit, which also shows through in countless places in her letters. For example, there is this passage from her general letter of May 3, 1941, which came at the time summer appointments were being made: "The fatal day is at hand. Some will be happy, I know, and some will be speechless for a second, if such a thing is possible for Sisters."

In a letter to the Congregation after falling and breaking three ribs at the cornerstone-laying ceremony for Regina Dominican High School in Wilmette, Illinois, she wrote,

> *I do not know what reports you have been receiving regarding my fall. Some probably thought I just bowed low (too low, indeed) to the assembled group. Others may have thought that the somersault I took expressed my joy on this occasion. (December 3, 1957)*

Sisters who knew her also bring up time and time again in their stories about her how much she enjoyed swimming. It was a special pastime when she went to Florida on visitations to the Congregation's various institutions in that state.

"She loved to go to the beach," recalled Sister Winifred, who taught at Rosarian Academy in West Palm Beach for many years and often saw Mother Gerald during her visitations there. "I can see her now. She'd pull off her bathing cap and fill it with salt water and pour it over her head."

"Mother Gerald loved the water. We would go to the beach every week," said Sister Rosemary, who was missioned in Florida for ten years. In many other congregations of women religious, sisters were not allowed to wear ordinary bathing suits, but the Adrian Dominicans were, and Sister Rosemary thinks that had everything to do with what was certainly one of Mother Gerald's favorite leisure activities.

According to Sister Regina Marie Lalonde,

> *Mother Gerald loved to visit Barry College and she enjoyed the sea. Once on a beautiful sunny day, she decided to combine a swim in the ocean with her visitation of the Sisters. Each of us in turn swam to her side and had our little chat with her. We all warned her to keep her shoulders under water, but to no avail. She had reason to remember her "Great Atlantic Visitation" as we named it, for we had to call a doctor the next day to treat her terrible sunburn.*

Her love for the Sunshine State makes one trip there especially humorous because it came completely by accident. On April 24, 1948, Sister Benedicta Marie was rather startled to receive this telegram: *"ON WAY TO FLORIDA. SR. DOLORES MARIE[10] IS SENDING THIS MESSAGE. SHE WILL PHONE YOU TOMORROW FROM DETROIT."*

Sister Benedicta Marie subsequently wrote to Mother Gerald on April 26: "As you can well imagine, I was very much mystified by the telegram from Logansport, Indiana, but the tension was relieved and I had a good laugh when Sister Dolores Marie called on Sunday morning to give me the details."

Mother Gerald had been in Chicago and was supposed to be heading back to Adrian via train, but got on the wrong train and instead found herself on the way to Florida. She wrote to Sister Benedicta Marie on April 25 from Nashville, Tennessee.

> *By now you have some word from Sr. Dolores Marie of our wild exit from Chicago. "Wrong Way Corrigan" could do no better. Since by accident or Providence I was on the way to Florida, I thought it best to continue, but I wanted to get to Mass this morning and here I am after having communed with the Lord.*

She got off the train in West Palm Beach and walked to the convent. Obviously, the sisters were not expecting her. According to Sister Winifred, it was laundry day and they were outside hanging up the wash: "then suddenly here comes herself, strutting through the gate."

Diplomatic, but Determined

It may be that Mother Gerald's Irish bloodlines had a direct effect on her ability to work with others. According to author Dolores Liptak, writing about the impact Irish Catholics had on the American Catholic

Church and American society in general,

> *With a charm which engaged others, a great gift of humor, and an innate sense of the dramatic, [Irish Catholics] could negotiate the best arrangements not only with Protestants but among other Catholics as well. Their resourcefulness, moreover, could easily support their intellectual gifts.*[11]

Whether a distinctly Irish trait or not, a capacity for negotiation seems to have been fully formed in Mother Gerald. Her talent for diplomacy shows throughout her correspondence, especially with people like the parish priests with whom she often had to deal.

But that diplomacy could certainly be mixed with steely determination. The history of the Congregation from 1924 to 1933 by Sister Nadine Foley[12] contains an extensive account of Sister Gerald's handling of a complicated issue that arose in 1928 concerning Father V.F. Kienberger, pastor at St. Dominic Church in Detroit, and another story of her face-off in 1936 with Father Vincent Balcer at Detroit's St. Lawrence Church. A prolonged issue with Father Balcer had started during Mother Augustine's tenure.

Mother Augustine, who clearly trusted Sister Gerald completely with Congregation matters, regularly dispatched her to take care of such problems. It did not take long for her reputation as an advocate for the sisters in her charge to become well known. A letter written to her by Archbishop Michael Curley of Baltimore dated December 21, 1931, refers to the earlier situation with Father Kienberger.

> *I am really glad that you have not changed much since the old days in Palatka.*[13] *I was really afraid of you then because I knew that you could give a man a right upper cut and knock him out for the count. Well those are qualities that a person need not drop. You certainly brought that particular quality into fine play when you silenced the O.P. in Detroit [Father Kienberger] and threw the whole bunch of Dutchmen into a scare from which they have not yet recovered.*
>
> *Bishop Gallagher said that he would give ten dollars for a ringside seat and would bet anything in the world on you in combat with the whole crowd of them. You certainly stand high in the Bishop's estimation.*

The Chancery had ended up involved in the difficulties with Father Kienberger, and such was the case in the situation with Father Balcer too. Mother Gerald clearly was not afraid to speak her mind about this priest. In a letter to Archbishop Edward Mooney of Detroit as the matter played out, she wrote,

> *If it is really impossible for him [Father Balcer] to make arrangements, I might, by continuing my game of checkers succeed in sending him a teacher for each of the eight grades. I have transferred and retransferred until I am almost bewildered in trying to release this group of sisters from assignments previously made. . . .*
>
> *I have done this for one who has been my sworn enemy.*

Hands-On Leadership

In the pre-Vatican II world in which she lived and led the Congregation, Mother Gerald was in complete charge. She personally decided where sisters would be missioned for the coming year. She gave detailed instructions in her letters on how the sisters should act in public; how they, as well-mannered women, should sit, stand, walk, and even eat; and how they should interact with their students. There are exhortations to the sisters in these letters about remembering the way they should behave in keeping with their vows: how to properly wear the habit and warnings not to stay away from the convent past the permitted hour, not to have excessive personal correspondence or telephone conversations, and not to have too much contact with "seculars." She decreed that the daily Office was to be intoned in A flat instead of A because A was too high for many of the women. Occasionally, she even gave grammar lessons:

> *I notice in your letters to me that some of you often forget to use a subject in a sentence. Such as the following is the procedure: "Met Sister John down town the other day." You should use the subject. Punctuation is very poor also and the difference between the nominative and objective cases is not a part of your understanding it seems. Letters and conversation, too, come out with such expressions as "They invited my sister and I to be present at the assembly." You really would not say that they invited I if you were thinking only of yourself and yet that is what you are doing although you do speak of your sister.*

> *Now, my dear children, I did not expect to be teaching grammar when I started this letter but you can take what I have said as an incentive to do the studying and the correcting. Prepare your reading and read with thought when you read for the community and when you present to your classes the lessons that you are required to give them. Make use of the best English for your conversation and your writing. American slang is very snappy and, I know, very contagious, but let us avoid it and be promoters of the best English.*
> (October 13, 1946)

She could be very blunt about having her instructions followed. In a July 1953 letter to sisters whom she had named as superiors, she gave a number of directives and then wrote: "If you do not intend to follow the directions given above then I would have you be honest enough to return this letter to me telling me so."

It seems, however, that Mother Gerald was willing to give some "wiggle room" on occasion. Sister Rosemary Ferguson gave an account of the time she was missioned in Chicago and asked for permission to take some visiting sisters to see Notre Dame. This would have been prohibited because sisters were not allowed to drive anywhere that was more than forty miles away. Mother Gerald refused permission but then, as Sister Rosemary was almost out the door, said to her, "Sometimes it's better if you don't ask."

Mother Gerald was clearly conscious of needing to be a spiritual guide to the sisters under her leadership. Her letters are filled with reminders to the sisters to live out their faith and to always seek God. She obviously sought to bring the sisters closer to God in her personal encounters with them as well. Of course, on many occasions her role as spiritual mentor meant warning the sisters not to allow contemporary things to find their way into religious life.

> *I fear our perfection is impeded by the presence of radios. One radio in the community room is absolutely all we need and all others should be denied us. Now, Sisters, turn in your radios, and Superioresses, do your duty too. See to this.*
> *(September 10, 1947)*

> *I learned that popular songs are often given at Christmas plays when the people really expect the lesson of Christmas, and that with great dignity even if only the younger children are the actors and actresses. Using slangy methods before a false microphone to entertain people is not the result of good thinking and good teaching either at Christmas or another time. . . .*
>
> *Hymns at church and sodalities in some places and cases are shockingly jazzy in air. Surely there is no need for this. . . .*
>
> *Superioresses, be sure to stand guard over these glaring educational and spiritual mistakes.*
>
> *In a few places I observed the luxury of television sets installed in the convents. You must either give these back to the donors or closet them except for a special performance such*

> *as something from the Cathedral or the Vatican or maybe a good Notre Dame game rarely. . . . We see enough of the world around us. We hear enough too, and you know I took the radios from you to safeguard your minds. I now protest the television and do not want it blinding you to your obligations as religious women consecrated to the service of God and hidden with Christ. 'Tis bad to hear some things on the radio but 'tis worse to hear and see the things that some actors and actresses put before the world. We are in the world but not of it.*
> *(December 8, 1949)*

A few years later, she was restricting the use of the television still further.

> *If you have a television set in the convent, it will either have to be returned to the kind donor or it will have to be set up in the school where its use must be regulated and restricted.*
>
> *The only programs you would be permitted to see or show to the children on television would be those pertaining to the Holy Father, to Bishop Sheen, or those featuring religious or educational interests. This definitely does not include ball games or the like.*
>
> *. . . My previous letter to you was clear enough on this point, Sisters, and I hope you will now understand that you are not permitted to have a television set in the convent. Nor are you to suggest to anyone to ask me for a special permission.*
> *(November 28, 1952)*

All that changed, however, a few years later. The General Chapter of 1957 approved the use of televisions in the convents and the acceptance of donations of TVs, for viewing of "programs of good solid nature . . . educational, religious, civic, and other programs that would be beneficial to the Sisters."[14]

Honored for Her Contributions

The Adrian Dominican Sisters thought highly enough of their Mother General to elect her to five terms of office. They were not the only people who held her in such regard. Priests and bishops alike, to say nothing of countless lay people, regularly sang her praises, and in 1949, she was awarded the first of three honorary degrees. It was from the University of Santo Domingo in the Dominican Republic, which conferred upon her an honorary Doctor of Philosophy degree. The distinction was in recognition of her contribution to Christian education and culture in that country through the work being done there by the Congregation.

Mother Gerald received the news of the University's decision with a humility that would not have been surprising to anyone who knew how much God and her sisters always came first with her: "The University of Santo Domingo has honored the community and not the individual," she wrote to the Congregation on March 6, 1949. ". . . I do not see why there should be such a fuss over the matter but the University has its own way of doing things and we are glad to comply.

"A Truly Valiant Woman"

Let us be quiet and happy about it all in the meantime and let us work for God in a manner that will be pleasing to Him. Working for Him is the greatest honor that we could ever have."[15]

She also received an honorary doctorate in 1952 from the University of Notre Dame and again in 1961, from Loyola University in Chicago. After the latter was conferred upon her, she wrote to the Congregation with sentiments that echoed those of 1949: "I never would have received the honor were it not for all that the Community has been able to accomplish through each of you and your dedicated service to God and to the Church."

Mother Gerald receiving an honorary degree from the Vice Rector of the University of Santo Domingo, Dr. Oscar Robles Toledano.

The Lateran Canons[16] honored her as well, by awarding her the Lateran Cross on February 26, 1950. An English translation of the citation's Latin text, filed in the Congregational archives along with the actual document, indicates that a recipient of this medal was a person "who had deserved well of the works and adornment of the Archbasilica."

A Woman of Vision

In her reminiscence about Mother Gerald cited earlier, Sister Corinne O'Connor also wrote,

> *In a conversation on the remarkability of each congregation having recognizable family traits I asked her [Mother Gerald] if she could choose the characteristic by which Adrian Dominicans would be known by [sic], she responded without hesitation, simplicity. It said it all.*
>
> *In consideration of Mother's gifts—religious, intellectual, administrative, literary, humanistic, et al.—the trait that best characterized her was her "simplicity." She walked and talked with the great and humble; she always remained a true Dominican sister.*

But that "simplicity" belied the fact that Mother Gerald was a woman who had the foresight to see what her Adrian Dominican Sisters could accomplish in the world and the leadership to bring it to pass. During her time in office, Adrian Dominicans educated thousands of children, began to provide health care, and did much to reach the poor and disenfranchised.

She also impacted the Catholic Church itself as everyone from priests to cardinals looked to her for advice and assistance. Sister Thomas Annette Burns wrote about a time she, and the other sisters missioned in Bad Axe, Ruth, and Gagetown, Michigan, attended the confirmation of children at Sacred Heart Parish, Bad Axe:

> *Bishop [Allen] Babcock [at the time the Auxiliary Bishop of Detroit] was the confirming prelate. He came over to the convent to meet all the Sisters. After the introductions were completed the Bishop said, "All of you are Adrian Dominicans*

and I want to tell you that in the day of the General Judgement, I believe, the Lord will take the miter from the head of one of us and place it on the head of Mother Gerald. She has been a real shepherd to so many of us and we are in her debt."

The chapters that follow examine the history of the Congregation through the twenty-eight years Mother Gerald served as its Mother General. It was a time of expanding and sometimes pioneering work, a time when the Congregation extended its reach beyond the United States, and a time when the Adrian Dominican Sisters more than doubled their numbers. Much of this development was directly due to the vision of Mother Mary Gerald Barry.

1. See pp. 252-256 for more about Father Vincent Reginald Hughes.

2. This term was used until 1972, when the term "Prioress of the Congregation" became, in a return to early custom, the title of the elected head of the Congregation. The woman so elected continues to be called "Sister" as opposed to "Mother."

3. The Vicaress, as she is known today, assumes the responsibilities of the Prioress if that sister is unable to continue her duties.

4. When it came time for the 1940 U.S. Census, a March 20 letter from Mother Gerald to the sisters informed them that all of them would be registered through the Motherhouse and that they did not need to give any information to census-takers themselves. In this letter, she mentions that she had been appointed to handle this registration "under my family name, Catherine Barry."

5. Kerby A. Miller, *Emigrants and Exiles: Ireland and the Irish Exodus to North America* (New York: Oxford University Press, 1985), 407 and 514: ". . . between 1856 and 1921 about half of the Irish emigrants were women. . . . a disadvantage peculiar to the majority of post-Famine emigrants was their extreme youth. Most were in their teens or early twenties . . . "

6. The Stations of the Cross, located along the chapel walls. At that time, there were fourteen Stations.

7. The first phase of formation, typically lasting six months to a year.

8. Although the term "nun" is often used interchangeably with "sister," they are canonically not the same thing. A nun has taken solemn vows and lives an enclosed (cloistered) contemplative life. A sister has taken simple vows, lives communally but is not cloistered, and engages in active ministry.

9. Making the venia involved prostrating oneself upon the floor, not necessarily as a penance although it was occasionally prescribed as such. It was one of the nine ways in which St. Dominic was known to pray, and therefore was practiced in the Dominican tradition.

10. Sister Dolores Marie Ferguson.

11. Dolores Liptak, *Immigrants and Their Church* (New York: Macmillan, 1989), 82.

12 Nadine Foley, *Seeds Scattered and Grown* (Adrian: Adrian Dominican Congregation, 2006), 114-123.

13 This is apparently a reference to a much earlier connection between the two of them due to the relationship between Archbishop Curley and Mother Gerald's brother Patrick. Both were priests in Florida in the early twentieth century, with then Father Barry serving at St. Monica's in Palatka from 1903 to 1913, and they clearly knew each other. In 1917, Curley became Bishop of St. Augustine, Florida, and appointed Father Barry as his Vicar General. Bishop Curley was named Archbishop of Baltimore in 1922, and Father Barry succeeded him as Bishop of St. Augustine.

14 On August 6, 1957, the Sacred Congregation for Religious issued a document on the use of radios and televisions. These were permitted for religious in the "active life," such as the Adrian Dominicans, but they had to be in a common area and their use had to be monitored, both for the type of programs watched/listened to and for the time spent in this activity.

15 Her reluctance to accept this honor was even more evident in the course of several letters to Sister Mary Philip Ryan, superior of Colegio Santo Domingo at the time. At one point, she wanted the whole thing called off. On May 2, 1949, following several delays in actually conferring the degree, which was to be done in Adrian, she wrote a letter typical of others she had sent to Sister Mary Philip. It was in response to a new plan to have the degree conferred at the Siena Heights College commencement, a suggestion she rejected out of hand as embarrassing. "Have them mail the document to me without fuss or feathers," she wrote. "Then whenever the Rector or the Vice Rector can come, we will give them a royal welcome and a big show, and I shall enjoy the occasion because I shall be out of the limelight. Now, Sister, understand, I am not joking. I am in deadly earnest and if my wishes are not carried out and if arrangements are made for either of these men to come to Adrian with the intention of giving the degree publicly, I shall not be here. I shall take flight to Ireland . . ." But, after the event had finally taken place, at the Siena Heights commencement as planned, she wrote to Sister Mary Philip on May 27 that she had "thoroughly enjoyed" the ceremony: "No one knows more than yourself how much I dreaded this, but I must say that it was one of the grandest days of my life."

16 The Lateran Congregation was originally established at the Basilica of St. John Lateran. This basilica "is the mother of every church edifice because it was the first Christian basilica in history; it is the head, because Rome, the see of St. Peter,

is the principal local Church in the world, and the Lateran is the principal Church of the Diocese of Rome. The Lateran, not St. Peter's, is the Pope's Cathedral, where his *cathedra*, the chair symbolic of his teaching authority, rests. The Lateran, not the Vatican, is where the Popes resided for the first millennium of legalized Christianity" (www.catholicity.com).

Chapter Two
Mother Gerald's First Term: 1933-1939

Through the Great Depression

As Mother Gerald began her leadership of the Congregation in 1933, the country was firmly mired in the Great Depression. But while the financial troubles of the time had their impact on the Congregation, one of the major reasons the sisters were able to weather the storm dates back to the actions Mother Augustine Walsh and Sister Gerald had taken two years earlier.

The history of the Congregation from 1924 to 1933 by Sister Nadine Foley[1] recounts the steps taken to secure the Congregation's finances in the first part of the decade as the Great Depression worsened and banks began to fail. What is especially striking about this account is how shrewd Mother Augustine was in her understanding of what needed to be done to protect the Congregation's finances. Also noteworthy is her trust in Sister Gerald to handle the matter.

Letters between Mother Augustine and Sister Gerald in September 1931[2] tell of how Sister Gerald was dispatched to withdraw all of the Congregation's funds from five different banks and place them in safety deposit boxes. Mother Augustine also charged Sister Gerald with seeing to various matters of paying down Congregational debt.

Bank failures were becoming more and more common, and Mother Augustine's distrust of banks was only heightened when, as she mentioned in one of those letters to Sister Gerald, an employee of a Chicago bank was caught embezzling three million dollars from the institution. All this was before federal deposit insurance was instituted, and Mother Augustine realized that if the banks failed and the community's resources were all in deposit accounts, the money would be lost.

Between placing funds in safety deposit boxes, keeping a considerable sum at the Motherhouse instead of in one of the banks the Congregation used, and paying down indebtedness, what Mother Augustine, Sister Gerald, and Sister Pius Wagner, the Congregation's treasurer, did in September 1931 surely saved the Congregation from financial ruin. At the same time, the Congregation was able to make donations to help people whom the Depression had left in distress.[3]

Mother Gerald's letters to the sisters in the early years of her tenure as Mother General offer little hint of the Congregation's financial picture, but some "reading between the lines" gives a few glimpses of the issues she faced. On November 21, 1933, she wrote a general letter instructing the sisters to tell family and friends not to send them any gifts for Christmas or Easter. If someone desired, however, they could send the money they would have spent on a gift and it would go into the common fund to be used "for whatever the superior would decide." She suggested that at least some of the money could be donated to The Society for the Propagation of the Faith.[4]

It is certainly true that such admonitions were rooted in the fact that the sisters were vowed to live simply. Additionally, as she reminded the women in this same letter, being given a gift by their relatives might well mean that the family could not take care of some need of its own as a result. It is also true, however, that the monetary gifts would be a most welcome help to the Congregation. "The needs of the community are many. . . . The subjects[5] will please help the superiors to provide the dues[6] that are owed to the motherhouse," Mother Gerald's letter continued.

Another reference to the financial difficulties the Congregation had at this time is found in her general letter of the first Sunday of May 1935, in which she notes that each of the convents needed to send to the Motherhouse the money needed for the sisters to attend summer classes, for "I cannot coin money to meet the bills and last summer I was thousands of dollars in debt for bills for the summer school."

In the aforementioned letter of November 21, 1933, Mother Gerald also reminded the sisters that she needed to provide an accounting of what each parish owed the community as salary for the sisters teaching in their schools. In the 1920s, this amount was typically $25 per sister per month, an amount which over the next several years increased to $50 per sister. Each convent sent to the Motherhouse half of the money provided by the parish. These funds were used for such needs as supporting the formation of young sisters and covering health care and administrative costs.

Parishes that were facing their own financial woes could not provide what was due the sisters, which obviously created problems for the Congregation. Sisters raised money for their salaries and students' tuition through such means as hot dog lunches, raffles, and sales of candy and Christmas cards.

Mother Gerald deplored these practices. On January 8, 1937, she sent a letter to Dr. Carroll Deady, superintendent of the Detroit diocesan schools, to address the situation.

Father Carroll Deady

> Dear Father Deady,
>
> It seems that you were not born to escape from burdens so I am placing my heaviest on your shoulders with a prayer to Him Who can make it light. This racketeering for money in the schools is the weightiest problem I have, and what I write now concerning it I am intrusting [sic] to you in strictest confidence and with the greatest confidence. You know as well as I do that the Sisters are at the present time just sublimated "hucksters" clothed in the Religious Habit. I not only abhor the abuse but I fear the grave consequences that commercialism will bring to Christianity.
>
> For a long time I have been a witness to the evil influences in this country, but I saw the situation with a new and terrible force while I was in Europe. If the Sisters continue to drive and drill for money in the classroom in these communistic winds, certainly they will fast drive the children to the public schools. All the activity and organization that could be so strong a means of making good citizens for this world and the Kingdom

of Heaven seems in the light of present conditions to be in conspiracy with Antichrist.

I know that none of this is new to you or due to you, but I know you can be a power in removing some causes and I want you to be sure that I am willing to sacrifice anything. I am thinking not only of our Community but the Church. I know many things that we shall have to correct as far as our Sisters are concerned, but I know that it will need a stronger force than I can provide to correct the abuse and remove the causes from other sources. I know that we who embrace the vows must and can certainly live healthy lives with the salary that should be provided for us by the parishes, as well as I know that these sales, parties and other activities that make the Sisters tyrants in the classroom, wrenching money and embarrassing the children that they came to "instruct until justice" can be discharged by adult organizations. It seems to me that you will take a step in the right direction to correct this so that the Sisters, free from the bonds of money-making, can be restored to the dignity of Christian teachers seeking "first the Kingdom of Heaven".

This situation has alarmed and distressed me a long time. I think you can enkindle a spark somewhere that may start a conflagration throughout this diocese and others, and I am promising a campaign of prayer for this cause. . . .

Sincerely in the Sacred Heart
Mother Gerald

To Fields Near and Far

But the Congregation also did its part to help students attend St. Joseph Academy and Siena Heights College by raising money that it put toward providing scholarships. Mother Gerald also came up with a very successful idea for a view book about the schools which was sold for a dollar apiece. Not only did the book raise money for the community, but it also increased enrollment at the various educational institutions covered in the publication.

Ever-Expanding Reach

Even though the Depression and the recession that followed in 1938 took their economic toll, the Congregation's work continued apace. During Mother Gerald's first term, the Congregation continued to expand its outreach by beginning, or taking over, a variety of missions in Illinois, Florida, New Mexico, Arizona, Ohio, and several Michigan cities. The Adrian Dominican House of Studies in Washington, DC, was also established, and Archangelus Hall and Benincasa Dining Hall were built at St. Joseph College.[7]

Mother Gerald was determined to open new schools and staff parish schools wherever possible because of her firm belief in the impact Catholic education had on America's youth. To her, Catholic schools were a means of winning souls for Christ, and the sisters themselves were doing "God's work."

Sister Corinne O'Connor, who taught at several schools during her professed life, and served as the first mistress of the Congregation's preparatory school in the 1940s, wrote after Mother Gerald's death: "I was reminded of [St.] Dominic in her confidence in the sisters, often sending young and inexperienced women to far-off places to spread the Word of God, and stressing singleness of purpose: we came to serve God."

Mother Gerald's personal blend of education and evangelization was a constant theme for her, as in this excerpt from one of her letters to the Congregation.

> *Never forget the real purpose of our schools and the cause that brought you to the Convent. In these days we have a grave responsibility to prepare youth to be "soldiers of Christ" to fight the forces, which each day grow more treacherous and strong. (September 24, 1936)*

Constantly expanding the Congregation's educational outreach made filling all the needed teaching positions a considerable challenge. Mother Gerald regularly exhorted both her sisters and the parish priests to send postulants from their schools to Adrian so that new teachers would be available. As Mother Augustine had before her, however, she often had to tell priests that they would need to hire lay teachers to supplement the ranks of sisters. If a priest insisted on having only sisters on his school's faculty, Mother Gerald was known to remind him that he had not done his part by sending enough postulants her way. Her May 3, 1941, general letter includes this comment: "It is interesting to note that the greatest demands from parishes are sometimes made by those who have few to their credit in the Community. Remind the pastors of this and keep them at bay and postulant minded."

The pressures of providing enough teachers meant that postulants found themselves in the classroom when they were as young as sixteen, and often teaching classes of fifty, sixty, or even more students. It was a situation that Mother Gerald and the Congregational leaders who preceded her all deplored but which they found unavoidable given the demand for teachers. As time went on, she did her best to ensure that the sisters would become better prepared by sending them for further education. The list of institutions from which they earned degrees came to include not only the Congregation's own colleges but schools across the country and around the world as well.[8]

Part of her motivation for getting the sisters an exemplary education, particularly when it came to graduate degrees, was similar to her philosophy that educating children in parochial schools helped win souls for Christ. She wrote on December 30, 1935, to Sister Ann Joachim,[9] who was working toward her doctorate at the International Catholic University in Fribourg, Switzerland.

Sister Ann Joachim

> *I realize that it is a great strain and sometimes I wonder, as you often must, if it is worth it all. But if it helps us to propagate the faith through our College and brings even one soul a bit nearer the Master, it will not fail of its reward.*

Mother Gerald's First Term: 1933-1939

Sister Regina Marie Lalonde was in Fribourg during the 1930s as well, studying at the University of Fribourg. Her work in languages also took her to universities in Peru, Cuba, and the Dominican Republic, where she earned her doctorate.

One of the many other sisters who studied overseas was Sister Helene O'Connor. She was sent to Rome in the mid-1930s to study art, and spent some four years there developing her talents. According to a story kept in the Siena Heights University archives, "Bishop Gallagher [Michael Gallagher, the bishop of the Diocese of Detroit] saw a small portrait she had painted and told Mother Gerald, 'Either you send her to Rome to study, or I will.'"

Sister Regina Marie Lalonde in her academic regalia, holding her mortarboard and her newly received doctorate.

Sister Helene kept a detailed account of her time there. Today, that journal could serve as a tour guide to 1930s Italy, with its colorful descriptions of Rome's churches, museums, events at the Vatican including audiences with the Pope, and much more. She also made observations about daily life. For instance, she wrote at one point: "All Italian cars are sound propelled—they go when the horn goes."

Her artist's training also led her to comment upon what she saw around the Eternal City.

Sister Helene O'Connor

"On route [to visit a Rome church] we passed the [Fontana del Mosè], the central figure of which is a horribly disproportioned statue of Moses. It is said that the sculptor, realizing his mistake, killed himself rather than face the popular criticism. What a pity he didn't do away with the statue, too," reads one excerpt.

A number of sisters studied in Ireland over the years, including the trio of Mary Paul (Noreen) McKeough, Philomena Murray, and Marie McGowan, who went there together in the late 1930s. Sister Philomena studied at the National University of Ireland in Dublin to earn her Licentiate in Music. Sisters Marie and Mary Paul both studied at University College, Dublin, part of the National University of Ireland. The former did graduate work in history, while Sister Mary Paul earned her master's degree in English.[10] She did her doctoral work there as well, although the outbreak of World War II brought her back to the United States where she completed her dissertation *in absentia*.

Sisters Mary Paul (Noreen) McKeough, Philomena Murray (with Rita Barry), and Marie McGowan.

Two particular letters from Mother Gerald to these sisters during that time reflect her desire for a sister to earn a PhD from Dublin for the honor it would bring to the Congregation. When Sister Marie learned that a master's degree in history would take her longer than anticipated because of the requirements involved, Mother Gerald wrote that she should return to Adrian. Mother Gerald did not want Sister Marie to spend several years overseas and have just a master's, not a doctorate, to show for all that study. The coursework "would, of course, benefit Sister personally but that is not the purpose I had in mind in sending her to Dublin," Mother Gerald's letter added. "If she would get a Ph.D. by remaining two years longer, it might be worth while for it would have a great deal of prestige on this side of the water."[11]

On the other hand, Sister Mary Paul was later told to stay in Dublin to earn her doctorate because she could meet the requirements more easily than if she came home. "I find that the Sisters here find it increasingly difficult to obtain this degree and, as Sister has done good work there and is known, no doubt it would be advisable to go on with the work where she will encounter the least difficulty. It will also add to the prestige of the Community to have a Ph.D. from Dublin," Mother Gerald wrote on February 24, 1939.

While Sister Helene wrote voluminously in journal form about her experiences in Rome, the three sisters in Ireland recounted their adventures in lengthy letters to Mother Gerald. The tales began with the voyage across the Atlantic, during which they wrote about everything from the lifeboat drill (which, they wrote, left them feeling "very buxom and giggly" as they wore their life vests over their habits, cloaks, and shawls), to descriptions of the meals, to observations about the passengers they met. Then, throughout their stay in Dublin, they wrote about their classes, people who came to call on them, the sisters with whom they were living at the St. Mary Dominican Convent, and visits to other locales in Ireland and on the Continent.

Other religious communities also benefited from Mother Gerald's desire to ensure that Catholic schoolchildren had the best teachers possible, for she generously opened wide the doors of Siena Heights College and Barry College to members of other congregations.[12]

Her zeal for education came from very early in her life. "I always felt that her love for and energy around education stemmed from her background in Ireland," Sister Rosemary Ferguson said about Mother Gerald. It was Sister Rosemary's belief that education became especially important to the Irish because for many years the country's British rulers tightly controlled the schooling Irish children could receive.[13]

When Sister Attracta Kelly, a native Irishwoman like Mother Gerald, was asked about the same topic, she agreed with Sister Rosemary. "Education was important to us because we had been denied it," she said.

By the 1830s, "national schools" had been established as "a concession, in a way," said Father Liam Kelly, Sister Attracta's brother and the retired pastor of St. Paul's Catholic Church in Jacksonville Beach, Florida. Mother Gerald's own education in the Inagh National School would have been typical of the schooling received by an Irish child in the late nineteenth century. According to a form kept in the Congregation's archives, she attended the school from the age of five through fifteen and studied English, history, science, Latin, sewing, mathematics, religion, and what was called "manual training."

What would today be considered a high school education was not something accessible to all Irish children, for many towns were too small for a high school and therefore children would have had to go to a boarding school. But, Sister Attracta noted, by the time Mother Gerald graduated from primary school, "she would have learned more than a typical eighth-grader here [in America]."

Father Kelly emphasized that the British decided what the children would learn, particularly when it came to history. Such a restrictive system is why Sister Attracta thinks that Mother Gerald "would have had a strong desire to get everyone as educated as possible." And, she added, she believes Mother Gerald "had a real understanding of the role educated women"—including the Adrian Dominican Sisters—"could play in society."

Rosarian Academy

Rosarian Academy in West Palm Beach, Florida, began in 1925 as St. Ann on-the-Lake, a girls' boarding school although boys could attend as day students.[14] It was opened largely because parents from the St. Ann and Lake Worth parishes wanted to have such a facility for their older children.

Rosarian Academy

The Adrian Dominicans had since 1923 staffed the school at nearby St. Ann Parish at the invitation of Mother Gerald's brother Bishop Patrick Barry. Then, when Palm Beach casino owner and prominent racehorse breeder Colonel Edward Bradley donated seven acres of property on Lake Worth to the Bishop with the idea that it be turned into a girls' academy, the Bishop in turn deeded the property to the Adrian Dominican Congregation.

St. Ann on-the-Lake, named at Bradley's request for his mother, opened its doors in 1925. In 1928, Bradley Hall, which was then the only Academy building, was badly damaged by a hurricane. Although repairs were made, the building continued to suffer water damage whenever it rained. The site also took on uses other than the one intended for it: the first floor was converted for use by students from the parish school as a locker room and shower facility, and the front lawn was used as a baseball diamond.

Edward Bradley, Bishop Michael Gallagher, Mother Gerald, and Sister Mary Alice Collins, principal of St. Ann on-the-Lake.

Mother Gerald's nephew Gerald, an architect who drew up the plans for many of the Congregation's buildings, beginning with Mount St. Mary Academy in 1924, was sent to assess the situation. Ultimately, Bradley Hall was repaired, renovated, and returned to its original purpose as the Academy. It reopened for classes in 1934. In 1939, the school's name was changed to Rosarian Academy to distinguish it from the parish school.

Over time, Mother Gerald invited any number of prelates to come for extended stays in the warm Florida weather. The most notable of these was the Apostolic Delegate[15] to the United States, Archbishop Amleto Cicognani, who visited often, complete with his retinue of secretaries and assistants. Mother Gerald and the Archbishop developed a friendship that impacted the Congregation favorably in many ways.[16]

Muldoon High School

Opened in 1930, Muldoon High School in Rockford, Illinois, was originally staffed by the Dominican Sisters of Sinsinawa, Wisconsin. In 1933, the Bishop of Rockford, Edward Hoban, asked the Congregation to purchase both the school and convent from the diocese, a process begun by Mother Augustine and completed by Mother Gerald.

Bishop Edward Hoban

Hoban was one of the many priests, bishops, and archbishops who were great friends of the Congregation. As Bishop of the Diocese of Rockford, he was already well acquainted with the sisters through their operation of Mount St. Mary Academy in St. Charles, Illinois, when he asked them to take over Muldoon High. He developed a friendship first with Mother Augustine and then with Mother Gerald, and years of affectionate correspondence took place between them. He often sent items for the Congregation's use including statues, artwork, and relics. In turn, Mother Gerald's letters to him regularly came with gifts or contained invitations to visit Adrian (or Rosarian Academy, to take advantage of the warm Florida weather) or to take part in a Congregation function.

He was appointed Coadjutor Bishop of Cleveland in 1942, became Bishop of the Diocese in 1945, and as a personal honor from Pope Pius XII was named an Archbishop in 1951, even though Cleveland was not (and is not) an archdiocese.

When the Congregation established a high school in Cleveland in 1951, it was named Hoban Dominican High School in his honor.

The Adrian Dominican House of Studies

When Mother Gerald visited three sisters—Agnita Reuter, Evangela O'Hare, and Agnes Cecile Prendergast—who were studying at The Catholic University of America in October 1934, she was so impressed by the University that she wanted to make it possible for the Congregation to take greater advantage of its programs. The result was the Adrian Dominican House of Studies, which housed Adrian Dominicans as well as sisters from other religious communities both for the academic year and for summer sessions. Because of it, not only could more sisters study at the University, but they could do so more economically than having to be housed elsewhere in Washington. Mother Gerald was confident that the new building would pay for itself in time.

It was constructed on a parcel of land owned by the University's Catholic Sisters College on which Mother Gerald took out a 100-year lease.[17]

The Adrian Dominican House of Studies.

St. Theresa Home for the Aged

This home for the elderly in Cincinnati, Ohio, had existed in some form since 1910, and was staffed by the Sisters of the Precious Blood from 1920 until 1936 when they withdrew. The Archbishop of Cincinnati, John McNicholas, OP, asked the Congregation to take over the home's administration, something that returned the community to its early days as a provider of care to the aged and pointed forward to its eventual expansion into hospital work.

Mother Gerald wrote about this new venture in a letter to the Congregation on December 8, 1936: "It seems that I have never told you that . . . we adopted a family of about 90 old people at St. Theresa's Home for the Aged in Cincinnati. . . . Sisters Rose de Lima, Reynolds [*sic*], Pauline, Celeste and Helen Agnes[18] are enjoying their labors among the little old children, and I think many of you will be picking this mission out as your favorite in the future."[19]

St. John's Parish, Albion, Michigan

In September 1937, St. John's Parish in Albion, Michigan, began what the local newspaper termed "an experiment in Roman Catholic activities"—a convent school designed to supplement the parish students' regular education in the public schools. The school, which was the brainchild of the parish priest, Father A.J. Olk, brought in students, from preschool age to twelfth grade, for at least one hour per week. The children studied religion along with such areas as music, elocution, painting, sewing, needlework, and "domestic science." Three Adrian Dominican Sisters taught the classes: Mary Aurelia Gray, Thomas Marie Keenan, and Ursula O'Neill.

Sisters Thomas Marie Keenan, Ursula O'Neill, and Mary Aurelia Gray.

According to the newspaper story about the opening, "Indications are that its progress will be watched by [Catholic] leaders with a view to establishing similar schools in other communities too small to warrant a general parochial school."

Over time, the parish grew so that a school did need to be established. St. John's parish school, staffed by the Congregation, opened in 1959. The Congregation withdrew in June 1971, and the school closed in June 2002.

Siena Heights College Expansion

Continuing growth at St. Joseph College led the General Council in 1937 to consider building a new dormitory that Mother Gerald envisioned as including not only student rooms but lounges, parlors, a kitchen, and a dining hall. She wrote in a May 23 letter to the sisters that the project would allow the students "the joy of eating their bread and syrup while at the same time they could get a glimpse of the beautiful scenery God provides for them here."

By October of that year, she was able to announce that plans were in the works, and what actually became two buildings—Archangelus Hall and Benincasa Hall—were dedicated in September 1938. The *Michigan Catholic* newspaper wrote of the dedication in its October 6 issue.

> *The resplendent beauty of an Autumn day lent an appropriate setting for the magnificence of the liturgy and the colorful array of vestments as Archbishop Edward Mooney, escorted by six*

> bishops, a score of monsignori, some 175 priests, 300 nuns and laymen, blessed and dedicated the two recently constructed buildings of the Sisters of St. Dominic, here, yesterday morning.

"The Dedication was a gala day to be remembered for a long time," an October 24 letter from Mother Gerald to the sisters noted. After describing the work still being done to the buildings and to an art department on the fifth floor of Sacred Heart Hall, she continued: "Between the liberal and fine things we are a saucy sandwich. We have had compliments from many quarters—mostly on our nerve."

The art department's genesis is a story in itself. It became the domain of Sister Helene O'Connor, who had been teaching art in a room on the fourth floor of Sacred Heart Hall. After Sister Helene returned from study in Rome in 1938, Mother Gerald wanted her to find a place for a studio. The opportunity came when Gerald Barry, the architect, was in Adrian supervising the completion of work on the new buildings.

As Sister Helene later wrote, "I was on the fourth floor of Sacred Heart when my code clattered on the intercom phone. Mother Gerald was on the line. She asked me to stay right where I was, because she was sending Gerald over. I was to show him the fifth floor," which was an attic space she had mentioned to Mother Gerald as a possibility.

> By the time the tired "puffing" Gerald arrived, he was in the mood to take the elevator. I got the nerve to show him the dark hole with its wooden ladder. One must climb up. A 30 watt

bulb hung where it gave us enough light to show how to collect a handful of splinters. When we neared the top of the ladder, I switched off the bulb. Gerald fairly flew up the last rungs. Neither of us knew what to expect.

What they found was a long, narrow hall, running the full length of the building, that was floored with black asphalt tile . . . and two very large rooms with high ceilings. The studio that arose in that space was named Studio Angelico, after the great fifteenth century Dominican artist Fra Angelico.[20]

And Soon to Come . . .

In her general letter of March 7, 1939, Mother Gerald made the momentous announcement that the Congregation was going to found another college, this one somewhere in the Miami area. For the time being, however, the sisters were to keep the news a secret "until the time is ripe for advertising."

On May 18, 1939, the Congregation purchased forty acres of land in Miami Shores, with the help of a donation from Mrs. Margaret Brady Farrell. She was a parishioner at St. Patrick, which was the Miami Beach parish of Mother Gerald's priest brother William. Ultimately Mrs. Farrell was a very generous benefactor of the new college in many ways. Her financial help included funding in its entirety the construction of the College's chapel, Cor Jesu, when she learned that a shortage of finances was postponing the work.[21]

Gaining Pontifical Status

The effort to have the Congregation changed from a diocesan to a pontifical congregation spanned much of Mother Gerald's first term in office.

It had been the intent of Mother Camilla Madden to secure this status because of the benefits of being a pontifical, rather than a diocesan, congregation. When active congregations fell under the jurisdiction of the local bishop, there was always the possibility that, as bishops changed, the congregation could be subjected to the new prelate's whims.

Bishop Michael Gallagher

Mother Camilla died before being able to take any real steps toward her goal. It fell to her successor, Mother Augustine Walsh, to set the wheels in motion.[22] Mother Gerald took up the cause after Mother Augustine's death, but an unexpected problem arose. It was discovered that in 1923 the separation of Adrian from its "parent" Congregation in Newburgh, New York, had been approved by Bishop Michael Gallagher of Detroit and Archbishop Patrick Hayes of New York, but apparently no one had realized that Rome needed to approve the separation. Therefore, in the eyes of the Vatican, the Congregation did not exist.[23]

Mother Gerald's First Term: 1933-1939

The letter that started the separation process was written on June 15, 1923, by Mother Emmanuel Phelan of the Newburgh congregation to Bishop Gallagher.

Your Lordship,

In respectful deference to Your Lordship I wish to submit the matter of our separation from the Dominican Community in Adrian, before we conclude the arrangements.

Before the Community at Adrian was able to meet its needs the necessary assistance was given it from New York.

For the past thirty years or more the Adrian Branch progressed so admirably, under the wise and energetic guidance of Rev. Mother Camilla, that there was no need of help from the Parent House.

Our connection, therefore, has become rather independent on both sides although still claiming unity.

To prevent complications later on I think we ought to arrange for a complete separation while Mother Camilla is living, except as far as friendship and mutual good wishes hold us together.

I have consulted Mother Camilla, she agrees to the separation.

I herein petition Your Lordship to give your consent, then there shall be no further dependence of one on the other. Our

> Most Rev. Archbishop and Rt. Rev. Bishop Dunn[24] have given their consent for the separation.
>
> I take this occasion to express my sincere gratitude to Your Lordship for your great kindness and solicitude for the welfare of the Community in Adrian.
>
> Mother Camilla and Sisters give high compliments to your hearty cooperation with them in their religious and educational efforts.
>
> Hoping my petition will meet with your approval and asking Your Lordship's blessing
>
> I am
> Yours humbly in Christ
> Mother M. Emmanuel
> (Mother General)

The Bishop replied on July 26, 1923.

> *Rev. and dear Mother Emmanuel:*
>
> Your letter of June 15th in which you suggest that the Sisters of St. Dominic at Adrian, Michigan, be completely separated from the Mother House in New York, was received and in accordance therefore with your wishes and the consent of Mother Camilla of Adrian, We gladly give Our hearty approval.
>
> We extend to you Our deep appreciation and sincere gratitude for the assistance you have rendered in the distant

past, and We trust that the same friendly relations will continue to prevail in the future.

With kindest personal regards, I remain,

Cordially yours in Xto.,
Michael J. Gallagher,
Bishop of Detroit

As Mother Emmanuel had noted in her letter, Archbishop Patrick Hayes of New York had already given his consent.

A decade later, as Mother Gerald was working on moving the papal approbation process forward, the problem with how the separation had been handled came to light. Father Louis Nolan, OP, of the Dominican Master General's staff in Rome, who was assisting Mother Gerald, wrote to her about the issue on November 6, 1934.

There is one point about which I am somewhat preoccupied, and about which I spoke to the Bishop in Detroit [Bishop Gallagher], and that is the permission of the Holy See for the separation of Newburgh and the erection of your new Congregation. The Bishop says he knows nothing of such permission, and he did not think that such was necessary. If you are in good relations with the Newburgh Sisters will you please ask them if they have any documents on the question in their archives. My feeling is that the Holy See was not asked for such permission.

This "canonical defect" was the topic of a January 4, 1935, letter from now-Cardinal Hayes to Mother Mary Blanche Dorsey, Prioress

General of the Newburgh Dominicans at this point. Cardinal Hayes wrote that he was seeking "any reference to the foundation and the permission which should have been obtained from the Holy See." Mother Mary Blanche promptly provided all the correspondence in Newburgh's files, writing in the accompanying letter, "I think these few letters prove the neglect to have been unintentional and, most likely, due to the fact that our Superiors put the establishing of the new foundation in the hands of the Authorities in Detroit."[25]

On March 15, 1935, Father Nolan was able to report to Mother Gerald that a rescript providing the requested sanation[26] had been issued. "You need not tell the Sisters, officially at least, that there has been any defect in the erection of the Congregation, as it might upset some of them," he added in the letter.

Meanwhile, Bishop Gallagher was pressing forward with the effort to secure papal approbation for the Congregation. On November 18, 1934, a letter had gone from Monsignor Augusto Fidecicchi of the Sacred Congregation for Religious to Bishop Gallagher, noting that the two men had spoken about the topic in Rome in 1925 and that Fidecicchi had given the Bishop a list of the required documents. But things had not gone ahead at that time. The Monsignor noted in the letter that two days after their 1925 conversation, he had called on Bishop Gallagher at the hotel in Rome where the Bishop was staying—as was Joseph Schrembs, the Bishop of Cleveland. "Both he and you had a long speech, the result of which was that you cancelled any order you gave me to care after the 30 copies of the Constitution," he wrote in the letter.

If by "a long speech" the Monsignor meant "a long discussion," the conjecture could be made that Bishop Schrembs had been expressing his views on the proposed change in status to Bishop Gallagher. It is known that Schrembs did not support the idea, because he believed women's congregations should be under diocesan control. Each bishop in whose diocese the Adrian Dominican Sisters were serving would need to support the change in a letter, and with Schrembs not approving of the idea, it would not have moved forward.

Bishop Schrembs had been at odds with the Congregation even before going to the Cleveland diocese in 1921. He had previously been bishop of the Diocese of Toledo, Ohio, and he continued to hold the position that women who wanted to enter religious life in his diocese must join a congregation there, rather than one outside the diocese. Mother Camilla, however, would accept any qualified young woman regardless of her hometown, meaning that women who might otherwise have joined a congregation within the Diocese of Toledo could, and sometimes did, come to Adrian instead. The Bishop's animosity toward the Congregation because of this practice continued well after he had moved on to Cleveland. When Mother Augustine sought the required letters of approval from the various diocesan bishops, Schrembs was the only bishop who did not provide one.

Monsignor Fidecicchi, in that 1934 letter, directed that the work on pontifical status needed to start from the beginning. He notified Bishop Gallagher that the following documents were required: an application to the Pope from the Prioress and the General Council, a history of the Congregation, a report from the Prioress and Council called a Questionary because it answered a number of questions posed about the Congregation, and the testimonial letters from bishops. The answers to the Questionary, signed by Mother Gerald and Sister Bertha Homminga, the Secretary General of the Congregation, and a copy of the Constitution were sent to Father Nolan on December 18, 1934.

A year later, the Adrian sisters sought input from the Sisters of St. Dominic of Everett, Washington, on exactly what was needed to secure papal approval. A letter sent on December 2, 1935, to Sister Benedicta Marie Ledwidge from Mother Mary Frances Miller of Everett listed the necessary steps and the documents needed, and gave advice on what books of canon law to consult. Mother Mary Frances also wrote,

> *We are certainly happy to hear that you are going to apply for Papal approval for it is certainly a wonderful privilege and makes one feel secure. . . . We wish you every success in this glorious undertaking and pray that the coveted privilege will soon be yours. We waited two years but that is not long.*

Over the course of the next several months, Mother Gerald and Father Nolan corresponded concerning the gathering of the necessary materials, including the required letters of recommendation from the bishops of the various dioceses. Despite his previous issues with the Congregation, the letter Bishop Schrembs wrote at this point could not have been more laudatory. It reads in part,

> *Gladly do I recommend this Community for favorable consideration in this matter because for years they have served*

in the Diocese of Cleveland in three of our parishes, where they have brought the blessing of a sound Catholic education to the little ones of Christ and have, by their religious life, brought honor, respect and admiration upon themselves.

Accordingly, I heartily approve the request which they are about to make to receive for their Congregation Pontifical approbation.

Letters were also secured from the archbishops of Chicago, Cincinnati, Santa Fe, and Baltimore, and from the bishops of Rockford, Illinois; Toledo, Ohio; Marquette, Michigan; St. Augustine, Florida (Mother Gerald's brother Bishop Patrick); and Des Moines, Iowa.

On October 3, 1936, Mother Gerald, Sister Benedicta Marie, and Sister Raymonda Culhane, with all the required documents in hand, set sail from New York on a ship bound for Naples, Italy. They arrived there on October 10, and the next day the materials were in Father Nolan's custody in Rome.[27]

But there was one potential hurdle ahead. On November 20, 1936, Father Nolan wrote to Mother Gerald that

. . . your cause has gone on ahead. The Constitutions are now printed, the Votum[28] is written and printed and circulated to all concerned, and all the documents in order, and I have been able to have it listed for the sitting of the Commission to be held on 2nd December, so now set to praying hard for its success.

There is just one little shadow, which may cause a difficulty . . .

That "one little shadow" was that Father Nolan could find no record of a papal document authorizing the Congregation's change of status from Second to Third Order:[29] "I suppose you have no knowledge of such a document having ever been obtained by Newburgh Sisters at any time before your separation from them," he wrote.

Newburgh had voted to make the change to Third Order status on August 31, 1896, with the required changes made in Adrian immediately thereafter. When that occurred, Archbishop Michael Corrigan of New York had made the change official, so Mother Gerald asked Newburgh's Prioress at this time, Mother Mary de Lourdes Goan, to forward a copy of that document to Father Nolan.

On December 3, 1936, the priest was able to send an update to Mother Gerald.

> *You will be very happy to hear that yesterday, 2nd December, we discussed in Commission the petition with all the relative documents concerning the Apostolic Approbation of your dear Congregation and its Constitutions, and the result was unanimously favorable, thank God. The matter will now be discussed by the Commission of Cardinals, probably at their meeting at the end of January, but their decision, once the Commission of Consultors is favourable, is a foregone conclusion; and then a few days later the case will be brought before the Holy Father for the formal Apostolic Approval, and then the authentic text of the Constitutions with the relative Decrees of Approval of Congregation and Constitutions will*

be drawn up; so that by Easter I trust you will have all in your hands, please God.

This information which it gives me so much joy to send you will add to the Christmas happiness of yourself and your Congregation. And I now take this opportunity to congratulate you on the very happy issue of your visit to Rome, and what it has meant for your Institute and yourself.

"I proffer my sincere and heartfelt thanks for your part in bringing things to such a favorable issue," Mother Gerald wrote back on December 16. "I can scarcely make myself believe that this matter, which has caused me so much anxiety for a long time, has been so speedily taken care of. God was extraordinarily good to us in giving us such a capable 'friend at court.'"

Finally, on April 12, 1937, a telegram reached Mother Gerald as she was visiting Aquinas Convent in Chicago.

APOSTOLIC APPROVAL GRANTED CONGREGATION AND CONSTITUTIONS CONGRATULATIONS= NOLAN

What Mother Gerald had referred to in a March 1937 letter to Father Nolan as the "great cause" had finally come to a happy conclusion.

1. Nadine Foley, *Seeds Scattered and Grown* (Adrian: Adrian Dominican Congregation, 2006), 81-92.
2. Ibid., 85-90.
3. Ibid., 87-88.
4. The Society for the Propagation of the Faith is an organization that works to assist Catholic missionaries working in non-Catholic countries. Donations from the Catholic faithful fund its work.
5. The term "subject" was formerly used instead of "member."
6. Each house was supposed to send to the Motherhouse a certain percentage of what each sister earned. These funds were referred to as "dues."
7. In 1939 the name of the school was changed to Siena Heights College, honoring St. Catherine of Siena. The move was made to avoid confusion between the College and St. Joseph Academy "and the idea some people have that the same faculty operates both College and Academy," Mother Gerald wrote to the Congregation that March 7. The College became Siena Heights University in 1998.
8. Sister Bertha Homminga, who served for years as the Congregation's Directress of Studies and as Siena Heights College's Registrar, kept voluminous notes of which degrees sisters had earned and from where. A note contained in one of her record books indicates that as of December 31, 1956, the Congregation counted among its 1,945 professed sisters 1,373 bachelor's degrees, with teaching certificates; 488 master's degrees; 36 PhD's; 15 RN degrees; and 128 theology certificates.
9. Sister Ann Joachim, who wrote her doctoral dissertation on the comparison between the Swiss and U.S. constitutions, had earned her law degree, passed the bar, and become a partner in her law firm before entering the Congregation. In 1936, she was granted the right to argue cases before the U.S. Supreme Court, becoming the first woman religious—indeed, one of the first women at all—to receive that distinction. Her religious name was Ann Joachim and her family surname was Joachim, making her full name Sister Ann Joachim Joachim.

Mother Gerald's First Term: 1933-1939

10 A letter from the three sisters, written by Sister Philomena, to Mother Gerald on December 11, 1938, contains this line: ". . . Sister Mary Paul's subject for her thesis, 'The Blessed Virgin in English Literature,' sort of took them [the sisters at the Dominican convent in Muckross Park, Dublin, where they lived] off their feet since a religious subject hadn't been attempted by anyone among the nuns or priests in God knows when. They generally have selected a secular subject so Sister's lofty ideals put them guessing again about America. Her professor said, 'I believe they do that at Catholic U. in America but somehow, they haven't ventured that way here.'"

11 Letter dated October 29, 1938.

12 In another example of her continuous desire to assist other religious communities, in 1958, Mother Gerald "loaned out," as she put it, Sister Mary Paul (Noreen) McKeough to Marillac College, a Sister Formation college in Missouri. "In the charity of Christ we and other religious communities have sacrificed a highly-degreed teaching sister to help the cause along," Mother Gerald wrote to the Congregation on September 29, 1958. See pp. 163-164.

13 Under the Penal Laws, until late in the eighteenth century Catholic education was forbidden in Ireland. This led to the rise of the so-called "hedge schools." Children were educated in secret, sometimes literally behind hedges or walls and sometimes in barns.

14 Today, Rosarian is a co-educational day school serving elementary and middle school students.

15 This was the title for the Vatican's representative to a country with which it had no diplomatic relations.

16 See pp. 275-279 for more on Archbishop Cicognani.

17 Sisters continued to live there and study at the University until a variety of factors made it advisable to re-think the whole arrangement. The minutes of a November 23, 1970, legal affairs meeting between Sisters Jeanne Burns, the Vicaress General; Ann Joachim, the Congregation's legal counsel; and Marie Wiedner, the Secretary General, list two concerns in particular: "At present the House of Studies is not being used by sister-students of C.U. due to discontinuance of the bus service to the University as well as discontinuance of dining facilities." In 1971, the property was returned to the University in exchange for scholarships for sisters.

18 This refers to Sisters Rose de Lima Birch, Mary Reynold Darga, Mary Pauline Baske, Mary Celeste Graham, and Helen Agnes McDonnell.

19 In the late 1940s and into the 1950s, some communications took place between the Archbishop (both McNicholas and his successor, Karl Alter) and the Congregation regarding a potential purchase of the home by the community. Mother Gerald and the rest of the General Council decided against this course of action because the Archdiocese wanted to be consulted on policy matters and because the home was in a great deal of debt. The Congregation, however, continued to administer the facility until withdrawing in 1982.

20 Fra Angelico (c. 1395-1455) was an Italian painter and Dominican friar whose works can be seen in numerous galleries and religious institutions throughout Italy, including at the Vatican. He was beatified by Pope John Paul II in 1982. His most extensive project was the painting of numerous frescoes at the convent of San Marco in Florence, which today is a museum. Today, Studio Angelico at Siena Heights University has grown to be housed in its own two-story building.

21 From Barry University's website, www.barry.edu. According to this source, when Mrs. Farrell died the College received a gift of a chalice decorated with her personal jewels.

22 See Foley, *Seeds Scattered and Grown*, 158-174, for a discussion of this early pursuit of papal approbation and of the reasons this status was beneficial.

23 Ibid., 206-207.

24 Bishop John J. Dunn was an Auxiliary Bishop in the Archdiocese of New York.

25 Foley, *Seeds Scattered and Grown*, 207.

26 The word "sanation" refers to a step taken to correct an error.

27 The trip also included a lengthy audience with Pope Pius XI, tours of many key sites in Rome and elsewhere in Italy, stops in Paris and Lisieux, and a visit to Ireland. Mother Gerald's general letter of December 8, 1936, about the experience is a fascinating travelogue as well as a very interesting glimpse at her human side as she reflects on the places she and her companions visited.

28 In this context, a Votum is a document asking that a specific action take place.

[29] See Mary Philip Ryan, *Amid the Alien Corn* (Adrian: The Sisters of St. Dominic of the Congregation of the Most Holy Rosary, 1967), 11-13, for a discussion of the differences between Second Order and Third Order status.

Chapter Three
Mother Gerald's Second Term: 1939-1945

At the Congregation's fourth General Chapter in June 1939, Mother Gerald was elected overwhelmingly to a second term of office with 107 out of 118 votes. It was to be another eventful six years for the Congregation.

This period in the Congregation's history coincides with the Second World War, which began September 1, 1939, when Germany invaded Poland. Mother Gerald had witnessed the gathering storm clouds of war when she visited London in late summer 1939. Once the United States entered the war two years later when Pearl Harbor was bombed, the sisters were affected by the conflict as were so many other Americans. As their relatives and family friends, both men and women, served and even died in World War II, the Congregation did what it could for the war effort.

Siena Heights College students in helmets and gas masks for a civil defense drill during World War II.
PHOTO CREDIT: SIENA HEIGHTS UNIVERSITY ARCHIVES

Mother Gerald noted in a May 8, 1942, general letter that many of the sisters' relatives had suggested that home visits[1] be put off due to rationing of gas and tires. "I think you ought to look with favor on this suggestion," she wrote, adding, "Do not be too disappointed if you are not allowed by the government to enjoy any kind of transportation that is not absolutely necessary. Let us be ready at all times to make sacrifices."

Then almost exactly a year later, on May 5, 1943, she wrote,

> *You will be disappointed when I tell you that there will be no home visits this summer. You must see our reason and set yourselves and your parents to feel that we ought to do something in the way of sacrifice for world peace. We are rightly expected to show our patriotism by following the advice of the government and doing as little traveling as possible so that the space may be given the men in the service who are constantly being transported—they know not always where.*

She also regularly exhorted the sisters to serve God and country through their faithfulness to their vows, and to pray for peace and for "the poor and starving of the terrified countries of Europe."[2] Additionally, the General Council, in response to an appeal from the National Catholic Welfare Conference, created a way to help sisters in the war zones by sending material for clothing.[3] But the war did not slow down the Congregation's work. In fact, during those years it began to look to new ways of ministering to the world.

Parish Visitation and Census-Taking

Parish visitation was an early form of social work for the Congregation in which teams of sisters went door-to-door in Catholic parishes, taking a census of the Catholic residents and in the process talking to them and hearing their concerns. The practice actually began in the 1920s in Cincinnati, Ohio, due in large part to the work of Sister Marie Dominic Bjerring.

The New York City-born Olga Bjerring became a Dominican tertiary[4] early in life, following in the footsteps of her father. Eventually she made the acquaintance of Father John McNicholas, OP, the national director of the Holy Name Society,[5] and began assisting him in his work.

Olga Bjerring (Sister Marie Dominic), third from left.

Later, she joined a group of English tertiaries, known as the Dominican Sisters of Corpus Christi, when they came to the United States to engage in social work. Father McNicholas had by this time become Bishop of Duluth, Minnesota, and he arranged for these women to be based in Duluth and work in a variety of missionary activities. They worked primarily among Native Americans, African Americans, and Chinese immigrants. Olga took the name Sister Mary Andrew when she joined the Corpus Christi sisters, and was especially drawn to work with the Chippewa Indians of the area.

After Bishop McNicholas became Archbishop of Cincinnati, he was approached by Father Raymond Meagher, OP, Provincial of the Dominican Province of St. Joseph. Father Meagher wanted to organize an American group of Dominican sisters to work in dioceses around the country in missionary work and parish visitation. Archbishop McNicholas suggested that the Adrian Dominican Sisters, with their "good, simple spirit,"[6] might do such work. He thought that the Adrian Dominicans could supply an initial group of sisters who would in time form the basis of a separate congregation, and offered to start them off in Cincinnati. Meagher then asked Mother Augustine Walsh to provide these sisters, while Archbishop McNicholas suggested that Sister Mary Andrew be accepted into the Adrian Dominicans to help form this new congregation.

Although the idea of a separate group did not prove feasible, Olga did indeed become an Adrian Dominican, although for a different reason from what the Archbishop had suggested. The Corpus Christi sisters decided to join with the Carmelites and Olga, desiring to stay in the Dominican tradition she loved, left them. At the age of fifty-two, she became an Adrian Dominican postulant.

After she professed her vows, taking the name Sister Marie Dominic Bjerring, she and two other Corpus Christi Dominican tertiaries who had become Adrian Dominicans—now known as Sisters Marie Regina McDonald and Marie Jane McGoldrick—began full-time parish visitation work in the Cincinnati archdiocese. Sister Marie Dominic began her ministry in October 1929, with Sister Marie Regina joining her in January 1930 and Sister Marie Jane arriving a few months later. The ministry thrived there for more than twenty years.

Mother Gerald's Second Term: 1939-1945

In 1940, Archbishop Samuel Stritch of Chicago asked Mother Gerald to supply some sisters to do census work for St. Matthew Parish, where the Adrian Dominicans were already teaching. The plan developed in a roundabout way. St. Matthew's pastor, Father Henry Matthew Shea, had discussed with Sister Andrew Marie Podsedly, the superior, the idea of asking for a group of sisters from a religious community in New York, the Parish Visiting Sisters of Mary Immaculate, to do the work. Sister Andrew Marie told Father Shea that her Congregation had sisters who did such work and that he should contact Mother Gerald. When he did, however, Mother Gerald turned him down because she had no one available to send.

Father Shea then went to Archbishop Stritch to ask for the sisters from New York, but when the Archbishop discovered the parish already had Adrian Dominicans teaching there, he personally went to Mother Gerald. Suddenly, two sisters became available.

As time went on, the parish visitation ministry spread to communities across the country. In some cases, sisters were assigned to this work full-time, as was the case in Chicago for a number of years. But since the primary work of the Congregation was still education, sisters were needed to teach during the school year, so in many places parish visitation was done only in the summertime.

Sister Agnes Raphael Roche making a home visit.

To Fields Near and Far

The success of the work in Cincinnati led directly to the Congregation's involvement in the founding of the Glenmary Sisters, a story that is told beginning on page 121 of this book.[7]

A New College

By early 1940, work was under way on both Barry College in Miami Shores, Florida, and on a new school the Congregation was building on the east side of Detroit, Dominican High School. The high school opened that September with an enrollment of 494 students and was dedicated on the Feast of the Most Holy Rosary, October 7.[8]

A view from the Dominican High School rooftop of the June 1950 graduation ceremony.

Barry College, which became Barry University in 1981, was named after Mother Gerald's brother Patrick. Since 1922, he had been the Bishop of the Diocese of St. Augustine, which at the time encompassed virtually the entire state of Florida.

By all accounts from those who knew him, Bishop Barry was a kind and generous man and one who worked tirelessly to propagate

Bishop Patrick Barry
PHOTO CREDIT: BARRY UNIVERSITY ARCHIVES AND SPECIAL COLLECTIONS

the faith in Florida. The fourth oldest of the Barry children (and the third son), he was ordained in 1895 and immediately thereafter went to the mission fields of Florida, where he had volunteered to go even before his ordination. A zealous young priest, he battled swampland, anti-Catholicism, and more to minister to Catholics and to cultivate people of other faiths. He was initially at Immaculate Conception Parish in Jacksonville as curate to the Vicar General of the Diocese of St. Augustine.

When the church, along with a large section of Jacksonville itself, burned to the ground on May 5, 1901, Father Barry helped raise funds locally to rebuild the church and the facilities associated with it before being assigned to St. Monica Parish in Palatka. From there, he was assigned to Jacksonville and then to a post as rector of the cathedral in St. Augustine, where in 1917 he was named Vicar General of the Diocese and, later, Administrator. In February 1922 he was named the fifth Bishop of St. Augustine, from which vantage point he oversaw a tremendous growth in the Catholic Church in Florida.[9]

It is difficult to ascertain from the Congregation's archives exactly when Mother Gerald, or the Bishop perhaps, began thinking about the need for a Catholic college in that state. By March 1937, however, the Bishop had made some inquiries about a tract of land owned by the Florida East Coast Railroad, according to a note he sent to Mother Gerald on the nineteenth of that month. Additionally, an April 25, 1937, letter from Mother Gerald to her brother Monsignor William Barry opens with a note of appreciation for his counsel concerning "an acceptable site for a potential college."

After several possible properties were explored, on May 18, 1939, the forty acres of land for the new institution was in Congregation hands. The transaction was handled by Miami attorney John Thompson,[10] who negotiated the sale and dealt with other necessary legal matters.[11] He also offered his assistance in other ways: volunteering to help procure books, making suggestions as to the form of the official seal, and seeing to it that payment was made for the design work on the seal. In a February 21, 1940, letter to Mother Gerald, he asked her to send the bill for this work to him because "I have made arrangements for this to be taken care of locally."

John Thompson
PHOTO CREDIT: BARRY UNIVERSITY ARCHIVES AND SPECIAL COLLECTIONS

His enthusiasm for the new college led him, at one point, to even suggest a name: "Gerald College." A May 25, 1939, letter from him to Mother Gerald with his idea observed, "You will no doubt recall that as we left Father Barry's house the afternoon you were here, you told me that my next job was to find a good name for the new college." Whether Mother Gerald was really serious about that or not, he certainly took the comment seriously.

The letter went on to note that Monsignor Barry thought the name should be Latinized to "Geraldi College." "I realize that you may not agree with my suggestion," Thompson continued, "and I think that I can put my finger on the reason and that is that any person who has been as unselfish and untiring in her work as you have, might think that a name as similar as this is to your name (and, of course, that is the source of the idea), might tend to counteract the years of service that you have given. However, my reaction is—what better tribute could be paid to you than to use this name?"

Mother Gerald responded tactfully on May 30, 1939: "I am most grateful to you for your gracious letter and I am happy that you took seriously your duty of selecting a name for our College. It is very kind of you to think of my name as one fitting for the new College. I deeply appreciate your thoughtfulness but you well understand why I cannot let this come to pass." The letter included a list of potential names and requested that he and Monsignor Barry select "the most becoming name for our purpose."

Thompson replied on June 5 that he had asked others to weigh in on her list, which included names such as Ponce de Leon College, Christ the King College, Salvae [sic] Regina, and Dominican College of San Patrice, which Mother Gerald had noted in her letter would likely be the preference in Adrian. Personally, he wrote, he liked the latter although he thought perhaps simply "Dominican College" would be appropriate.

He was not quite ready to give up on his first idea, however. "In spite of the list of names and what you said, I still like my original suggestion and wish there was some method by which I could override your decision in the matter," his letter continued. "It appears that the final decision of the name is going to have to lie entirely with you."

According to the Congregation's records, the General Council held discussion of what to name the institution at its January 2, 1940, meeting, and "Barry" won the vote.

Mother Gerald wrote to her brother the Bishop on January 8: "I wonder whether you got my wire saying the new college was named for you. I had nothing whatever to do with the matter and was told that it really was the business of the Congregation in this instance, so you might as well be happy about it." "I got your wire naming College and, of course, my head has swelled over it," Bishop Barry replied in a January 22 letter.

Margaret Brady Farrell
PHOTO CREDIT: BARRY UNIVERSITY ARCHIVES AND SPECIAL COLLECTIONS

The design work on the buildings was carried out by Mother Gerald's architect nephew Gerald, and the school became reality with the help of donors including Bishop Barry himself, Monsignor Barry, and the ever-generous Margaret Brady Farrell. But as successful as the institution ultimately proved to be, Mother Gerald's writings show her early trepidation about the massive undertaking.

On February 5, 1940, she wrote in a letter to Sister Gonzaga Greene, who was supervising the construction, equipping, furnishing, and decorating of the campus buildings, as well as interviewing potential staff and working hard to recruit students:

Mother Gerald's Second Term: 1939-1945

I sometimes feel that I am taking an awful plunge and that I will not rise above the waters, but I know it is the Lord's work and He will complete it in His way and not in mine. If I fail, it will be His will. If it succeeds, it will be His doing.

The legendary Sister Gonzaga, who became Barry's first Vice-President, played a significant role in the construction of the initial buildings. After her death on July 31, 1956, the *Miami Herald* ran this account of her role in the construction of the new college.

She was known among founders of the college as "the woman who knew more about blueprints than the man who drew them." An efficient supervisor who didn't believe in "staying on the sidewalk," she rapidly earned the respect of construction workers. A flowing white habit did not stop her from climbing ladders to make certain that plans were being followed to the letter. Painters and carpenters became surprisingly more conscientious upon finding a 56-year-old nun peering over their shoulders to inspect their work—even when they were 20 feet off the ground.[12]

Sister Gonzaga Greene
PHOTO CREDIT: BARRY UNIVERSITY ARCHIVES AND SPECIAL COLLECTIONS

The *Miami News* carried an article when Barry celebrated its twenty-fifth birthday that also made note of Sister Gonzaga's role.

She lived at St. Patrick's convent [on Miami Beach], but she spent her days at the building site, climbing ladders to check up on the construction workers. She admonished them soundly when they attempted to circumvent the specifications.

Although she was a tall, heavy woman, she walked on the roof with graceful agility, her black veil and white habit flapping in the breeze. When it rained, Sister Mary Gonzaga returned to St. Patrick's wrinkled and muddy. The Dominican Sisters who staffed the grammar and grade school [sic] there checked her shoes, polished them, and saw to it that she had a fresh habit. She arrived at the construction site each morning tidy and crisp.[13]

Barry had not been Sister Gonzaga's first experience with supervising major projects involving buildings. In 1929, she had directed the Herculean task of moving the entire Aquinas Convent building in Chicago, lock, stock and barrel, across 72nd

Bishop Barry blessing the Barry College cornerstone. PHOTO CREDIT: BARRY UNIVERSITY ARCHIVES AND SPECIAL COLLECTIONS

Street to facilitate an addition to the high school. Building Barry College was an even more immense task. But under her direction, five of the College's buildings were constructed from the ground up and ready to open in the space of roughly eight months.[14]

Mother Gerald's Second Term: 1939-1945

When Mother Gerald appointed Sister Gonzaga superior of the sister-faculty not long before the official opening, she wrote back,

> *Since it has happened, the responsibility seems greater than it did during these months when I have been your humble agent in this grand and glorious project, but Mother dear, all I can say is I accept what is God's will for me and I will give the best that is in me to the present and future development of Barry College. May God reward you for the choice of a grand group of Sisters and I trust that each one of us will be faithful to the trust and confidence you have placed in us. I assure you I will endeavor to make both Sisters and students happy in their work.*

Unfortunately, Bishop Barry did not live to see the opening of the institution that bore his name. On August 13, 1940, one of the sisters at St. Joseph Academy in St. Augustine, Sister Thomasine of the Sisters of St. Joseph, sent Mother Gerald a letter in which she expressed concern about the Bishop's failing health. She recounted his reluctance to see a doctor but noted he had acquiesced just that morning, and she urged Mother Gerald to come to see him.

By the time Mother Gerald received the letter, it was already too late. The same day the letter was sent, Bishop Barry died suddenly, at the age of not quite seventy-two. Mother Gerald began her September 6 letter to the Congregation with these words,

> *Dear Sisters, I owe you fervent thanks for your great kindness and large-hearted sympathy at the death of my best loved*

> brother, Bishop Barry. He was and is your brother too, and I know you will remember him as such. It made him happy to see and hear you and learn of you in this life and now I hope you will make him happy by your prayers and good works for him.
>
> In all our sorrows let us remember that death must come so that we may have joys that will not end. Let us remember, too, that eternity will be what we now want it to be.

The letter quickly turned to Congregational matters, however, including mention of both Barry College and Dominican High School. "You have good reason to be proud of these two projects so far as their buildings are concerned," Mother Gerald wrote. "They are yours and the credit is due you but they are your interest also and you are to beg God to send students so that His work may be done in the hearts of His children in this Western World."

The College opened on September 16, 1940, with forty-four students and a faculty of eleven sisters, two lay people and a priest.

Health Care

Not long after the dedication of Barry College on February 4, 1941, the Adrian Dominican Sisters officially embarked on a completely new ministry endeavor. They agreed to take over the operation of a hospital in Santa Cruz, California.

The seeds of this new direction for the Congregation[15] were planted in December 1940 when Mother Gerald contacted the

Bishop of the Diocese of Monterey-Fresno, Philip Scher. Two letters exist dated December 18, 1940, from her to the Bishop. It has been impossible to determine, other than speculatively, which one of the two went to him. They each contain similar information, so it cannot be that both were sent. Each letter apologizes for Mother Gerald's not being able to keep a scheduled appointment with him while she was visiting the Congregation's missions in Arizona and New Mexico, with one explaining that she had had the flu and the other simply referring to "unexpected circumstances." Both also offer sisters to staff a school in his diocese.

Sisters Hospital Photo Credit: Dignity Health

One of the letters is relatively short and to the point, stating that "a good friend of mine," Mother Catherine of the Dominican Sisters of Grand Rapids, Michigan,[16] had suggested that Mother Gerald communicate with him "in regard to the possibility of obtaining a school in California."

"I have many demands on the Community but I would like a house on the Pacific and I think I could spare four or five Sisters for a school next year," this letter continues. "I understand, of course, that you might not have any such opening, but I am simply offering our services if you would care to avail yourself of them."

The other letter in the file is lengthier and contains a rather humorous reference to the sisters' capacities.

> *Sister Marie Catherine of Nazareth, Albuquerque suggested that you had likely a need for Sisters, Your Excellency, and it is through Sister's recommendation that I wish to offer the services of our Community if such should be your desire and need. On our part, there is the hope of doing apostolic work for the strengthening of the faith among your people, but there would also be a healthful reward and a part of the "hundredfold on this earth" to have a house near the ocean. I confess that I would like the Pacific Coast for such good reasons; but I boast in the same breath that our Sisters are not the kind that sink should you see fit to put us in a school near the mud puddles. We shall be entirely at your disposal. In the event that you need us, I shall be glad to reserve Sisters for next fall, if you let me know on time.*

Whichever of these letters made it to Bishop Scher, Mother Gerald certainly had no way of knowing the response her offer would generate.

The Bishop replied on December 31, saying that her "kind and generous offer . . . came as a pleasant surprise," but that at the present time it did not appear there were any openings for a school. He added, however, that he would check with the mother superior of the congregation serving at a school in Taft, a city some distance south of Fresno. She had planned some years earlier to remove her sisters but had not done so because no other teachers were available to take over.

This letter likely would not have reached Adrian until after a very surprising telegram from the Bishop arrived on January 2, 1941.

> *FULLY EQUIPPED FIFTY BED HOSPITAL AT SANTACRUZ [sic] VALUE EIGHTY THOUSAND AVAILABLE TO NUNS WHO WILL ACCEPT LEAN [sic] OF TWENTY FOUR THOUSAND DOLLARS NO CASH PAYMENT OR OTHER OBLIGATION ARE YOU INTERESTED WIRE RESPONSE VIA POSTAL TELEGRAPH.*

Mother Gerald wired Bishop Scher back that same day to decline, saying "we are not at all equipped to take hospital work at present." But just two days later, she had had second thoughts, and wrote him a letter "to give you a fuller picture of our situation."

She informed him that hospital work was outside the scope of the Congregation's mission at that time and that it only had two registered nurses, although a number of others had experience as practical nurses. But she asked for more data on the hospital and admitted that she had often thought of branching out into hospital work.

It was obvious that her interest was piqued. She reflected that the pressure for sisters in the schools was unrelenting but that a number of sisters were completing their college studies and would offer some relief. While she still preferred to staff a school, she thought that with two registered nurses and several practical nurses the Congregation might be able to undertake the project the following year.

She concluded the letter by asking him to write "very frankly" to her about the situation. "It may well be that it would be unwise for us to undertake hospital work at all until we have a larger number of nurses trained, and I should be glad to take your advice in the matter."

A reply came to her via telegram on January 14 from the Chancellor of the diocese, Monsignor James Culleton, informing her that the price of the hospital had been reduced to $16,000 with no cash necessary. It had been closed by the mortgagor, he wrote, and had no nursing school. And, the telegram continued, occupation was necessary within two months.

Mother Gerald's reply was swift: "I am inclined to take up proposition," she wired Culleton on January 15. "Must present to Council meeting Saturday after which likely two Sisters will be appointed to see property."

While the Council did indeed decide to investigate the matter further, the inspection was to be delayed until after the Barry College dedication on February 4. When the Congregation informed Monsignor Culleton of the necessary delay, saying that no one from the Council could get to Santa Cruz before February 15, the Chancellor replied that he had to give the mortgage holder an answer on January 27.

When this letter arrived at the Motherhouse on January 24, Sister Benedicta Marie Ledwidge passed on the information by telegram to Mother Gerald, who was on her way to Barry. "We will take hospital provided we are satisfied it is a good proposition," was Mother Gerald's reply to the Monsignor.

For his part, Monsignor Culleton asked the Sisters of Mercy, a group of hospital sisters from Burlingame, California, to look over the facility and give their opinion of what the diocese and the Adrian Dominican Sisters would face if they took on this endeavor. Mercy Sister Mary Paschal made the trip with another sister and the chief engineer of St. Mary's Hospital, the Mercy Sisters' hospital in San Francisco, and the result was fairly pessimistic.

Their report noted the hospital's poor construction, the lack of soundproofing, no basement, absence of a water circulating pump to ensure a good supply of hot water, and generally obsolete equipment. The trio had seen only five modern beds. They estimated that fifteen thousand dollars would be needed for initial repairs and wondered why a city the size of Santa Cruz would need the facility at all when there was already another hospital there.

The Monsignor forwarded the letter to Monsignor John Galvin of Holy Cross Church in Santa Cruz, the person who had first brought the hospital's availability to Monsignor Culleton's attention and who helped with the proceedings that followed. The Mercy Sisters' report, Culleton wrote, "is not very encouraging on the face of it. However, the Sisters of Mercy conduct hospitals of a type which we cannot very well hope to possess in this diocese. All their hospitals are built according to Class 'A' specifications. We have to contend [sic] ourselves with about Class 'C.' I still think the proposition is good and that the Sisters from the East will take it."[17]

In mid-February, Mother Gerald herself, along with one of the General Councilors, Sister Thomasine McDonnell, headed to Santa Cruz to inspect the hospital, which was called Hanly Hospital.[18] On February 26, she wrote to the Congregation: "We saw it and we were not frightened, so we promised to take over this work, and very soon, when the title is cleared, a few Sisters will be sent there to Santa Cruz to supervise some repairs and remodeling."

Later on in the same letter came these words.

> *I believe the prospects are good in spite of the fact that we have not an army of nurses ready to take over the operation of it. With your prayers and interest and enthusiasm I know it will be a success as is every other work you take up. Let us look to the good we can do and help one another in this project to do it as we do in all others. There will be many souls we can help to die a happy death and there will be others we may help to recover and to go out into life seeing the goodness of God and striving to make Him known and loved.*

On March 4, 1941, Bishop Scher wrote Mother Gerald that he expected to have a clear title within about a month. By June 5, however, no further word had come to the Congregation. This led her to write, with her typical dry wit, to Monsignor Culleton.

> *Since I have had no word in regard to the property in Santa Cruz, I am wondering if some wanton wind may have toppled*

the hospital into the sea, or if the Federal Government has taken it over in the cause of National Defense. Truth to tell, I should not be too disconsolate if this were the case, for as I look into the immediate future, I am appalled by the demands made on the Community, and I need a new kind of multiplication table that could be applied to the Sisters.

It turned out, the Monsignor replied, that clearing the title had required some untangling. While he expected that the transfer would be complete shortly, he suggested that Mother Gerald send him a separate letter informing him that the Congregation needed everything to be completed by July 15. "I understand your position but both the Bishop and the people of Santa Cruz are anxious to have you," he continued. "I am sure you will be happy and successful at Santa Cruz and that from this point you will be able to spread out in California as quickly as the number of nuns permits."[19] He also instructed her to avoid mentioning in this letter that he had written to her.

Mother Gerald did as he wished. On June 14, 1941, she wrote to him,

The time when I must appoint the Sisters for the coming year is fast approaching so, if the property cannot be handed over to the Community by July 15, 1941, free of all legal entanglements, we must withdraw all offers to purchase the place.

Will you kindly notify the owners that the above mentioned date is the dead line and that, if the transaction is not completed by that time, the negotiations must be called off?

Over the next month, all the legal issues were settled. On July 16, Monsignor Culleton wired Mother Gerald that the hospital title had been transferred the previous day and that the sisters could take possession at any time.

Sisters Ann Patrick Shields, who was to be the superior; Rose Dominic LeBlanc; and Cyril Therese Quinlan, along with Virginia Duggan, a postulant who was a registered nurse, left Chicago for Santa Cruz on August 5 to get the hospital ready for re-opening. They found a daunting challenge when they arrived on August 9. In a commentary on the experience, Virginia (who became Sister Georganne at her religious reception)[20] later said, "Everywhere I looked increased my panic. Having come from one of Chicago's most modern and beautiful hospitals [Little Company of Mary Hospital] made it difficult to even imagine how this cottage-like building would ever become functional as a hospital."[21]

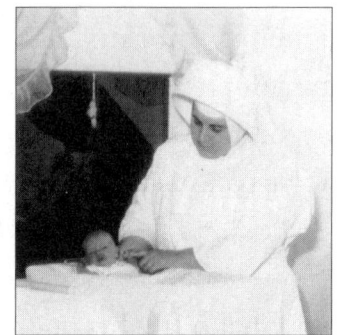

Sister Georganne Duggan

The previous occupants had left the place in disarray. "It looked as though someone had rung a bell and they had all dropped everything and rushed out," Virginia said.[22] But when Mother Gerald arrived on September 2, the sisters had completely turned things around. According to the hospital's 1941-1942 annals, "At first the task seemed impossible, but in due time, scattered linens were sorted, rusty and stained instruments were made to look new, mattresses were overhauled, and new drapes and curtains were made for the windows."

Once Mother Gerald arrived, which the annals note "added sparks to the machinery already in motion," workmen began making repairs, painting the exterior, and installing a new roof on the building.

She brought with her three companions, one of whom, Sister Maura Padraig McGeever, stayed on to join the hospital staff as the assistant dietitian. A sixth member of the Congregation, Sister Marie Augustine Seissiger, arrived on September 13. A registered nurse by training, she had stayed behind in Chicago to spend time observing in various hospitals and to renew her license, since she had not been working in nursing until Mother Gerald summoned her to go to Santa Cruz.

What Mother Gerald later wrote to the Congregation, on October 6, 1941, about the events surrounding the dedication and opening of what became known as Sisters Hospital has already been quoted in part in Chapter One of this book. The letter, however, bears further quoting here.

> *On my arrival there I felt that a great transformation had taken place since I viewed the remains of lay management last February when we promised to take it over. 'Tis a great thing to have the living Community at hand. In this case it treated us to enthusiasm, zeal and the highest type of ardor for the honor and glory of God and respect for our ideals. Every place seemed in order; cleanliness met the eye and hope rose to great heights. . . .*

> *Surely it was the most inviting little hospital I ever visited.*
>
> *. . . it was decided that the dedication would be September fourteenth, the feast of the Holy Cross, and, naturally, I was expected to remain for the first big event; and the hospital was to open for business the next day.*

But that timetable for opening was pushed up.

> *. . . soon after the dinner on the evening of the dedication, I discovered, on taking a walk from the room where the Bishop was holding court, that we had visitors in the office and, on inquiring, I was met with the statement that they were our first patients. . . . The two leading doctors of the city had been vying with one another, it seems, as to who would have the first patients registered with us. One of these doctors is a Protestant and a call from the dinner table almost placed him as our first patron until his opponent, a Catholic doctor, must have heard some whispers and rushed to bring in his two immediately.*
>
> *. . . I need not tell you that the Sisters are most enthusiastic and, I am sure, between the nursing and serving of meals and attending switchboard and typewriter and all the other odds and ends, they have little time for dreaming, but they have made reality of what seemed impossibility. God bless them one and all. They are Sisters Ann Patrick, Rose Dominic, Cyril Therese, Marie Augustine, Maura Padrig [sic], and Virginia Duggan, postulant, without whom I should never have been able to shine the many articles of silver found among the treasures left us.*

By 1942, more work was being done to train sisters as nurses. After Mother Gerald made her annual appointments of where sisters were going for summer placement, she wrote on May 8, "Some of you are appointed to a practical nursing course at Providence Hospital, Detroit, not with the idea that you are immediately to do hospital work but that we have some Sisters getting ready to be of use if needed. The Community may be called upon and the Community must be ready."

Within just a few short years, the call indeed came. By 1946, sisters were working in nursing at Providence Hospital which, Mother Gerald reminded those assigned there, was "a big opportunity . . . to draw people closer to God."[23] But, the far bigger mission of operating yet another hospital, this one in Nevada, was still to come.

Sister Marie Augustine Seissiger, postulant Virginia Duggan, Sister Cyril Therese Quinlan, Mother Gerald, Bishop Philip Scher, Sisters Rose Dominic LeBlanc, Ann Patrick Shields, and Maura Padraig McGeever, at the dedication of Sisters Hospital.

A New Social Service Ministry

On January 26, 1942, the Congregation embarked on a type of social service work that came with a twist. It began operation of Casa

Francesca in Miami Beach, a residence for women that charged five dollars a week at the time.

Casa Francesca was the idea of Sister Mary Henrice Binder, a social worker at St. Patrick Parish in Miami Beach, where Mother Gerald's brother Monsignor William Barry was the pastor. Sister Mary Henrice and the Monsignor saw the need for a home for young women of all faiths who had come to that area looking for work. Sister Henrice and Sister Rose Eileen Ferguson, who arrived the next year, operated the home for many years.

The facility had everything from maid service, a laundry room, and a barbeque pit to a full schedule of activities for the residents, including parties, dances, and speakers on topics ranging from Catholic religious practices to "Wartime Marriages." But it was far more than just a spot for young women to live and socialize. The sisters helped the young women get jobs, gave them money for food or to return home when needed, and acted as counselors.

Over the years, young women ended up at Casa Francesca with all manner of issues, typified by a letter dated March 11, 1968, by

Casa Francesca and its interior.

Sister Rosaleen Marvin, the superior at that time. Writing to Mother Gerald's successor, Mother Genevieve Weber, Sister Rosaleen provided a sampling of recent incidents that "hardly come under 'running a hotel.'"

The cases she detailed included those of a girl "who claimed her clothes had been stolen in New York and that she rode to Miami Beach in a car with a man she met in New York"; one that involved the police phoning Sister Rosaleen at 4 a.m. and shortly thereafter bringing to her a young woman who "was a mess" and "undoubtedly mentally disturbed," whom the sisters were able to put on a bus for home; two girls who had given blood to get money for food; and two who had come to Miami Beach with their boyfriends, with both young men ending up in jail.

The Congregation ran Casa Francesca until July 1, 1969, when the sisters withdrew. Another community of sisters operated it until 1986, when the facility closed.

Marking the Golden Jubilee

The Feast of the Holy Rosary on October 7, 1942, was a grand day: the celebration of the Congregation's fiftieth anniversary.[24]

It was quite the event by any measure. Hundreds of clergy and sisters from many congregations arrived in Adrian for the festivities. Detroit's Archbishop, Edward Mooney, celebrated a High Mass, with the sermon preached by Bishop Edward Hoban of Rockford, Illinois.

After dinner, a pageant was presented in Walsh Hall at Siena Heights College depicting the Order's history from the time of its founding by St. Dominic seven centuries earlier.

Mother Gerald recounted the day in her general letter of November 26, 1942, in words that, even coming as they did seven weeks after the celebration, clearly reflected her profound happiness about the day.

> *The jubilee was all that could express golden beauty and glory and happiness and enthusiasm. The galaxy of color, the procession, the singing during the procession, the order, the magnitude, cannot be described by my weakness and all I can say is that my eyes and ears and heart rejoiced in the Lord. I rejoiced because the day was so beautiful, because so many distinguished people came to do honor to our wonderful community. I rejoiced more especially because every sister of our community here had the smile of heaven on her face as a greeting to those who honored us. I rejoiced at the very many Masses offered on our grounds here—fifteen altars being made available. I rejoiced at the sermon—a classic—preached by our beloved Bishop Hoban whose voice rang out with the sincerity and devotion that we all know were in his heart. I rejoiced with a fervent joy at the Pontifical Mass and the singing of the sisters. It was all so magnificent that we were lifted out of ourselves.*
>
> *Those who laid the foundations of our community were surely present in spirit, and those who were privileged to be*

here physically reflected joy all around them. . . .

You know that we had the honor to have with us on that day two archbishops, five bishops, fifteen monsignori, about two hundred sixty of the clergy, which included many Dominicans, Franciscans, Jesuits, Vincentians, Benedictines, Augustinians, Redemptorists, Passionists, Precious Blood Fathers. We had representatives from eight different groups of Dominican Sisters as well as from the Immaculate Heart Sisters, Sisters of St. Joseph, Mercy Sisters, Franciscan Sisters, Felicians, Ursulines, Sisters of Charity of Cincinnati, Sisters of Charity of St. Vincent de Paul, and others, and some of these sisters came from afar—New York, Florida, Columbus, Cleveland, Sinsinawa, etc.

Also to mark the jubilee, the Congregation published a book of poems that had been written over time by several of the sisters. The contributors included Mother Gerald, who in the book is simply Sister Mary Gerald. The book was titled—after a line in her included poem—*On the Strings of Time*. Sister Mary Philip Ryan wrote in the foreword that the book

. . . is a volume of verse playing on the 'strings of time,' a volume of fifty poems gathered for the Fiftieth Year of our Community's life.

These are poems that not only play on the strings of time; they are the strings. Some of them are the mystic strings that

To Fields Near and Far

bind a Sister's soul to God, the threads of her contemplation caught in the clouds.

Others are the lyric strings of the rushing wind that unloose themselves and wait for neither harp nor lute as the Sister hurries along in the way of her vocation.

All are ancestral strings, the cords of Christian heritage, the ends of which have been gathered up in this little volume and given to Saint Dominic to hold for us in Heaven.

The Preparatory School

In June 1943, the Congregation started a new venture designed to attract more potential members by providing them with both an academic program and formation training—the preparatory school.

Preparatory school students, 1946.

Girls, who needed to be recommended by their teachers and parish priests, came in the summer after their eighth-grade year to begin what was a two and a half year process. The goal was to give them all the education found in a traditional high school program in just those two and a half years. Ideally, of course, they would enter the Congregation upon graduation.

Sister Corinne O'Connor

Sister Corinne O'Connor was the first "prep" mistress, serving in that capacity from 1943 to 1953 when Sister Jean Patricia McGowan succeeded her. An account of those early days written by one of the school's first "alumnae," Carole Dawson Webber, which is contained in the Congregation archives, remembers Sister Corinne as

> . . . a demanding taskmaster and disciplinarian but a loving and gentle teacher.
>
> I can only say that she has been the most influential person in my life and strange as it may sound she has taught me most about being a mother. Sister harassed us with proverbs and sayings, much like my own mother, but I have never forgotten them (I heard them so often) and I badger my own children with them, knowing they in turn will pass them on.

The accelerated academics began each summer in June at Innisfail, the Congregation's retreat on Lake Allen in the Irish Hills near Adrian. Girls spent summers there because the accommodations at the Motherhouse were in use during those months by sisters attending Siena Heights College.

In the course of just their first summer, the preps' curriculum encompassed everything that a traditional high school student would study in an entire freshman

Innisfail

year. It made for a very rigorous schedule. The girls were in classes all morning and most of the afternoon as well. And "we had classes anywhere you could imagine," said Sister Rose Celeste O'Connell, who came to the school in June 1953. She was part of a group of fourteen girls, seven of whom were new and seven of whom were in their second year.

Webber wrote about her first summer at Innisfail, "No one ever had a nicer summer than any of us had that year. We learned much academically in a very intense, structured program but the real gain was in our relationship with the Sisters and each other—a definite closeness and maturity was developing in us all." After the class work was done for the day, the girls were able to spend time doing what any other youngsters would do at summer camp: swim, boat, hike, roast hot dogs, sing around the campfire, and much more.

Once the sisters who were in Adrian for the summer left in August, the preparatory students came to the Motherhouse, where they lived while taking classes at St. Joseph Academy. While Sister Rose Celeste was at the school, she and the other students lived on the top floor of Madden Hall in a common sleeping area with the bathroom and shower facilities at the end of the hall. Occasionally, they would sneak into the attic, where mattresses were stored, climb into the rafters, and jump onto the mattresses. "The whole building would shake," said Sister Rose Celeste, "and word would come up from Mother Gerald: 'What are those preps *doing*?'"

"We were always in some kind of trouble," she said, for offenses ranging from talking to the St. Joseph Academy students to—as she and some other preps once did—going into town where they spent all their money eating at a restaurant.

But there was not much time for true escapades, other than small matters such as the mattress-jumping, or the occasional nighttime sneaking into the bakery or out of the building down the fire escape. Days began at 5:30 a.m. and were as rigorous as they had been in the summertime. The girls had classes all day, followed by recreation time in the evenings, and it was lights out at 9 p.m. Furthermore, each student had a particular chore, or "obedience," to be tended regularly.

The preps wore uniforms consisting of blue dresses with Peter Pan collars and white cuffs, plus lisle stockings. "It made us look like department-store elevator operators," said Sister Rose Celeste. The girls were in the same classes as the Academy students, but the two groups were quite separate. "We couldn't talk to the Academy girls, and we couldn't hang out with the nuns, so we were neither fish nor fowl," she said.

But at the same time, "the nuns were great. They were our confidantes. You'd tell them your woes and they'd give you milk and cookies." She also thinks Mother Gerald had "a soft spot in her heart" for the preps.

The students were often called upon to perform for visiting clergy. "Mother Gerald thought it would be really lovely if we learned how to do the Irish jig," said Sister Rose Celeste. "That became the preps' claim to fame."

For her, the prep school was the perfect place. Her parents may have thought she would only last there for two weeks, but she found it to be a wonderful opportunity, with teachers who cared about the girls' education and made sure they learned.

"I never had a second thought in the world," she said. "For me, [the school] was exactly what it was supposed to be" in leading her to enter the Congregation.

Others, however, changed their minds, making the "return on investment" for the community considerably less than ideal. Out of those fourteen students who were in the program during Sister Rose Celeste's first year, only she and two others went on to become members of the Congregation. And, some who entered did not stay, including Carole Dawson Webber, who became an Adrian Dominican in 1946 and left just six years later.

As Webber put it in her reminiscence,

> *As I look back now, spiritually, it was exactly what I needed at that time in my life. Without it, I wonder what I would have done. . . . Academically, it was an accelerated program but as I see what my own children are accomplishing in four year high schools today, I cannot fault our program. It was definitely hard work but a solid background in a good basic liberal arts education.*
>
> *. . . I can only say this: many of us were probably too young*

to have entered the religious life when we did, too young to appreciate the serious commitment involved as evidenced by how many preps from the original number have remained Dominicans. Although many of us have gone in different directions, I am sure there is always a part of us that never forgets what it is all about. We were truly called and belonged there. It was the training ground for the next vocation. I have nothing but love, affection, and gratitude to the good Sisters of Adrian who gave their time and selves so that we could grow.

The preparatory school closed in 1956.

The *Liturgical Meditations*

On August 30, 1943, Mother Gerald included this note in a general letter: "I am very anxious to compile a set of meditations for each day of the year, written by our own sisters and emphasizing the Dominican Saints and Blesseds. There are many capable sisters who could help do this work.... Do not fear this work but simply contribute and God will inspire you." Later, on December 8, she sent each convent its assigned subject matter.

The resulting two-volume work, titled *Liturgical Meditations for the Entire Year*, was edited by Sisters Patrick Jerome (Mary) Mullins and Ellen Vincent McClain. Published by the B. Herder Book Company, St. Louis, Missouri, in 1949 and reprinted in 1961, it was widely used not only by the Adrian Dominicans, but by other congregations as well. Its reach even extended overseas, according to a note sent to a vacationing Mother Gerald by Sister Benedicta Marie on August 21, 1953, that included this sentence: "I had a letter from Sister Margaret Helen [Lynch] yesterday and she asked me to tell you that she had forgotten to mention in your letter that she had found copies of our 'Liturgical Meditations' in a London Bookshop and that the clerk told her they sold quite well."

"I think the *Liturgical Meditations* are beautifully done," Mother Gerald wrote to the Congregation on May 8, 1949. ". . . I am grateful to you all and I hope to enjoy your gifts."

Overseas Missions

As far back as the mid-1930s, Mother Gerald had begun considering missions abroad. In a letter to the Congregation dated October 10, 1935, she wrote,

> *During the past two weeks I received requests for Sisters for China when Bishop O'Gara from China called here, and for Puerto Rico—Father Putters, O.P.,*[25] *called here also. I am sure that a large number of Sisters would be offering their services, and some day perhaps they will be called upon. Pray for what is best to be done on these requests.*[26]

Although plans did get under way for a middle school in Changsa, China, civil unrest broke out in the country and eventually both bishops involved in the planning, Bishop Cuthbert O'Gara and Bishop Hyacinthe Stanchi, the Vicar Apostolic of Changsa, were imprisoned.

Mother Gerald's Second Term: 1939-1945

As for Puerto Rico, a proposal from the Dominican friars in Holland to build a college for women became instead a program in which scholarships were offered to young women to study at Siena Heights College.[27]

Sisters Thomas Ann (Eileen) Burke, Mary Philip Ryan, and Rudolf (Dorothea) Beuttenmuller, ready to leave for Santo Domingo.

Then came the opportunity to work in the Dominican Republic. The groundwork for what became known as Colegio Santo Domingo was laid sometime in 1943, when Mother Gerald met with Archbishop Cicognani.

According to an account written by Sister Mary Philip Ryan,

> . . . when Pius XII pointed to the great need in Latin America,[28] the Adrian Congregation had only one question: 'Where should we go?' Mother Gerald and her Council decided to consult the Apostolic Delegate to the United States, who at that time was His Excellency, the Most Reverend Amleto Giovanni Cicognani. As the story is told, he brought out a globe of the world and suggested that she indicate the country of her choice. Asking the Lord to direct her, Mother Gerald placed her finger on Santo Domingo. . . . curiously enough, the Delegate had already received a request for American sisters from His Grace, the Most Reverend Richard Pittini, Archbishop of Santo Domingo.

The story about the globe may be more legend than fact. But it is true that Mother Gerald herself received a letter forwarded to her, via the Delegate but sent by Archbishop Pittini, from Father Antonio Mendoza in Ciudad Trujillo (the present-day city of Santo Domingo). He offered the Congregation a school he had been running. She wrote back to Father Mendoza and to the Archbishop, who replied to tell her that this school had in the interim been taken over by some local sisters but suggesting that they build a school in the town of La Romana instead. Her brother, Monsignor William Barry, was then asked by the General Council to go to the Dominican Republic and investigate matters, and he reported back that the school should be built in Ciudad Trujillo, the capital city.

Colegio Santo Domingo.

A site was settled upon, and in November 1944, Mother Gerald, Sister Benedicta Marie Ledwidge, and Father Andrew McEntee, chaplain at Dominican High School in Detroit, went to the Dominican Republic themselves to inspect the property. It was Mother Gerald's first time in an airplane, which she later reported in a December 17, 1944, letter to the Congregation as being "very calm and smooth and not at all terrorizing," but still quite the experience. "Later on I felt

Mother Gerald's Second Term: 1939-1945

that we were really very far away and close to the stars and now and again I would look out to see what the heavens looked like, only to feel a great awe coming over me and I turned my eyes away from the scene they had quickly scanned."

Mother Gerald and Sisters Benedicta Marie Ledwidge, Magdalen Marie Weber, Angeline Steele, Bertha Homminga, and Margaret Helen Lynch, at the University of Santo Domingo in 1949.

They were hosted very graciously by the Archbishop during their visit. The little group toured the site of their new foundation and called upon the American ambassador, Ellis Briggs; the country's president, Rafael Trujillo; and its secretaries of State and Education. Of President Trujillo, Mother Gerald wrote in her December 17 letter, "He promised to do big things for the foundation and we left him convinced that he was the soldier and leader that he is reputed to be."[29]

"There is great work ahead and I know that you are all interested," the same letter continued.

> *You can do many little things to make homey the new foundation and we will be collecting the items that will show the unity of spirit that abides among us. The work to be launched is not the work of a few but of the whole Community; let us go forth in the name of God and in the name of Saint*

> *Dominic to bring new life to the land of his name and his fame. May the mountains ring with gladness at our coming and may the sea pour forth praise to the Lord.*[30]

As plans moved forward for the Colegio, in June 1945 the Congregation held its fifth General Chapter—and uncharted territory ensued.

Mother Gerald's Second Term: 1939-1945

1. Prior to this privilege being suspended, the sisters were permitted to visit home for one week every three years. These visits usually took place in late summer. Mother Gerald allowed the practice to resume in the summer of 1946.

2. General letter of November 26, 1942.

3. Over time, monetary donations also went to alleviate suffering in Europe caused by the war. In April 1948, Mother Gerald reported to the sisters that the funds sent to date totaled $11,127.61. Of that, $6,533.75 was received from various missions of the Congregation and from its houses, while $4,604.86 was taken from the general Community fund.

4. Generally, a Dominican tertiary is a secular Third Order Dominican. Tertiaries are not vowed members, as Dominican sisters are, and do not live together in the same type of religious community. However, they undergo their own form of religious training and upon making profession promise to live their everyday lives in the spirit of the Order. They are under the supervision of the Master of the Dominican Order, although indirectly as the Master appoints a priest to oversee them.

5. According to the Society's website, www.nahns.com, the Society, whose formal name is the Confraternity of the Most Holy Names of God and Jesus, "promotes reverence for the Sacred Names of God and Jesus Christ, obedience and loyalty to the Magisterium of the Catholic Church, and the personal sanctification and holiness of its members." The Society's apostolate includes a great number of "Works of Mercy" involving meeting people's physical and spiritual needs.

6. Letter from Archbishop John McNicholas to Father Raymond Meagher, July 3, 1927.

7. It turned out that parish visitation also laid some important groundwork for the Congregation. In 1968, the General Chapter of Renewal began looking toward new ways for the Congregation to engage in ministry. The parish visitation ministry had been an eye-opening experience for the sisters themselves as they listened to people's issues and became aware of the needs that existed in the wider world. When the renewal process led to the possibility of new ministries, the sisters already had a greater understanding of where they were most needed because of what they had seen in forty years of visitation work.

8   A middle school program was added in 1990. Dominican High School and Academy closed in 2005.

9   Includes information taken from *A Long Hot Day*, Sister Mary Philip Ryan's unpublished biography of the Bishop.

10 He later served as mayor of Miami Shores, in 1943-44.

11 Because of the amount of work he did on behalf of the new college, John Thompson is considered one of its founders, and is honored at Barry College each year on Founders Day along with Mother Gerald, Bishop Barry, and Monsignor Barry.

12 From the August 1, 1956, issue.

13 From the November 14, 1965, issue.

14 Years later, Mother Gerald called upon Sister Gonzaga's construction-supervising skills yet again. When it was time to build the new library and science facilities and Lumen Ecclesiae Chapel (now St. Dominic Chapel) at Siena Heights College, Sister Gonzaga oversaw the projects and was able to see most of the work to completion before her death in 1956.

15 Of course, since in its earliest days in Adrian the Congregation had operated a facility for the elderly and infirm, in a sense it was going back to its roots with this new effort.

16 This is a reference to Sister Catherine Clayton of the Dominican Sisters of Grand Rapids. According to that congregation's archivist, Sister Rose Marie Martin, Sister Catherine was an Irishwoman who joined the Dominicans in Portugal. Eventually, after many twists and turns in her life's journey that included being part of several different communities of women religious, she transferred to the Grand Rapids Dominicans. In the 1940s, she was administrator of Nazareth Sanitarium, the Grand Rapids congregation's hospital in Albuquerque, New Mexico. She apparently obtained the title "Mother" during her earlier time with the Kenosha, Wisconsin, Dominicans. It is unknown how she and Mother Gerald became friends.

17 Letter from Monsignor James Culleton to Monsignor John Galvin, February 7, 1941.

18 There are discrepancies between various sources as to whether it was "Hanly" or "Hanley" Hospital. References dating from the time the hospital was in existence

indicate it was "Hanly."

19 Letter from Monsignor James Culleton to Mother Gerald, June 10, 1941.

20 Sister Georganne Duggan went on to administer Dominican Santa Cruz Hospital and later St. Rose of Lima Hospital in Henderson, Nevada.

21 Nadine Foley, ed., *Mother Mary Gerald Barry, OP: Ecclesial Woman of Vision and Daring* (Adrian: Adrian Dominican Sisters, 2000), 27.

22 Ibid.

23 General letter of May 5, 1946.

24 The fifty years dated from 1892, the year Mother Camilla Madden arrived in Adrian to serve as Provincial of the newly formed St. Joseph Province.

25 The bishop referenced here was Bishop Cuthbert O'Gara. It is more difficult to ascertain precisely who Father Putters was. A reference on http://www.enciclopediapr.org titled "More than a Century of the Dominican Friars' Presence in Yauco (1904-2010)" mentions a parish priest named Alberto Putters, who in 1934 was inaugurating a new church in that area of Puerto Rico.

26 Over the years of Mother Gerald's tenure, the Congregation had an impact on any number of foreign missions even without actually sending sisters to them. She corresponded with many missionary priests and regularly included financial support in that correspondence. One such letter, sent September 13, 1957, to Father Louis Scheerer, a Dominican priest missioned to Pakistan, is typical in its sentiment: "Here at home we are trying to do our part to save Christian civilization through the means at our disposal and the enclosed check is a means of sharing those means."

27 Later, however, in 1946, a school in Guayama, Puerto Rico, that was owned by the American Redemptorists and which had been staffed by Sisters of Charity from New Jersey became available when those sisters were needed back in the United States. It was the first of two schools in Puerto Rico that the Congregation took over from the Sisters of Charity; additionally, sisters went to work in other apostolates there including teaching on the university level. The Puerto Rico story continues in the next chapter.

28 It is unknown to what exactly this phrase refers. Pope Pius XII did indeed call for missionaries to go to Latin America in his encyclical *Fidei Donum*, but that was not until 1957.

To Fields Near and Far

[29] The dictatorial way in which Rafael Trujillo ruled the country led to his 1961 assassination. Since he had gone after the Church itself, it is interesting to consider that perhaps Mother Gerald and her companions sensed, even at that early stage, the need to be on his good side.

[30] On September 13, 1945, Sisters Mary Philip Ryan, Thomas Ann (Eileen) Burke, and Rudolf (Dorothea) Beuttenmuller arrived in Ciudad Trujillo to supervise construction of the Colegio. It opened on October 17, 1946, and was dedicated on February 12, 1947.

Chapter Four
Mother Gerald's Third Term: 1945-1951

Postulation

The General Chapter of 1945 presented the Congregation with a new situation: what to do when the delegates re-elected Mother Gerald to a third term. According to the Constitution then in effect, a Mother General could be elected to two six-year terms. If she received at least two-thirds of all the delegates' votes for a third term, the resulting "postulation," as such a process was known, had to be appealed to Rome.

Given that Mother Gerald received 126 out of the 144 votes cast for prioress, the postulation rule was in effect. According to the minutes,

> *His Excellency [Bishop Stephen Woznicki, the auxiliary bishop of Detroit, who was presiding] read the total for each candidate. He then quoted the Constitutions of the Community which state that the Prioress General may have only two terms of office. He then explained that the present situation was regarded by the Church as 'postulation'. This meant that the Community must have recourse to the Holy See inasmuch as more than two-thirds of the delegates voted for Mother Mary Gerald. Due to existing war conditions, however, the request for permission to extend Mother Mary Gerald's period of office for another six years, would have to be addressed to the Apostolic*

> *Delegate. Until such permission would be received, the Vicaress General, or first assistant, would preside over the Community. The Bishop announced that he would immediately wire the Apostolic Delegate for permission.*

The election for Vicaress General was then held immediately, and Sister Benedicta Marie Ledwidge, who had served in that capacity for Mother Gerald's prior two terms, was re-elected handily. But her leadership of the Congregation was to be short-lived. That same day, June 25, during the Chapter proceedings, a telegram arrived from the Apostolic Delegate, Archbishop Cicognani. It read: "GLADLY CONFIRM YOUR POSTULATION. ALL SEND PROMISED PRAYERS."[1]

That evening, at Holy Rosary Chapel in the presence of the community, Monsignor James Cahalan, presider at the Masses held during the Chapter, read this telegram sent by Archbishop Cicognani to Sister Benedicta Marie: "POSTULATION MOTHER GERALD HEREBY CONFIRMED BY APOSTOLIC FACULTY. RESCRIPT WILL FOLLOW."

It was the first of three times Mother Gerald's election was postulated.

Pioneers in Phonetics

Mother Gerald thought it important that the children in the Congregation's schools learn to read well, especially aloud. Her September 29, 1939, general letter is an example of how much she emphasized reading.

> *I insist on oral reading and good reading. Be sure you work on this. . . . I am very much afraid that you have forgotten your duty to the children and allowed silent reading to take the place of oral reading. . . . You must use READERS! Geography and History will not take the place of Readers. . . . Silent reading was never meant to take the place of oral reading. Cultivate in your children a taste for reading, and provide means for them as far as possible. You can offer a prize in my name, to be given at Thanksgiving to the best reader in each class. . . . Take a snapshot of each child who wins and send it to me, and I will write an individual letter to each of the winners.*

> *. . . P.S. In my drive for oral reading, I do not mean to neglect silent reading. Rather, I want you to encourage a taste for reading in the child's private life, which will have to come through silent reading.*

A reminiscence by Sister Mary Schmagner contained in the Congregation's Historical Area[2] shows that Mother Gerald was as good as her word about writing to the winning students. As a young schoolgirl, Sister Mary had received a letter from Mother Gerald.

> *It was a real thrill for me to receive this letter from Mother Gerald—and a vivid memory. (She had visited St. Philip Neri, so her image was "awesome" to me.) I was in fourth grade.*
>
> *Dear Mary:*

I think it is great that you have won the reading race in your room, and I know that your parents and teacher are proud of you with me.

It is a wonderful thing to be a good reader, but you know there is no use in being only a good reader. You must be a good child. And you must be a good pupil in all your other studies. Your reading must teach you how to know and love and serve God with your whole heart. It must teach you how to help at home and in school, and it must teach you fair play with the other boys and girls.

If it does all this, then you will win the real contest in life, and you know that is Heaven. God bless you, and may He bless your reading all your life.

Affectionately,

MOTHER M. GERALD, OP

Mother Gerald's emphasis on reading skills led to a groundbreaking effort by two Adrian Dominicans, Sisters Leonita Noetzel and Rose Norine Gauthier. The pair were supervisors of the schools staffed by members of the Congregation in Michigan, Ohio, New York, South Carolina, and Georgia. In 1945, they were commissioned by Mother Gerald for a special task. It changed the course

Sisters Leonita Noetzel (left) and Rose Norine Gauthier.

of reading instruction not only in the Congregation's schools but in other parochial, and even some public, schools as well.

During her visitations to schools at which Adrian Dominican Sisters were teaching, Mother Gerald had become aware that many of the children were having trouble reading. Concerned, she asked the two sisters to develop a better approach to teaching reading than the traditional method. The result was a phonetic method that proved to be so successful that, according to Sister Leonita's biography, it surprised even the two sisters themselves. It was used for about forty years, in both parochial and public schools, and it came a full decade before the 1955 publication of *Why Johnny Can't Read*, Rudolph Flesch's book discussing why the "look-say" method was not working and advocating "a return to the old phonetic method still used in Europe."[3]

Mother Gerald's concern about the topic extended to older children as well. She wrote in a September 10, 1947, general letter that she wanted the sisters teaching in the upper grades to focus on proper reading. "I notice a great lack of correct pronunciation, interpretation, and clarity in the young sisters coming to the community," the letter read. "They are the victims of poor teaching in this subject. Raise reading to its proper place."

A New Community

At the end of December 1945, Mother Gerald received a letter from John McNicholas, the Archbishop of Cincinnati, asking for sisters to help with a new venture. McNicholas had been contacted by Father Howard Bishop, the founder of the Home Missioners of America. Father Bishop had asked for some sisters to assist him in forming a community of sisters who would work in rural areas, paralleling what his priests and brothers were doing. The Archbishop had had an extraordinarily positive experience with the work the Adrian Dominican Sisters had done in creating the parish visitation ministry in Cincinnati, so he asked if they would assist in this formation process.

In her reply on December 31, 1945, Mother Gerald wrote that the letter from the Archbishop "held a little surprise for me." She could not turn down such an opportunity, she said, "if there is the least possibility of my being able to say 'yes.'

"It will give me joy, therefore, to set aside a couple of sisters for this very important work, and I hope they will help lay the foundations of a great missionary society," she continued. She then added something

Sister Anne O'Connor and the Glenmary Sisters.

that seems to reflect her own early years in Ireland: "I agree heartily with you in regard to the necessity of turning our attention to the rural areas where people have more time to think of God, to admire the works of His hand, and to rear their families in simple faith and love. 'Man made the cities but God made the country.'"

By mid-August 1946, Sisters Kevin Campbell and Immaculata Ebbitt were at the eighty-seven-acre farm[4] near Glendale, Ohio, that served as the headquarters for the new endeavor. "Greetings and love from THE CHICKEN AND COW FARM," wrote Sister Kevin in an August 22, 1946, letter to Mother Gerald. At the suggestion of the Archbishop, the farm was known as "Glenmary," and eventually the new community took on the name Glenmary Sisters.

Sister Kevin's correspondence with Mother Gerald over the next several years recounted all the news of what was going on at the farm and often expressed her dismay with Father Bishop. His vision of what he wanted his new group of sisters to do clearly did not correspond with what Sister Kevin thought she was there to teach them. Nor did his idea of what he expected them to become. Would they be Dominican, or something else entirely?

Mother Gerald's correspondence was full of advice, encouragement, and news from Adrian. Taken as a whole, both women's very affectionate letters create a descriptive and often witty chronology of what was happening both with the Glenmary effort and around the Congregation.

Sister Kevin Campbell

Sister Immaculata, whose failing health Sister Kevin related with great concern to Mother Gerald on several occasions, died of a heart attack in April 1947. Sister Kevin continued the work by herself, making a truly heroic effort with the Glenmarians and in the process suffering a heart attack herself in April 1949.

She stayed on until August 1950, when Mother Gerald, deeply aware of the ever-growing challenge Father Bishop posed, wrote to him that she had appointed Sister Kevin to a faculty position at Siena Heights College.

Upon hearing the news, Sister Mary Dorothy of the Glenmarians wrote to Mother Gerald, "We deeply appreciate [Sister Kevin's] motherly guidance and her splendid example of generous self-sacrifice. Nothing we can say or do can possibly repay even in a small measure her efforts in our behalf. God grant that our lives will reflect the spirit of Christ which she has tried to instill in our little Community." Wrote Glenmary Sister Mary Catherine to Sister Kevin: "Your service to our community and to each of us individually, can be neither measured nor repaid."

Father Bishop requested that Mother Gerald appoint someone to take Sister Kevin's place. Archbishop McNicholas had died earlier that year, but the priest's request was seconded by the auxiliary bishop of Cincinnati, George Rehring, when he wrote to Mother Gerald on August 20, 1950: ". . . I do not think they [the Glenmary Sisters] are ready to launch out on their own; they still need Sister Kevin or some other equally capable Sister."

Mother Gerald ultimately assigned Sister John Joseph (Anne) O'Connor, who was in charge of parish visitation for the Archdiocese of Cincinnati, to take Sister Kevin's place. She stayed until August of 1955, after the Glenmary Sisters had held their first General Chapter and elected their own leadership.

Another Overseas Mission

With the Congregation's first overseas venture well under way in the Dominican Republic by 1946, Mother Gerald quickly accepted the challenge of a mission in another Caribbean locale when the opportunity arose.

On March 18 of that year, she received a letter from Reverend Joseph Murphy, Vice Provincial of the Redemptorist Fathers. Father Murphy informed her that the Sisters of Charity, who were staffing two schools in Guayama, Puerto Rico (in the Diocese of Ponce), and St. Thomas, Virgin Islands (which at the time was part of the Diocese of San Juan, Puerto Rico), needed to withdraw because of a sister shortage at home in New Jersey. Murphy asked her to consider taking over one or both of the schools. It was a request that was followed by a March 26 letter from Bishop James Davis of San Juan, inviting the sisters to the school in St. Thomas. On May 1, 1946, Mother Gerald wrote to the two men and to Mother Mary Benita, the Mother General of the Sisters of Charity, to inform them that the Congregation would take over St. Anthony School in Guayama.

Sister Colette Martin was the superior of the group of sisters who arrived in Guayama in August. She later wrote that, when she had seen "Puerto Rico" on her appointment card, she had gone to Mother Gerald and asked if they were going into the jungle and what to expect. With her were Sisters Mary Hyacinth Adelson, Mary Nicholas Fojtik, Regina Marie Lalonde, Ann Felice Flowers, Petra Baxter, Donald Marie Flores, Mary Noel Kelley, and Rose Clare Britz.

They received a warm welcome and found their services much in demand. Not only were they teachers in the school, but they also provided catechetical instruction. The latter took them into the *campos*, exposing them to the way of life there.

Meanwhile, Bishop Davis was still trying to get Adrian Dominicans for his diocese, the Diocese of San Juan. He wrote Mother Gerald again in December 1946 about having the sisters take over another school from which the Sisters of Charity were withdrawing. This one, Academia Sagrado Corazón, was in Santurce. She replied that they could not staff the school for the 1947-48 school year, as the Bishop had asked, but in a postscript added that the Congregation would be there in 1948. The ten sisters assigned to the school[5] arrived at the end of June and

Sister Mary Jean Walsh and first communicants in Guayama.

began teaching in September. Like their counterparts in Guayama, they also taught catechism to poor children.

As time went on, still more work was to be done in Puerto Rico. The Bishop of Ponce, James McManus, preparing to open a new Catholic university in Ponce, rather slyly asked Mother Gerald for faculty members.

> *Last year during a visit that I made to Adrian you gave me the following bit of advice in regard to a project that I had in mind regarding a new college or university: "Don't be timid. Start the university yourself. The Lord will help you."*
>
> *Your advice was good, but it has gotten me into trouble as I have not enough professors. Can you do anything about it besides giving advice—even good advice?*[6]

Mother Gerald sent two sisters, both of whom held PhD degrees: Sister Loyola Vath to teach Latin, history and sociology, and Sister Cyril Edwin Kinney to teach philosophy and English. The Bishop went on to make a series of additional requests for help, which were met by almost equal replies of "no" from Mother Gerald. Finally, however, two more sisters followed, Rose Concepta Loftus in 1949 and Aquiline Pety in 1951.

The presence of the sisters in Puerto Rico almost expanded to another college and even something more. In early 1951, Mother Gerald visited with Bishop Davis and spoke with him about her desire to open a college in San Juan. After her return home Davis sent her a letter, dated March 16, 1951, in which he said that her idea put him "truly at a loss for words."

At a meeting of the General Council on March 3, 1951, Sister Benedicta Marie read a letter sent by Mother Gerald on March 1 from San Juan. The letter informed the Council that a building in Santurce might be available that "could be well adapted for establishing a girls' college."[7]

The Council voted unanimously to purchase the property. But at its regular meeting of March 19, 1951, Mother Gerald informed the Councilors that the owner of the house was a doctor who, after she sent that March 1 letter, had told her that he had a one-year contract with the government and therefore was not interested in selling at that point. So, for the time being, the project was dropped.[8]

Over the next several years, however, work progressed on the Bishop's idea to have the sisters not only open a college, but staff a hospital as well. Neither project ultimately came to fruition.

St. Rose Dominican Hospital

The Congregation had had great success in Santa Cruz with Sisters Hospital, and more sisters were being trained as nurses or even entering the community with nursing training. Consequently, a May 20, 1946, letter from the Bishop of Reno, Nevada, Thomas Gorman, met with a very different response from the initial one Mother Gerald sent to Bishop Scher about the Santa Cruz hospital.

At the suggestion of Detroit's Archbishop, Cardinal Edward Mooney, Bishop Gorman offered the Adrian Dominican Sisters the opportunity to operate a hospital in "the mild desert climate" of Henderson, Nevada.

The hospital had been built and operated during World War II by the Defense Plant Corporation to serve the workers at Henderson's magnesium plant. It was named Basic Hospital because of its association with the plant, Basic Magnesium, Inc. Bishop Gorman wrote that the government now wanted to turn the facility over to a private entity, "preferably a community of sisters."

Rose de Lima Hospital. Photo Credit: Dignity Health

"The whole plant would be turned over to begin with at a nominal lease of one dollar per year, which would include free water and power," his letter continued. "The sisters would be expected to operate the hospital without [governmental] control and any profit from its operation would belong to them. What makes this proposition so attractive is the more than likely possibility of acquiring complete ownership within a reasonably short time."

Mother Gerald replied immediately that she was interested. In very short order, on May 30, 1946, the General Council voted to accept the proposal. It then fell to Father Peter Moran, pastor of the Church of

St. Peter the Apostle in Henderson, to do the work of dealing with the government and many of the other concerned parties. U.S. Senator Patrick McCarran of Nevada[9] helped the hospital become available to the sisters, and what Father Moran referred to in a July 23, 1946, letter to Mother Gerald as "government red tape" aside, everything came together relatively smoothly.

One potential problem required some special attention, however. As Father Moran wrote to Mother Gerald on October 1, "the present medical staff, consisting of four doctors, have been enjoying a lucrative income, not only from their practice but from a basic salary paid by the government. You can easily see that these men are reluctant to give up the benefits they have enjoyed."

The physicians would not be able to block the transfer in the long run, he continued, but he thought they might try to put up roadblocks in order to keep the status quo as long as possible. In fact, they had already made an unsuccessful effort to separate the medical clinic from the hospital in order to operate the clinic themselves.

Father Moran suggested that Mother Gerald write a letter to the head of the Clark County Medical Society asking for its support of the management transfer, and to invite the four doctors to remain. She carried out both tasks, and shortly thereafter the Medical Society unanimously endorsed the change. The doctors, and the dentist on the staff, responded with a group letter indicating that they wanted more details of the plan before giving a definitive answer. Two of the physicians, however, actually sent Mother Gerald separate letters telling her they planned to remain in the area. Other doctors contacted her to offer their services as well.

Eventually, things were settled and the transfer was accepted by the government on May 1, 1947. Under the terms of the final agreement, within a couple of years the government would give the Congregation the property outright in exchange for the establishment of a nursing school. If the school was not opened, five percent of the appraised value should be paid by the Congregation over time. "I don't want you to worry about this aspect of the matter at all, because we can get around it at a later date, and it is only a technicality anyway," Father Moran wrote to Mother Gerald the next day.

On May 16, Sisters Mary Carolyn Harrison, who was to be the superior and administrator, and Marie Daniel Lundy, a registered nurse, left for Henderson to begin the process of getting the facility ready.[10] Sister Carolyn, one of the two Adrian Dominicans who started the census-taking effort at St. Matthew Parish in Chicago, had long had an interest in hospital ministry. After graduating from high school, she had gone into nurses' training in Chicago, her hometown. Some thought she might join one of her sisters in the Daughters of Charity of St. Vincent de Paul as a nurse, but she chose the Adrian Dominican Sisters instead. Once she did so, any dreams she had of going into health care had to be put aside for teaching, which she did for the next eleven years.

As the plans for the hospital in Henderson unfolded, Mother Gerald sent Sister Carolyn to complete an internship in administration at

To Fields Near and Far

The Rose de Lima Campus of Dignity Health St. Rose Dominican Hospitals today.
PHOTO CREDIT: DIGNITY HEALTH

St. Mary Hospital in Milwaukee. She was there, preparing for her new role, when Mother Gerald summoned her to return to Adrian so that she could then travel to Nevada.[11]

An extensive set of letters between Sister Carolyn and Mother Gerald, housed in the Congregation archives, makes it clear that the new superior had her work cut out for her. Her correspondence details the difficulties she had with certain physicians and nurses who were not happy about the change in management. There were also issues with local politics regarding control of the hospital, a great number of financial problems, and the fact that the hospital had a rather "unsavory" reputation as far as care was concerned.

"Basic Hospital has been noted for its very poor nursing care and service," she wrote Mother Gerald in a June 11, 1947, letter. She went on to note that some of the nurses probably would not stay on because they had not previously been expected to work very hard. With sisters in charge, however, that situation would change, and quickly. In fact, Sister Carolyn continued, the expectation from others seemed to be that the sisters would change things overnight, "which perhaps we could do if we had enough Sisters."

This comment seems to have been a response to a previous letter from Mother Gerald in which she wrote that she did not know how many sisters she would send by June 27, the date scheduled for the official transition. "But even if I didn't send any, I am sure that you could take over anyway," that letter continued.

Mother Gerald did send Sisters Daniel Therese Smith; Marie Augustine Seissiger; Felicia Haidysz, who succeeded Sister Carolyn as administrator in 1953; Marie Angelita Wasco; and, for a short time until she left to take a school assignment, Marie Joyce Smith, who was Daniel Therese's sister. Together with Sister Carolyn, they put things together in very short order. Father Moran wrote to Mother Gerald on July 30, 1947,

> *. . . the initial process of organizing the institution is brighter than I had anticipated. Sister Carolyn and her staff, with a very laudible [sic] desire for perfection wanted it to be running normally in a week or two after they took over. But they have done magnificent work and now after one month's operation they have it well in hand. If the Sisters could have set it up the first day they moved in in the manner that it is now, the institution would be running economically from the start.*

A few weeks earlier, as the June 27 date for the official transfer drew near, the question of what to re-name the hospital needed to be settled. Mother Gerald proposed to Bishop Gorman that it be named Gorman Hospital, a suggestion that drew the following response on May 2, 1947:

> *I feel deeply appreciative that you would even think of such a thing, but somehow the name sounds strange to me and I don't think I would ever feel too happy about it. There might be some justification for the institution suffering the handicap of such a name had I done something to get the hospital, but you and Father Moran accomplished that. St. Gerald's or St. Peter's [for Mother Gerald or Father Moran] would seem to me more appropriate.*

The original staff of Rose de Lima Hospital with Father Peter Moran. Front row, left to right: Sisters Marie Joyce Smith, Marie Daniel Lundy, and Daniel Therese Smith. Back row, left to right: Sisters Marie Angelita Wasco, Carolyn Harrison, Felicia Haidysz, and Marie Augustine Seissiger.

He went on to make several other suggestions including St. Rose of Lima, a Dominican saint whose feast day fell on his birthday. The sisters thought that using this name was a spectacular idea, and decided that the new institution was to be called Rose de Lima Hospital. According to the history which the hospital prepared for its fiftieth birthday celebration in 1997, the "St." was originally left off the name deliberately so that people of all faiths would feel comfortable going there for medical care.[12]

Bishop Gorman was pleased with the choice. ". . . I appreciate very deeply the fact that you selected one of the names which I suggested for the new hospital," he wrote Mother Gerald in an undated letter which continued,

Mother Gerald and Bishop Gorman with a cake shaped like Rose de Lima Hospital.

> *St. Rose of Lima has always been a favorite saint of mine, I suppose mostly because that happens to be my birthday. I assure you that it will also be a great happiness for me to know that name has been selected by you for the hospital in the diocese of Reno. I shall always consider that it has been named for me, so that brings a great satisfaction to me.*

The subsequent history of Rose de Lima Hospital had its ups and downs as population shifts took place in the area and competing health care facilities made their appearance. But the hospital was fortunate to have on its board an influential woman who became a personal friend of the sisters as well as a guiding light for the hospital through turbulent times. Her name was Selma Bartlett.

Selma Bartlett came to Henderson in 1954 having earned a business degree at Hill Business School in Oklahoma City, Oklahoma. Her business acumen enabled her to rise in the banking business in Henderson and in the state of Nevada. She came to be regarded as instrumental in the tremendous growth of Henderson through her sixty-year career. Her association with Rose de Lima Hospital remained constant and supportive.

Expansion in Santa Cruz

The need to expand Sisters Hospital in Santa Cruz came quickly. By 1946, the hospital annals reported that the place was "filled to capacity at all times," that patients not requiring emergency care were being placed on waiting lists, and that the physicians were being asked to discharge "nearly well" patients to make room.

The dedication of Dominican Santa Cruz Hospital.

The situation was confirmed for Mother Gerald personally in November of that year, when she visited the hospital and met with several of the doctors. She took those concerns to the General Council meeting that November 26, and the Council initially voted to purchase a neighboring house and move it to the hospital property. The Councilors, however, later decided against this move, and were reluctant to assume the risk of building a new building, so any expansion was put on hold.

The hospital's annals of 1948-1949 indicate that various donors were coming forth to offer their property to the Congregation but that for one reason or another none of these offers ended up being suitable. Then, at the General Council meeting on March 5, 1949, Mother Gerald informed the Council of a new possibility. Dr. Anthony Allegrini, a physician in Santa Cruz, had told her that another hospital in the city, Santa Cruz Hospital, was for sale for "a sum between $80,000.00 and $100,000.00."[13] She went on to note to the Council that Sisters Hospital

Dignity Health Dominican Hospital today. PHOTO CREDIT: DIGNITY HEALTH

"could always be used as a convalescent home, for which there is great need."[14] The Councilors voted to make the purchase, which would involve buying out the shareholders.

As it turned out, not all of the shareholders, most of whom were doctors, liked the idea. The reason does not seem to be spelled out in any of the archival documents. A report published in the Santa Cruz *Sentinel* on July 11, 1949, however, describes the physicians as not objecting on religious grounds but feeling "that there should not be a hospital monopoly in the community."

Despite the opposition, the Congregation gradually purchased shares, and took control of the facility on July 25 although it took until December 1950 for the sisters to finally own all the shares. The hospital, renamed Dominican Santa Cruz Hospital, was dedicated on May 5, 1951. Initially, both facilities were operated by the same staff of sisters, but on July 31, 1953, the two were placed under separate administration, each with its own staff.[15]

Early Political Involvement

Mother Gerald often requested prayers from the sisters for one political situation or another. Over the years, her general letters asked them to pray for causes ranging from a case before the U.S. Supreme Court regarding the practice of allowing public schoolchildren to be released for religious instruction, to defeat for the Communist party in Italy in an upcoming election.

But the first apparent instance of taking an active political stance occurred in late 1946. It would be only a precursor to the Congregation's later commitment to issues of peace and justice.

In September of that year, the Archbishop of Zagreb, Aloysius Stepinac, was put on trial in Yugoslavia for alleged war crimes and collaboration with the enemy. The trial, which may or may not have been fair and balanced, led to the Archbishop's being convicted and sentenced to prison.

Mother Gerald's general letter to the Congregation on October 13, 1946, likened Stepinac's trial to that of Christ himself, with testimony coming from "the people of his own household" and featuring people cheering when the sentence was handed down. And, she said, the Congregation was protesting the Yugoslav government's actions.

> *In this mail we are sending a letter to the President of the United States asking intervention for the persecuted Shepherd and his flock in Yugoslavia. It can do no harm. I do not think we should sit in comfort and complacency and hear of the sufferings of our brethren in other less-favored climes without offering our sympathy and our protests. Our prayers will be pleasing to God Who knows well how the suffering need sympathy and help.*

She went on to write that "there have been countless nuns and priests and faithful whose lives have been taken because of their faith. Wars and their aftermath are always days of gluttony for Satan. He is very fat these days . . ."

To Fields Near and Far

On December 5, 1946, she reported in a general letter that they had received a reply from the State Department: "Assistant Secretary Patterson[16] said that a statement had been made to the press by Acting Secretary [Dean] Acheson, and he gave us a copy. The statement, however, was not a very strong or insistent one so we wrote again calling attention to the need of absolute assertion on their part."

A New Type of Work

As is well documented elsewhere in this volume, Mother Gerald held priests and bishops in very high esteem. Writing to the Congregation on May 19, 1940, she noted that she had just attended the first Mass celebrated by a new young priest, Father Henry Kenowski, brother of a deceased Adrian Dominican Sister, Agnes Michael Kenowski.

> *I was impressed anew by the greatness of God's goodness in raising the weak creatures of this realm to the dignity and the power of the priesthood. In spite of the weakness of persons they are made strong and great by being priests and we must recognize this fact always. Let us respect them; let us regard them as holy and in a place all their own. They are other Christs and their names and actions are not to be drawn into light or gossipy or critical conversations.*[17]

She also put action to her words by extending the hospitality of the Congregation to these men on innumerable occasions. But in the late

1940s, the community went one step further in the service it rendered to the clergy. At the request of Detroit Cardinal Edward Mooney, Mother Gerald provided a staff of sisters to do domestic work at the new St. John Provincial Seminary in Plymouth, Michigan. While this was not the sort of work she wanted for her sisters, a request from the Cardinal Archbishop in the diocese in which the Congregation was at that time located[18] could not be refused.

Exactly when the two first discussed this arrangement is unclear. It seems as though the Cardinal made the request on October 8, 1947, during a personal visit to Adrian, for a letter from Mother Gerald sent to him the next day refers to "our happiness that you asked us to do something." Clearly the Congregation was involved by mid-1948, as there is a letter in the files from the architect to Sister Benedicta Marie Ledwidge containing the plans for the new seminary's kitchen and asking her to review them "to make sure that we had not overlooked any piece of equipment." Sisters served at the seminary from its opening in August 1949 until 1988, when it closed.

Earlier in 1949, Mother Gerald had assigned two sisters to do domestic work for the Bishop of Des Moines, Iowa, Dominican Bishop Edward Daly, who had been a friend to the Congregation ever since becoming a part of the Apostolic Delegate's staff. During that time, he had lived in Washington, DC, and became acquainted with the sisters who were at the Adrian Dominican House of Studies located at The Catholic University of America. As the Delegate's canonist, he was often called upon by Mother Gerald to settle questions of canon law.

When he became the Bishop of Des Moines, he asked Mother Gerald if she could find him "a cook and a companion for her" for his residence there. "Just know that I am not fussy and the good ladies do not even have to speak English," he wrote on August 20, 1949.

Mother Gerald replied on August 25 to let him know that "two nice sisters, both of whom speak English—though perhaps not with an Oxford accent—" had departed Adrian for Des Moines the previous evening. They were Sisters Marie Catherine McDonald and Martha James Hoffman, with Sisters Jean Mildred Kirk and Marie Kevin Scanlon later succeeding them.

Bishop Edward Daly and Mother Gerald.

By all accounts, the Bishop was a kind and generous benefactor. He sent occasional contributions to the Congregation in addition to providing the salary for the sisters who worked for him. These women themselves also benefited. He sent them on visits to Chicago, for example, and he once surprised Sister Paul Mary Radtke, who did secretarial work for him along with teaching at St. Augustine school, by asking Mother Gerald to assign her to summer school at The Catholic University of America at his expense.

It was a warm relationship among all concerned that lasted until November 23, 1964. Bishop Daly was on his way home from a session of the Second Vatican Council when his TWA flight crashed upon takeoff from Rome, and he and most of the others on board were killed.

A Time of Growth

By any measure, Mother Gerald's third term saw tremendous expansion in the Congregation's ministries. Some three dozen new schools, foundations in the Dominican Republic and Puerto Rico, one new hospital and the expansion of another, and the work with the Glenmary Sisters, Bishop Daly, and St. John Provincial Seminary are all counted among the missions begun during those six years. Still more growth was on the horizon, but first came another General Chapter and yet another postulation, this time for a reluctant prioress.

1. Possibly, it helped matters that for many years beginning in 1937, Archbishop Cicognani was a regular winter visitor to Rosarian Academy. Mother Gerald extended the invitation because his health was affected by the Washington, DC, winters.

2. Located in Madden Hall, this area houses a public display of materials on people and events key to the Congregation's history.

3. "Education: Why Johnny Can't Read." *Time* magazine, March 14, 1955 (online reference).

4. In her first (undated) letter to Mother Gerald from the farm, Sister Kevin describes it as a 160-acre farm. The acreage given here is from *The Glenmary Story*, a booklet prepared by that community probably in the early 1950s.

5. The group consisted of Sisters Mary Agnita Reuter, the superior and principal; Thomas Ann Burke; Mary Petra Baxter; Ruth Ann Stiglitz; Mary Nicholas Fojtik; Ann Lorraine Horback; Louis James Creighton; Arthur Marie Zahn; Joseph Loretta (Elaine) Lederer; and Michael Patrice Gallagher.

6. Letter to Mother Gerald, July 17, 1948.

7. Minutes of the General Council meeting, March 3, 1951.

8. Minutes of the General Council meeting, March 19, 1951.

9. Senator McCarran had two daughters who were Holy Names sisters: Margaret Patricia and Mary Mercy. Both came to have some connection to the Adrian Dominicans, living at the Adrian Dominican House of Studies while attending The Catholic University of America.

10. Sister Marie Daniel spent the next twelve years there as Director of Nurses and in charge of obstetrics. Then after spending three years at Sisters Hospital in California and three years at St. Clement Infirmary in Adrian, she returned to Henderson for another twelve years. After she retired in 1976, she continued to work at the hospital as a volunteer in the Medical Records Department.

11. In 1953, Sister Carolyn was sent to The Catholic University of America to earn a master's in hospital administration, and went on to direct and teach at the Barry College nursing school when it first opened. Because she had not gone beyond her first year of nurse's training herself, all those years earlier in Chicago, she studied right along with her student nurses and became a registered nurse. Then, in 1963,

she was sent to Santa Cruz, California, to become the administrator of Dominican Santa Cruz Hospital. She remained there until 1976.

[12] It was added, however, in 1974. In 1989, a year after becoming part of a multi-congregation organization known at the time as Catholic Healthcare West, its name became St. Rose Dominican Hospital. Catholic Healthcare West is now known as Dignity Health. Today, Dignity Health St. Rose Dominican Hospitals is composed of three campuses: Rose de Lima (the original hospital site) and Siena, both in Henderson, and San Martín in Las Vegas.

[13] Minutes of the General Council meeting, March 5, 1949.

[14] Ibid.

[15] Land was purchased in 1964 for the construction of a new facility, and the resulting building opened in December 1967. Today the hospital, which has been greatly expanded since it opened, is part of Dignity Health (formerly Catholic Healthcare West) and is known as Dignity Health Dominican Hospital.

[16] From 1944 to 1946, Richard C. Patterson was Ambassador Extraordinary and Plenipotentiary to Yugoslavia. If this is the same man to whom Mother Gerald is referring, his title may be incorrect in the letter. An online search of the U.S. Department of State's Office of the Historian Web page naming the principal officers and chiefs of mission (http://history.state.gov/departmenthistory/people/by year/1946) lists no one named Patterson as an assistant secretary at this time.

[17] Still, her general letter of September 5, 1950, contained this comment: "Never are you to be critical of priests and their duties (or their lack of duties, for that matter)."

[18] Lenawee County, in which Adrian is located, was part of the Diocese (or, beginning in 1937, the Archdiocese) of Detroit until June 1971, when it was transferred to the Diocese of Lansing.

Chapter Five
Mother Gerald's Fourth Term: 1951-1957

Second Postulation

When the next General Chapter convened in late June 1951, Mother Gerald seemed to have had every intention of refusing a fourth term. She wrote the following letter and read it at the Chapter.

Adrian, Michigan
Friday, June 22, 1951

Sisters:

I am here now to ask a favor and some of you may guess what it is. I have thought and prayed and in a queer way, perhaps, suffered, before coming to this point. I think I made a good retreat and I would like to feel all of us in the spirit of the retreat the rest of our lives, but especially do I ask your prayers that I may not lose its spirit.

This is a time in the life of the community that the eyes of the world are on us. Good people, and some curious ones, are wondering what is going to happen and now comes my request.

Please keep my name off the ballot for Mother General. I have no desire for the office and for the common good I beg you to listen to my plea. I will still, please God, remain a willing and happy member of the community and the Order.

There is no need for postulation for me. Just elect a Mother General and leave out all postulation at this time and avoid the inconvenience of postponement of the Chapter—if that would be necessary because of postulation. You are here now from near and far. Let us love one another. Let us not be the object of worldly and even ecclesiastical gossip. Let us make it easier for Rome and for everybody. In other words let me especially practice what I have often quoted you—to be hidden with Christ in God.

You will be getting some instruction before the Chapter resumes and the elections begin this morning. All this is according to the duty of the Bishop, but I beg again and again that you do not postulate myself. Elect your choice and know I'll be grateful.

Listen to the advice of the Holy Ghost and remember that our community is glorious. Keep it so and I will do my part with the grace of God and your prayers.

Be united. Love one another in God and avoid animosities. All this I wanted to say before now but I did not know how.

Many Masses are being said all over the world for us and on my knees here before the Blessed Sacrament I submit my life to Him and His will and I am certain He wills this request and that you grant it to the last one.

Anything else you want me for and that I can do, I shall be delighted. You are all wonderful. I know it and God knows us all. Let us be happy, holy and united this blessed day and always.

Mother Mary Gerald Barry, O.P.

But the delegates paid no heed to her pleading. Later that day, she was re-elected with 144 votes out of the 194 cast. This meant another petition to the Holy See had to be made. Sister Benedicta Marie, in her capacity as Vicaress General, made the request in a letter to Cardinal Mooney.

The Chapter feels that Mother Gerald's genius for administration is much needed by our large Community in these critical days and her zeal in serving the cause of the Church is well known to you, our beloved Cardinal. During the six years that have passed since the last General Chapter, 493 novices have been received by Mother Gerald and this veritable little army of young souls has been prepared, or is being prepared, to take up the apostolate of Christian teaching in response to requests that pour into our Motherhouse from all over the United States and from foreign countries.

The Chapter, therefore, respectfully requests you to forward to the Holy See our petition that Mother Mary Gerald be permitted to continue in the office of Mother General and we humbly beg that you will add your recommendation to our plea.[1]

By mid-July, the rescript approving the request had been received.

This allowed the Chapter to be re-convened, which occurred on July 27. Just before it did, Mother Gerald wrote poignantly to Archbishop Cicognani:

> *As you can well imagine, I was more than willing to lay down the burden and have someone else put at the helm, but since the Sisters' postulation has been confirmed, I am submitting to what I am told is the will of God in the matter.*
>
> *I wish to thank you for your congratulations and for the promise of a remembrance in your good prayers. The thought that so many wonderful and holy friends are supporting me with their petitions gives me the courage and confidence I need at this time.*

The Sister Formation Movement

In the early years of her tenure as Mother General, Mother Gerald was consumed with the desire to educate her sisters. She had witnessed first hand the struggles of her predecessors, Mothers Camilla Madden and Augustine Walsh, to meet the demands of pastors and their parishes to provide teachers for their burgeoning schools. The practice of sending out unprepared postulants and novices to meet the critical needs was deplored by all of them; at the same time, they could conceive of no alternative. They had relied on the experience of seasoned teachers in the various schools to mentor the young untrained postulants and novices, a practice that often served the needs fairly well. At best, however, it was less than desirable. Not only was the education of the young teachers not solidly grounded but their formation as women religious was put on hold. As they were assigned to teach, in most cases they had not fulfilled the canonically required year of novitiate formation. That had to come later.

By the time Mother Gerald assumed office, the number of sisters who had completed undergraduate degrees and advanced degrees had been steadily growing and provided a well prepared faculty for St. Joseph College, established by Mother Camilla on the Motherhouse campus in 1919. This institution became the center of summer school education for hundreds of sisters returning from their missions. The summer session of six weeks was followed by an intersession of three weeks and often an additional one or two week session for the novices whose education and formation took place separately. All was geared toward education of the sisters to the undergraduate level in preparation for further studies. But under the circumstances the time required to complete a degree could vary from ten to twenty years.

In major cities such as Chicago, Detroit, Cleveland, Dayton, Toledo, Tucson, and San Francisco, sisters attended local colleges and universities after school and on Saturdays to complete undergraduate degrees, as well as to begin studies toward master's degrees. On the campus of the Sisters College associated with The Catholic University of America, as noted earlier, Mother Gerald built a spacious house of studies to enable sisters to pursue advanced degrees, particularly master's and doctoral degrees when sisters could be spared for full time study. The house could accommodate about thirty-six sisters and was filled to capacity with Adrian Dominican Sisters in the summer time. During the regular academic year there were usually about six Adrian sisters remaining there to study full time. The rest of the house was occupied by guest sisters of other congregations, a number of them from other Dominican congregations.

As a general rule Catholic institutions of higher learning were preferred by sisters for advanced study and in some cases were mandated by bishops. Among such universities were DePaul and Loyola in Chicago; Notre Dame in South Bend, Indiana; University of Detroit; John Carroll in Cleveland; University of San Francisco; University of Dayton; and others. Adrian Dominicans were graduates of all these institutions. In sending her sisters to study for advanced degrees, however, Mother Gerald did not limit herself to Catholic institutions. She sent them to the University of Michigan, Michigan State University, Columbia University, the University of Florida, Florida State, the University of Arizona, the University of Toledo and others in proximity to places where the sisters were missioned during the academic

Sisters at their MA graduation from the University of Michigan in 1944. Left to right: Sisters Helen Clare Doyle, Carmelia O'Connor, Jean Margaret Bowler, Marie Lucy Coressel, Helen Patrick Bartley, and John Therese Singer.

year. Furthermore, she sent individuals to study abroad in Rome, Switzerland, and Ireland as well as places in Latin America, including the Dominican Republic.

All of these movements were taking place in the 1940s and 1950s during Mother Gerald's long tenure as Mother General. Eventually, novices were no longer sent out to teach, although there were still young postulants assigned to teach as late as the 1960s. As the period of their postulancy came to an end, they returned to the Motherhouse for their canonical novitiate. In most cases these young women were better prepared than their earlier counterparts, having earned undergraduate degrees or at least having attended college for several years. Nonetheless both Mother Camilla and Mother Augustine had frequently expressed their dismay over the practice of sending out unprepared young women and yearned for the time when it would no longer be necessary. Mother Gerald had shared their concern and carried it with her. By the 1950s she had made great progress as the Congregation was growing in numbers.

These developments are backdrop to something that took place in the 1950s—the Sister Formation movement. This was a movement initiated by prominent sister educators who began to see that the practice of sending unprepared young women out to teach in the parochial schools was deplorable on at least three accounts. It was unfair to the young teachers, as well as to the students in their classrooms. It brought negative assessment upon the teachers in the parochial schools by those in the public school systems that over time were developing standards for their teachers. It relegated the religious formation of the new aspirants to religious life to a secondary concern and, in some cases, to regrettable neglect.[2]

As momentum grew to address the issues of adequate formation of young sisters, a constant question among those exploring the possibilities was why Mother Gerald was not involved. She was on the mailing list for all of the Sister Formation general communications and publications but usually did not respond in any constructive way. She did send Sister Benedicta Marie, and occasionally others, to attend some of the organizational meetings. Their reports kept her acquainted with the progress of the movement and of the Conference that eventually emerged. While written records of her position on Sister Formation are non-existent, it is clear that she did not support the initiative from the beginning. It is possible that she felt that she was doing enough with her own sisters to obviate the need to become involved. While she apparently did not directly respond to the various invitations she received, she had the practice of turning over letters to her assistants for reply. Several letters from Sister Formation have notes scribbled in the margins, for example, "Keep out of it" and "No!"

But the problems the movement was designed to address were quite real, and by the early 1940s serious attention was turning to them. In 1941 Sister Bertrande Meyers, a Daughter of Charity, published her dissertation, *The Education of Sisters*. Her study was based upon a survey of the educational practices among congregations of women religious. Many followed what was called a "twenty year plan," that being the usual time required to earn a bachelor's degree through a piecemeal education centered around summer school sessions. Recognizing that the problems were pervasive, Sister Bertrande made some recommendations for teacher education among the sisters. She proposed that a plan for education in each congregation be put in place to ensure that necessary education for sisters be carried out. She was particularly sensitive to the need that each plan be designed in accordance with the spirit of the congregation for which it was devised. While Sister Bertrande's study did not immediately produce the Sister Formation Conference, it was widely read and set many sisters to thinking.

The issues emerged with new urgency at the annual convention of the National Catholic Educational Association (NCEA) in 1948. In that year a Teacher Education Section was inaugurated in the College and University Department of the Association. There the issue of sister education found a new voice in Sister Madeleva Wolff, CSC, the highly respected president of St. Mary College, Notre Dame, Indiana. Her paper, "The Education of Sister Lucy," focused upon the problems attendant to placing a young sister without adequate professional preparation in the classroom. The impact of her words was transformative insofar as they were expressed openly and transparently. The gauntlet had been laid down and there was no turning back.

At the annual meeting of the NCEA in 1951 the agenda received impetus when members proposed that a four-year program for the education of sisters be instituted. The following year, in the

Teacher Education Section, a panel was set up to discuss "Counsel to Teaching Sisters," a document issued by Pope Pius XII. This was an address given by the Pope on September 15, 1951, at the First International Congress of Teaching Sisters. In it he emphasized the need to understand students in the culture of their times. He urged teachers to adapt their teaching methods and modes of expression to the understanding of their students without watering down the fundamentals of the faith. Educational work must be adapted to new circumstances, he said. He spoke of the religious habit as an "expression of inward naturalness, of simplicity and spiritual modesty." Worn in such a way, he said, it will edify everyone, even modern young people.

While the papal exhortation addressed teaching sisters in general throughout the world, one section in particular reinforced the issues being raised in the United States.

> *See to it, therefore, that they [teaching Sisters] are well trained and that their education corresponds in quality and academic degrees to that demanded by the State. Be generous in giving them all they need, especially where books are concerned, so that they may continue their studies and thus offer young people a rich and solid harvest of knowledge. This is in keeping with the Catholic idea which gratefully welcomes all that is naturally good, beautiful and true, because it is an image of the Divine goodness and beauty and truth. (#18)*[3]

One of the sisters who spoke to the document was a substitute speaker, Sister Mary Emil Penet, IHM, who galvanized the assembly with her analysis of the existing problems and proposals for a solution. She acknowledged that pressures upon the religious congregations of women were great and that correctives would require unusual methods at least for a period of time.

In the course of the discussions about what was needed in the ranks of sister-teachers, college and university administrators expressed concern that the young sisters lacked an appropriate intellectual background, that is, that they were in fact anti-intellectual. This expressed perception offended many major superiors, including Mother Gerald when she heard of it. But in her notes to her sisters, Sister Mary Emil addressed the issue forthrightly.

> *Are our Sisters intellectual? The vast majority of them have been educated, if they have earned degrees at all, on the twenty-year plan—that is, by an agglomeration of summer school credits for courses pursued in various institutions and in peculiar sequences. Those who hold B.A.'s of that kind will be the first to tell you that they do not really have college educations. If a Sister spends the years almost up to her silver jubilee painfully acquiring the training with which she should have begun, if she is conscious of her inadequacies during all that time and long after, if she is expected to mix with her teaching and class preparation a generous portion of cleaning, sewing, cooking and even janitor work, and if all of*

> *this must be crammed into the intervals between her spiritual and community exercises, is there any wonder that her love of learning is somewhat dimmed, and that she does not inspire scholarly enthusiasm in her pupils? Now there are many potential college teachers and many potential "distinguished scholars" in the Sisterhoods. Many of those Sisters are now teaching in the elementary school and will probably stay there—for a kind of accidental reason. By the time their undergraduate record has accumulated to indicate their power, they are almost too old to warrant the investment of Ph.D. training.*[4]

Her own congregation, the Sisters, Servants of the Immaculate Heart of Mary in Monroe, Michigan, had instituted a four-year degree program for the sisters preparatory to their assignment to teach. The program was relatively new and provided little data for analysis but Sister Mary Emil reasoned that three approaches were necessary to address the problem nationally:

1. that there be a uniform ratio established for the hiring of lay teachers to supplement the ranks of sisters as some left teaching to get their degrees;

2. that a study be made to determine how communities lacking in funds were to carry out the Holy Father's directives;

3. that there be some kind of organizational unity among motherhouses and colleges engaged in education in order to better understand the goals and current state of sister-education.

Mother Gerald's Fourth Term: 1951-1957

Among those attending the NCEA meeting, there were individuals representing various entities with a stake in the problems, notably the bishops of the United States, the major superiors of the congregations of women and men, superintendents of schools in the various dioceses, state accrediting agencies, parents, and others. While there were conflicting responses to the proposals of Sister Mary Emil, there was a fairly general agreement that a study needed to be made to determine the actual state of affairs. The sisters agreed to conduct the study. A highly professional and comprehensive plan was developed and carried out. Of 377 questionnaires sent out there were 255 responses. There is no record of a response from the Adrian Dominican Sisters.

As the Sister Formation movement gained momentum its agenda was embraced by many congregations of women, and received support from influential members of the clergy and hierarchy both at home and in the Vatican. It changed from being a "movement" to the status of "conference"—the Sister Formation Conference (SFC). The action formalizing this status took place in 1954. It capped six years of intense work on the part of scores of sisters under the leadership of Sister Mary Emil. One of its first actions was to set up an operating structure. For this purpose the organizers designated six regions corresponding to those of the NCEA. In each region a planning committee would work with a survey member to determine how the national agenda might be adapted to regional situations.

An important step in the growth of the Sister Formation Conference was the Everett Workshop, funded by a grant from the Ford

Foundation. It was intended to cover a fourfold process of research:

1. an exploration of the current and most effective practices in sister education in the United States and Europe;

2. drawing up an ideal curriculum on the BA level by a committee of selected sister educators;

3. regional SFC conferences to discuss the summer's work;

4. a cooperative project in which a religious community or two would try out the new curriculum to show the validity of the research.

The Everett Workshop was convened in the summer of 1956 to address the second of the proposed purposes. Everett, Washington, was chosen as the site for the workshop because of the investment of the Sisters of Providence of Everett in the work of the SFC. Author Marjorie Beane writes,

> *The Providence School of Nursing, operated by the Sisters of Providence in Everett, Washington, was finally chosen because of Everett's closeness to important education meetings scheduled during the workshop session, (TEPS, NCATE,[5] and state-certification officers would be in the area and therefore available to the sisters for consultation) and because of the state's climate and scenery. Disadvantages such as the lack of library facilities and the absence of an academic atmosphere were dismissed by the national consultors. That the libraries of Washington University, the University of Seattle and the*

University of Portland would be available would suffice. It was also seen as an advantage to be away from a campus atmosphere "to be absolutely free in our thought."[6]

The workshop began with analysis of data that had been gleaned from extensive visits to congregations of women both in the United States and abroad. Over 53,000 contacts with sisters had been made in the United States alone. As a result of study and analysis, the workshop produced an ambitious set of sixteen recommendations:

1. provide a five-year program of training for young sisters;
2. recommend college work through the bachelor's degree before sending the sisters into professional work such as teaching, nursing and social work;
3. place less emphasis on the purely professional and more on the educational;
4. emphasize joint planning of curriculum by personnel of the novitiate, college, and those concerned with sister formation and education;
5. advocate a study of the abilities and interests of the individual sister in order to determine the placement of the sister;
6. affirm the release of sisters full time to develop their overwhelming abilities, e.g., writing, research;
7. prepare elementary teachers to teach a foreign language in the grade school;

8. structure campus elementary schools with a forward look and prepare to carry out experimental programs;

9. promote community planning that includes plans for financing the programs;

10. stress special educational practices that include plans for graduate work for sisters able to undertake this study, including a year's study abroad;

11. explore cooperation in the education of sisters with other communities;

12. organize real curriculum planning and research. Plan for philosophy, theology, and social science courses in the curriculum. Devise a number of special courses geared to sisters' needs. Use television, music, and dancing in novitiates. Specially train faculties for the education of young sisters;

13. complete curriculum re-evaluation and planning;

14. start graduate study in juniorate;[7]

15. certify all teaching sisters whether certification is required or not;

16. when sisters are attending regular community colleges for women, establish special sections with well thought-out programs for them.[8]

Following the Everett Workshop, two colleges were identified to implement the curriculum as demonstration centers—St. Teresa College in Winona, Minnesota, and Providence Heights College in Seattle.

At the same time, plans were being set up to form three specifically Sister Formation colleges, one associated with Seattle University in Washington state and two others in the St. Louis, Missouri, area. In Seattle four congregations of sisters cooperated in forming a Sister Formation College—the Sisters of Providence, the St. Joseph of Carondelet Sisters, the Dominican Sisters of Edmonds, and the Dominican Sisters of Tacoma. Legal documents were drawn up to form the Sister Formation College of Seattle University. The agreement with the University was finalized by 1959. Each of the participating congregations had a site on their own grounds that was carefully visited annually by Seattle University administrators to ensure the quality of the education provided. One provision insisted upon by the oversight committee was that all those who taught courses had to have a PhD.[9]

Another Sister Formation College, Marillac College, was established in Normandy (St. Louis), Missouri, by the Daughters of Charity. The College had originally been a two-year college associated with St. Louis University. But now the Daughters of Charity desired to cut their ties with St. Louis University and take steps to form a four-year institution based on the curriculum developed by the Sister Formation Conference. Needing additional qualified faculty to further their plans and to seek North Central accreditation, the administration appealed to other congregations for assistance. Mother Gerald responded by sending two Adrian Dominican Sisters—Sister Mary Paul (Noreen) McKeough, OP, PhD, and Sister Agnes Cecile Prendergast, OP, PhD.

Sister Noreen wrote of her experience,

> *This was my first time on my own away from Adrians, and I was desperately lonesome. Even in my lonesomeness, however, I realized that it was a growing experience. I was teaching, praying, eating, walking, recreating, comparing notes with sisters of other congregations, and I had to open up to different styles and spirits in religious life. As time went on, I grew very comfortable with the Daughters and my non-Daughter colleagues, and I loved being with, and teaching, the young Daughters in formation (called "seminarians"). . . . The second year I was there, the college was accredited as a four-year institution, to the great joy and relief of everyone concerned. As I reflect on my Marillac years, I realize how important and formative they were in preparing me for post-Vatican II changes.*

Sister Noreen was at Marillac from 1958 to 1960, while Agnes Cecile was on the faculty for the 1961-1962 school year. It marks one of the few direct experiences at this time that any Adrian Dominican Sister had with the Sister Formation Conference. Sister Noreen once said[10] that Mother Gerald had later told her that, if she had known that it was a Sister Formation College, she would not have sent her.

The third Sister Formation College was founded by the School Sisters of Notre Dame in south St. Louis. Like the Daughters of Charity, the School Sisters had operated a two-year college for their young sisters and sent them to other major institutions to complete their degrees. But they then developed their junior college into a four-year institution based on the recommendations of the Sister Formation curriculum.

The proposals of SFC, recommending true education over professional training, with provision for philosophy, theology, foreign language, and study overseas, were intended to form a thoroughly prepared teacher for all levels of the school curriculum.[11] At the same time they addressed another issue that arose in the course of the ongoing explorations—that of anti-intellectualism. Many of the sisters were distressed over the accusation that anti-intellectualism was a common trait of the American sisters. Yet this perception of women religious rose during a time when the participants were asked to consider aiming for two years of preparation as an alternative to requiring a four-year baccalaureate degree before entering the classroom. The promoters of Sister Formation would not countenance such a "watering down" of their agenda for the formation of young sisters.

At the same time that the Sister Formation movement was gaining acceptance, another surprising initiative emerged in a letter from Rome. Up to this time, as has been noted, Mother Gerald and Adrian Dominican Sisters in general had been conspicuously absent from programs furthering sister formation.[12] Mother Gerald sent a representative to some of the meetings but never became personally involved. Now, however, a spotlight was focused on her in a letter from Rome, dated March 31, 1952. The Sacred Congregation for Religious was concerned that religious life needed deepening and strengthening as an effective antidote against the widespread evil and danger of the times. Rome was proposing that a national congress of women and men religious be convened at the University of Notre Dame on August 10 to 14 of 1952 to address their concerns. In the second paragraph of the letter she read,

> *The Sacred Congregation takes the liberty of asking for your valued collaboration as Executive Chairman [sic] of the National Committee for Sisters.*

Appointed to serve with Mother Gerald were: Reverend Mothers Rose Elizabeth Havican, CSC, Marie Helene Franey, SP, Mary Killian

The National Committee for Sisters, left to right: Mothers Joan of Arc Cronin, OSU; Mary Killian Corbett, CSJ; Mary Catherine Sullivan, DC; Gerald Barry, OP; Rose Elizabeth Havican, CSC; and Marie Helene Franey, SP; and Sister Madeleva Wolff, CSC.

Corbett, CSJ, Mary Catherine Sullivan, DC (who replaced Mother Caroline Collins, DC, the original appointee), and Joan of Arc Cronin, OSU; and Sister Madeleva Wolff, CSC. The latter was the only one who was not a major superior. Working under the pressures of time to carry out such a monumental project, the women and men religious set about the work of bringing it into being. In the end, the National Congress met with resounding success. Among the throng of attendees were over twelve hundred women religious. In addition there were approximately eight hundred men in attendance. Four hundred religious institutes in the United States were represented.

Father Francis J. Connell, CSsR, Dean of the School of Theology at The Catholic University of America, chaired the men's committee and addressed the assembly with some opening remarks.

> *The purpose of this Congress is to inspire us to a deeper love for our religious vocation, and a more ardent desire to fulfill the obligations we accepted on the day of our profession, to give one another encouragement, to exchange ideas about the problems common to all religious societies. Above all, it is the wish of the Holy See that we deliberate on the adjustment of the religious life to modern conditions, without violation of the principles on which the religious state is based.*[13]

In her welcoming remarks to those attending the Congress, Mother Gerald addressed the sisters directly. She rather subtly spoke to the issue of anti-intellectualism.

> *You, Reverend Mothers and Sisters, are likewise learned and cultured, and meek and humble, representing nearly two hundred thousand Sisters of the Western hemisphere. You are from every walk of the religious life. Where Christ has been a Stranger, you have taken Him into the lives of the little ones. The sick are nursed and visited by you; the poor are fed and clothed; the orphans are harbored, and on the highways and byways of Parish visiting, all are invited to the banquet. You represent the arts, fine and liberal. You are the authors of books and of poetry; and from the cradle to the grave, your words have been quoted. You know the gospels and you give testimony of the Light, and I am sure that Light and Our Lady of Light will keep you in the path that leads to Eternal Light and love.*[14]

Later, an intervention of Mother Gerald was noted in *Time* magazine. The writer, who was reporting on the Congress, cited a variety of topics to be discussed—whether or not religious sisters should use sleeping cars or sit up in coaches for rail travel, whether novices should watch television and be exposed to the "outer world," etc., and then said,

> *Before one of the sisters' discussion sessions, it was discovered that a priest was to address them on the subject of modern comforts and conveniences. Up rose a seven-member nuns' committee to protest. Said Mother Mary Gerald, O.P., "Why should any man tell us about our comforts and conveniences?" Four nuns were hastily scheduled to speak in the priest's place.*[15]

The four women who were chosen to address the issue of "comforts and conveniences" represented three of the recognized Orders of religious life and one more modern congregation. They were Mother Richarda Peters, OSB, Mother Mary Corona Wirfs, OSF, Mother Mary Evelyn Murphy, OP, and Mother Berchmans Reed, SC. Each of the sisters was able to respond to the issues through references to their longstanding traditions, in most cases to their founders or foundresses. Mother Richarda, for example, said,

> *... I would like to point out how the Rule of St. Benedict, and vows taken in accord with that Rule, allow for adaptation to present times—for the use of new and modern comforts and conveniences. Perhaps the most obvious proof is the actual existence of the Benedictine Order still fulfilling a vital function in the Church.*[16]

At the conclusion of the Notre Dame event the Sacred Congregation requested that the original committee remain in service to organize an ongoing conference. In due time two conferences were formed—the Conference of Major Superiors of Women and the Conference of Major Superiors of Men. The Canadian religious women and men had organized one joint conference, but this arrangement was rejected by the U.S. women. Initially, they had resisted forming any organization since for them the National Catholic Educational Association and the Catholic Hospital Association were sufficient for their needs of cooperation. But in the end they chose to follow the precedent being set in countries throughout the world in founding conferences of major superiors.

As the Sister Formation movement was taking on a comprehensive study of education and formation of young sisters in congregations throughout the country, they now had a new organization to deal with, one that might be a potential ally in their pursuits. But it was also one that introduced questions about jurisdiction over the responsibility for the formation of young sisters.

Sister Benedicta Marie kept up on information that related to the Sister Formation movement. In 1955 she wrote an undated memorandum to Mother Gerald in which she first acknowledged that the movement had done much good but then added that mistakes had also been made. She cited the experiences of four different congregations of women religious. In general each had found that, after completing a degree through the Sister Formation program, a number of the young sisters left religious life. In one case a congregation had twenty-five young sisters complete the Sister Formation program, after which eight of them left the congregation. Sister Benedicta Marie's assessment of the problem suggested that the reasons were twofold.

1. *The young sisters are, for a long period, engaged in acquiring an education and not giving any service to the congregation. This tends to make them selfish.*

2. *They are kept like hot house plants for five years and then suddenly transferred to an environment where they must work hard managing restless children and they do not have the stamina for this.*

Sister Benedicta Marie offered her own ideas:

It would seem to be a better plan, then, to keep our junior professed Sisters in for one year after their novitiate as soon as we can get caught up to this point, then let them go out to teach and complete the work for their degrees during summer sessions. They love to get back to the Motherhouse with their own "crowd". Here they are given instructions on Sunday by their former mistresses. They have an opportunity to consult with them and with the Mother General if they are at all unstable.

We have reason to thank God very humbly when we recall that we have between four and five hundred junior professed Sisters and that this year we lost only two of them and that one of these would have gladly stayed had we not advised her to go on account of ill health.

In January 1956, Mother Gerald was invited to a regional meeting of the Sister Formation Conference at Mundelein College in Chicago. Since she had scheduled visitation with her sisters in the Dominican Republic, she authorized Sister Benedicta Marie to represent her. Ill at the time, Sister Benedicta Marie in turn sent Sisters Margaret Helen Lynch and Cyril Joseph Cawley in her stead. It is unlikely that Mother Gerald would have attended in any case, especially since she was devoting time to the Conference of Major Superiors of Women. Sister Margaret Helen wrote a lengthy detailed report of the regional meeting to Mother Gerald.[17] What follows is based on that letter with some minor editing.

The two sisters found themselves among representatives of 125 congregations of the Midwest. There were mothers general and provincials (eighty-two), novices and postulant mistresses (fifty-two and nineteen respectively), juniorate mistresses (sixteen) and directresses of studies (forty-two). These numbers were approximations since, Sister Margaret Helen noted, some people came without having registered in advance.

The meeting began with an address by Monsignor J.D. Conway of Iowa City, Iowa, who was identified as having been a convent chaplain for fifteen years. His topic was, "The Integration of Spiritual and Intellectual Elements in the Formation of Sisters." Sister Margaret Helen summarized his talk in detail. It contained the following elements.

1. Americans in general do not pursue the Arts but prefer the professions.

2. The percentage of Catholic professors in American universities is woefully low.

3. This is not discrimination. American Catholics themselves, in choosing practical subjects, are lacking in culture.

4. While Catholics are rising in a material sense, there is a deplorable lack of intellectual Catholic Americans.

5. From a national survey of women's colleges some show a "bright light." He mentioned that Siena Heights of Adrian

ranked tenth. Nazareth and Grand Rapids also made good showings.

6. Sisters are the ones called to raise Catholic intellectualism, but they first must develop a love of it in themselves. They must have spiritual formation but ways must be found to integrate intellectual and spiritual formation. The SFC is a step in the right direction.

7. Intellectual growth should begin in the novitiate and spiritual growth should continue throughout life. "Is it not true that many sisters are fundamentally anti-intellectual?"

8. There is too much scrubbing of floors by novices who must go out to teach. "Is it not possible to train them in obedience by teaching the mind to obey, study habits, attention to intellectual interests?"

9. Wise choices for spiritual reading can advance the intellectual. They should not be confined to the preparation for the next day's meditation. Too many spiritual books are emotional and sentimental.

In the course of his presentation Monsignor Conway invoked Canon 565 of the then current canon law.[18] Answers to the questionnaire sent out by SFC indicated that some interpreted Canon 565 as forbidding study during the novitiate unless it related to theology. He was emphatic in asserting that Canon 565 does not forbid intellectual activities, but also does not emphasize them. While Pope

Pius X, who was pope when that Code of Canon Law was drafted, had de-emphasized intellectual formation in favor of instruction on the rule and virtues and a year-long retreat, he did not rule out intellectual formation. According to Monsignor Conway, the main purpose of Canon 565 was to prevent religious institutes from using novices in doing the work of the institute—not to utilize them but rather to prepare them.

Novices at work in the novitiate garden.

He went on to say that in 1929 the Sacred Congregation for Religious had found it necessary to give an instruction on Canon 565. It provided that examinations in religion be given to all postulants and novices, varying according to depth. Sister Margaret Helen then described a heated discussion around the topic of sisters' capability of teaching theology. The instruction stated that "Sisters can prepare for the teaching and study of theology 'in the nature of theology for laymen' without violating the Canon."

In the afternoon a panel of members of the clergy responded to the morning's presentation. They were: Walter T. Pax, CPPS, of DePaul

University; Edward J. Drummond, SJ, Academic Vice President, Marquette University; Robert E. Coerver, CM, Kenrick Seminary, St. Louis; Monsignor Reynold Hillenbrand, a noted educator in the Chicago Archdiocese; and Walter L. Farrell, SJ, West Baden College, West Baden Springs, Indiana. Sister Margaret Helen does not report on the content of their remarks but proceeds to the ensuing discussion that proved quite contentious on the issue of theological study and teaching by sisters.

She reported that one priest strongly objected to the charge that sisters were anti-intellectual. He said that he had yet to find one who fit that description. He had taught theology at Saint Xavier College in Chicago and found that sisters who taught there were universally well prepared and proficient. Later Sister Margaret Helen found that he was a Dominican, Father Reginald Masterson, at that time stationed in Dubuque, Iowa. She took the occasion to thank him for his defense of the sisters.

A panel of sisters also addressed the assembly. One was Mother Regina Cunningham, Provincial Superior of the Chicago Province of the Sisters of Mercy. She brought out the necessity of the study of theology by sisters but added, in Sister Margaret Helen's words, "... she did not mean that any sister with six summers of theology was capable of teaching it. Theology should be taught only by priests."

An unidentified Holy Cross Sister from St. Mary's, Notre Dame, objected vigorously. St. Mary's College in the 1940s had introduced a program of theological studies leading to the doctorate in theology for the express purpose of training sisters to teach theology, she said. Mother Regina then requested the opinion of a canonist and called upon Father Masterson. He, however, did not get involved. He said that every sister should have the three-year certificate in theology as part of her education and formation. He reviewed the course of studies required of priests (three years of philosophy, four of theology, and often two or more on the post-graduate level). He said that he could not speak to the purpose of the St. Mary's program.

The sister from St. Mary's pursued her cause. She said that their sisters who had attained the doctorate in theology at their institution taught along with the Dominican professors there. She mentioned that a Father Burke at The Catholic University of America had introduced a watered down course in theology for sisters, but after a week of it he threw away his notes and taught them the regular seminary course.

Mother Regina remained undaunted and insisted that a sister may teach theology only if she is given the same training that the priest is given. The next day the provincial of the Holy Cross sisters spoke at the meeting of higher superiors and said that, in the excitement, the sister who spoke said that they give a degree in theology. In fact the degree is given in religion, but its intent is to prepare teachers in theology. In this discussion Mother Regina held to her position.

This part of the program concluded with a discussion of secular reading. Do the sisters read *Time* and *Newsweek*?—most said "yes." Is a daily newspaper available to them?—many said "yes." Are they permitted to view television? "It was surprising the number who said 'yes,'" observed Sister Margaret Helen. Some regulated it; others did not. These questions centered around a statement that sisters often do not know what is going on in the world and therefore cannot properly teach students the moral implications of the issues, nor keep up adequately on social and related sciences.

Sister Margaret Helen's long letter concluded with a report on the election of officers. She added that Sister Bertrande Meyers, DC, had asked to be remembered to Mother Gerald and had said that "she thought much of you, that you didn't go off on such 'high-falutin' stuff as some of these people, but that you certainly knew what you were talking about."

Mother Gerald wrote from the Dominican Republic to thank Sister Margaret Helen for her detailed report of the meeting and said,

> *It seems that we are on the right track and I trust that we shall be able to reach the goal without getting into any fist fights. Thank God there was at least one voice to defend the Sisters against the charge of anti-intellectualism. I hope it didn't get into the papers this time as it did a year ago. It almost seems that we insist on presiding at our own scholastic execution in the eyes of the American people, and it is a shame after so much has been accomplished at the cost of such great sacrifice.*

In the last line of this comment no doubt Mother Gerald had in mind the extraordinary efforts she had been making to educate her sisters. At Siena Heights and Barry colleges women of exceptional competence were teaching with doctoral degrees. Among them were

To Fields Near and Far

Sisters Miriam Michael Stimson, contributor to early research on DNA; Helene O'Connor, a pioneer in liturgical art and renewal; Patrick Jerome Mullins, Latin and Greek scholar and expert on medieval Church history; Mary Paul (Noreen) McKeough, thoroughly grounded in the English language and literature and both a poet and writer; Cyril Edwin Kinney, philosopher; Mary Albert Lenaway, innovator in education; Mary Xavier (Katharine) Emery, distinguished teacher of English and the humanities; Dorothy Folliard, outstanding teacher of Latin and Greek; Denise Mainville, musician, composer, and artist; and Marie Carolyn Klinkhamer, historian and professor at The Catholic University of America. These women and many more were scarcely anti-intellectual. But there were no degrees in theology among them.

Mother Gerald had held to the view that teaching theology was the exclusive domain of the priests. Nonetheless the discussions around the issue of theology as an important discipline for sisters led Mother

Left to right: Sisters Miriam Stimson, Helene O'Connor, and Denise Mainville.

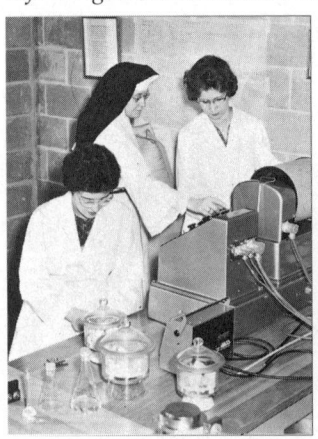

Gerald to reconsider. She chose not to send sisters to the program at St. Mary's, Notre Dame. Instead she sent sisters for study at Providence College where a summer program in theology for sisters had begun in 1948. In three summers a sister could earn a certificate in theology. She could then continue for two more summers and qualify for a master's level degree in theological studies. The College advertised that the program centered around the theology of St. Thomas Aquinas. The early courses utilized the multi-volumed *A Companion to the Summa,* by Walter Farrell, OP.[19]

When the program began in 1948 the large number of participants included four Adrian Dominican Sisters. Additional sisters were assigned in subsequent summers.[20] In a letter dated July 17, 1950, Father Robert J. Slavin, OP, President of Providence College, in announcing the extension of the program to include a master of arts in religious education, reviewed the purposes of the program. He wrote,

> *During the Summer of 1948, we began at Providence College a Theological Institute for Religious Women. We did this because we believed that the Sisters would benefit greatly both in their religious lives and in their teaching from a sincere study of the Master Theologian, St. Thomas Aquinas. Our purpose was and still is to stress the pursuit of knowledge rather than the acquisition of letters however learned.*

The title of the master's program was in deference to accrediting agencies that often did not recognize programs in theology in the transfer of credits. "Religious studies" was more generic and usually acceptable in the wider academic community. The title of the degree was often adapted to the needs of the recipient. Sister Carmelia O'Connor, on August 8, 1952, received a master's degree in "religious guidance." In fact, however, she had been studying the theology of St. Thomas Aquinas.

The Conference of Major Superiors

The committee held over from the Notre Dame conference continued to meet from time to time. One such meeting in Adrian on April 9, 1956, had its initial conversations recorded in a verbatim account now held in the Adrian Dominican archives. The membership had changed significantly by this time, although the congregations originally represented on the committee remained. Attending the meeting were the following:

> Mother Mary Gerald Barry, OP, Mother General*
> Mother Mary Catherine Sullivan, DC, Provincial*
> Mother Kathryn Marie Gibbons, CSC, Mother General
> Sister Madeleva Wolff, CSC, President of St. Mary's, Notre Dame*
> Mother Edward Marie Mahaney, CSJ, and Sister Grace Aurelia, CSJ,
>   representing Mother Eucharista Galvin, CSJ, Mother General
> Sister Rose Angela Horan, SP, representing
>   Mother Gertrude Clare Owens, Mother General
> Mother Marietta Marinen, OSU, Provincial
> Sister Benedicta Marie Ledwidge OP, Vicaress General (Adrian)

Sister Mary Kevin Campbell, OP, Councilor (Adrian)
Sister Mary Angeline Steele, OP, Councilor (Adrian)
These three were on the original committee.

Present for this meeting was Father Bernard E. Ransing, CSC, representing Father Arcadio Larraona, Prefect of the Sacred Congregation for Religious. Father Ransing was delegated to represent the interests of the Pope in the formation of national conferences of religious women and men in countries throughout the world. From the beginning Father Ransing made it clear, however, that his mandate was to facilitate dialogue about the advantages and disadvantages of a national organization of women religious. It was not to recommend it, nor to issue a requirement that such an organization be inaugurated. He said at the outset that there were special circumstances for women religious in the United States that did not pertain in other countries. The decision should be theirs.

As the conversations began there were clarifying questions about the relationship that a potential national organization of women religious would have with several existing entities, notably the Sacred Congregation in Rome, the National Catholic Welfare Conference (NCWC),[21] the National Catholic Education Association (NCEA), and the Catholic Hospital Association. Among a number of clarifications, largely put forth by Father Ransing, were the following:

1. The purpose of the proposed conference is to promote more efficacious cooperation ("organized charity") among religious in the attainment of their special ends.

2. The conference would have executive powers for all that concerns its own activities as an organization, but it would not have any jurisdiction over the internal affairs of the member societies or communities.

3. The conference would relate to the Sacred Congregation for Religious in Rome, possibly as it develops, through the Apostolic Delegate.

4. The pattern of organization could duplicate that of the National Catholic Welfare Conference, functioning through regional divisions and a national secretariat.

5. Membership would be restricted to major superiors of communities that fall under the Sacred Congregation for Religious. Major superiors that belong to diocesan congregations might secure membership with the approval of their bishops. Some congregations relate to the Vatican Congregation for the Propagation of the Faith and to the Congregation for the Oriental Church. The major superiors of these congregations may be members with the permission of the respective Congregations to which they relate.[22]

6. The conference might have an executive committee, elected by the members to provide implementation of the decisions of the conference. Under the direction of this committee, permanent committees might be set up, e.g., on religious discipline, financial administration, spiritual doctrine. Questions could be

submitted on such things as literature suggested for novitiates, formation of new members, etc.

7. There could also be a permanent secretariat in Washington, a central office where the various committees and agencies would function and to which the questions and matters that concern the conference could be referred.

In making these clarifications and suggestions Father Ransing was using the organizations of the NCWC and the Canadian Catholic Conference as references. The former was at that time an organization facilitating the work of the Catholic bishops in the United States and the latter was the new conference set up in Canada for both women and men religious.

Mother Gerald asked if they should be following the example of the Canadians and setting up one conference for both American women and men religious. Father Ransing replied that he thought it would be advisable. She then asked if it were true that the Canadian priests had done nearly all the work of the earlier Canadian Congress. Sister Benedicta Marie, who seemed to have some firsthand information, indicated that, while there had been committees for each constituency, "the men did most of the talking."

In response to a question posed by Mother Catherine about issues that might arise between a congregation and the local bishop, Father Ransing suggested that the problem would go to the secretariat who would then send representatives to the bishop to seek a solution. Mother Gerald's intervention at this point seems to have been immediate. "Papal communities go directly to the Sacred Congregation. We wouldn't have to go to the secretariat for these things." Those who knew Mother Gerald can only imagine the force with which she would make such an assertion.

The issue of the Sister Formation Conference was introduced by Sister Kathryn Marie, who said that this organization would be of tremendous help to the major superiors. She said further that Archbishop Ritter[23] was totally supporting the Sister Formation program and in favor of retaining the sisters at home until their scholastic preparation was completed. Father Ransing added that the Sacred Congregation for Religious would like to bring SFC under the proposed conference of major superiors. Mother Marietta thought that such an arrangement would be beneficial since "SFC is now in a very dangerous position." She did not elaborate.

The conversation then turned to the question of who was responsible for the formation of sisters.

Mother Gerald was quite direct. "A person has no right to be a Mother General if she cannot direct the formation of her own sisters."

Sister Madeleva, who had been with the Sister Formation Conference from the beginning, offered some information from a recent conversation that she had had with Sister Mary Emil Penet. She noted that no one had anticipated the trend being discussed and that Sister Emil was distressed about it. She reviewed the fact that voting members of SFC would be superiors general, directors of education, and mistresses of novices. Presidents of colleges would be included in their own group and have a vote.

Sister Benedicta Marie observed that in this arrangement the major superiors were permitted to vote by the sufferance of the officers of SFC which put them all on the same plane. Mother Gerald added, "The novice mistress is not an elected official."

She later asked, "Why do mistresses of postulants and novices have the right to govern?" It was probably not a question. It is obvious that among these major superiors there was concern about what they saw as an encroachment upon their rightful authority.

Another concern raised in the meeting was about communication with the bishops of the country. Mother Gerald observed that criticism from the bishops about the Notre Dame conference came to light only after the meeting was over. Some bishops claimed that they did not know about it, that their superintendents of schools went to it but left and reported back to their bishops that the religious had "something up their sleeves." She said, "Everything ought to be cleared with the local ordinary.[24] I wonder if there wasn't anything that should have been said to Cardinal Mooney about this meeting by the SCR [Sacred Congregation for Religious]."

Father Ransing, himself a member of a religious congregation, remarked that some bishops are always suspicious of religious congregations. "We always have to face that," he said. "They were all invited. Some of them seem to think that they were not invited. In this case, letters of courtesy were sent to Cardinal Spellman [New York] and

Cardinal Stritch [Chicago]." He said further that Cardinal Spellman was not pleased in 1952 because he was not asked to organize the Notre Dame conference. "I say that quite frankly."

Mother Catherine, wanting to be clear about procedures, asked, "When we go on with this, would not the bishops be advised?" Father Ransing was quite definite in his response. "The Sacred Congregation would inform the bishops that, with its approval, the religious of the United States are forming a conference of major superiors to more effectively work with them in the apostolate. The SCR did not think it necessary to inform all the bishops of the meeting of committees. Now it will write a circular letter." He said he thought that a meeting of major superiors would last about three days.

The tone of the record at this point suggests that the decision to form a national conference had been made. Now it would be time to call all the major superiors together to gain their acceptance. Mother Catherine said that the proposed meeting would have to be convened in the summer but Mother Gerald was quick to say that the major superiors are overburdened in the summer. She did not explain further but it was during the summer that she and those who assisted her spent long hours on the difficult task of assigning her sisters to the various missions for the following year.

After continued discussion it was decided that the national meeting of major superiors would take place the following year in Chicago possibly at Mundelein College. Father Ransing assigned the members of the committee geographical areas of the country in which they were to draw up lists of major superiors whose motherhouses were in that territory. He would take these lists to Rome to determine which congregations were pontifical and which diocesan. He reminded the group that diocesan major superiors could become members of the new organization with the approval of their bishops.

Mother Gerald continued to chair the National Committee for Sisters through a meeting that took place in Chicago at the Conrad Hilton Hotel on November 23, 1956, followed the next day by an assembly of 235 major superiors of religious congregations of women. This meeting had been decided on by the committee in a September 1956 meeting in lieu of the one previously proposed for 1957 at Mundelein College.

The Committee reviewed for the major superiors the entire sequence of events that had led to the proposal of a national organization of religious women's congregations in the United States and presented proposed statutes. Questions were clarified, especially the relation of the Sister Formation Conference to the new entity, and whether or not the new organization was tentative, i.e., in the nature of an experiment. The Committee believed that, since the SFC was under the NCEA, it was beyond the competence of the new organization to make decisions about the future of the SFC. Since the statutes had been approved by the Sacred Congregation, the new organization was not tentative.

The new conference of women religious, with its statutes, was unanimously approved and chairpersons for the newly established regions were appointed. The regions were Eastern, Midwest, New England, Northwestern, Southern, and Southwestern. The women appointed to chair these regions held temporary positions until the areas were organized and able to elect their own leaders.

Accordingly, the Conference of Major Superiors of Women (CMSW) was established in 1957. While Mother Gerald had chaired the National Committee for Sisters, she was not elected the first president of the CMSW, and indeed did not wish to be chosen. In fact, she had recommended that someone else be elected to head the Conference. The distinction of first president went to Franciscan Sister Alcuin McCarthy.

In the meantime the Sister Formation Conference continued respectfully acknowledging the rights of the major superiors to oversee the formation of their members, but preferring to operate under the arrangements that had first been made with the NCEA. An SFC newsletter was begun in 1957 and made available to sisters in general. Its editor was Sister Ritamary Bradley, CHM.

It is clear that the position held by Mother Gerald, that formation of sisters for religious life was the primary responsibility of the major superiors, became the established principle of the CMSW. SFC went through a restructuring process in 1964 which resulted in its becoming a committee of CMSW but it was an uneasy solution. An appeal was made to the Sacred Congregation for Religious who upheld the major superiors. Gradually, as Vatican Council II took place, and in its aftermath religious congregations of both women and men were directed to renew themselves, individual congregations took up the matter of formation programs.[25]

Second Trip to Rome

The Notre Dame conference ended on August 13, 1952. Less than a month later Mother Gerald, along with all the world's mothers general of congregations having pontifical status, was invited by Pope Pius XII to a meeting in Rome on September 11-13. Accompanied by Sister Kevin Campbell, Mother Gerald, as she reported to the Congregation in a letter upon her return, heard papers on "the education, preparation and life of the religious as in Canon Law."[26] While in Rome, however, she also became aware of the interest developing in establishing a university there offering preparation in theology for women religious. She looked on this possibility with approval.

The following year, on May 30, 1953, Mother Gerald received from the Sacred Congregation for Religious a notification that she had been chosen as a member of the commission of forty mothers general who would have "the honor and duty of representing the Superiors General of the whole world."[27] Two others from the United States were appointed to share this responsibility—Mother Marie Helene Franey, SP, and Mother Mary Bernardine Purcell, RSM. These three members of the World Committee met in Washington, DC, on August 18 to determine their responsibilities and to discuss the developing plan for the international university for sisters in Rome.

Their contact in Rome was with Mother Marie de St. Jean Martin, OSU, who was charged with overseeing the project. The initial needs were financial, for academic and housing facilities. Mother Marie de St. Jean proposed that if ten congregations could each contribute $10,000 over ten years, $100,000 would be available to advance the project. Mother Gerald immediately sent $10,000; later, $1,000 for the library; and still later, other smaller donations.

Mother Gerald was always supportive of the university, Regina Mundi Pontifical Institute, which opened in 1954. It achieved a measure of success, especially for sisters from Third World countries, until it closed in 2005. It is unclear, however, whether or not Mother Gerald ever sent any of her sisters to study there.

More New Schools

The 1950s were a decade of growth for the country and also for the Church. The population had emerged from the war years with a new sense of purpose and was enjoying a growing economy. The "baby boomers" had reached school age and were presenting challenges to the school systems, including those centered on Catholic parishes. Pastors were faced with the need to add to their parish schools or to build new ones. More importantly, they required teachers for their schools.

Mother Gerald was inundated with requests for sisters to meet the growing needs and she met the challenges as well as she could.

Mother Gerald's Fourth Term: 1951-1957

The Congregation was growing in numbers but scarcely fast enough to keep pace with what the schools required.

The 1950s also saw the completion of three Congregation-owned high schools for young women. The first, Hoban Dominican, was built in Cleveland and named for Bishop Edward Hoban, the local ordinary and longtime friend of the Congregation. A second, Rosary High School, opened in 1956 in Detroit, and a third, Regina Dominican High School, in Wilmette, Illinois, in 1958.

Hoban Dominican High School.

Regina Dominican seems to have been born out of a good-natured rivalry between two churchmen who had in common their friendship with Mother Gerald. One day in 1953, Cardinal Edward Mooney of Detroit and Cardinal Samuel Stritch of Chicago were dining with Mother Gerald at Rosarian Academy when Cardinal Mooney reminded Mother Gerald that she had promised him a new high school for girls. Cardinal Stritch pointed out that if she were to do this in Detroit, she had to do the same in Chicago.

Judy Zynda, the first student registered at Rosary High School, receives the American flag from members of the Veterans of Foreign Wars at the school's opening in 1956. She later joined the Congregation.

Mother Gerald committed to Cardinal Stritch that the Congregation would also open a high school in Chicago in about five years' time. Making such promises, for not just one but two high schools, would of course pose problems both in financing and in having enough sisters to staff these facilities. Indeed, on January 29, 1955, Mother Gerald sent a letter to the parish priests in whose schools the Congregation was serving, informing them that she could not add to their faculties in the next school year and would not be sending out postulants anymore.

> *. . . we have opened ever so many [parochial schools] with a beginning of four sisters and each year we have been pouring in increases with little or no returns in vocations. So, you can see that the end of the educational Marshall Plan is at hand. Perhaps some of you Reverend Pastors who have enjoyed bountiful treatment could turn back a sister or two to help in the current plight.*
>
> *I know the parochial school is the right arm of the Church and I love it, but please be patient with me now.*

The letter concluded by noting that the new high schools in Detroit and Chicago had been delayed by the shortage of sisters: "We have given those sisters who could staff them to the parochial schools. We are not sorry and wish we could do more."

But both high schools ultimately did take shape. Rosary High, the first to rise, was constructed on land donated to the Archdiocese of Detroit by the family of automotive pioneer Henry Ford. It opened in

Mother Gerald's Fourth Term: 1951-1957

August of 1956, with enrollment initially limited to freshmen only. The sisters on the faculty lived in the unused part of the school until their convent was built during the second year of the school's operation.

Sister Mary Philip Ryan, Rosary's superior and principal, wrote this about the school's beginnings.

> *When we occupied the building, the workmen were still completing pipe setting on the lower floor. There was a possibility of a break-in. Consequently, during that time, we were given police protection every hour in the course of the night.*
>
> *One morning as we went to chapel, we noticed a classroom door wide opened [sic] and clearly on the front blackboard written in large letters we read: "Sisters, write 100 times, We must close our classroom windows."*[28]

As for Regina Dominican, ground was broken in March 1957. More about its 1958 opening and the challenges the sisters there faced are discussed in the next chapter.

Undertaking such projects, and others as needed, obviously would come with a financial price as well as the need to have sisters to staff them. Mother Gerald's plan, which she unveiled in a letter on February 27, 1954, was to urge the sisters to make a special contribution to the cause.

In the letter, she outlined five projects: a building at Siena Heights College to house a chapel, the library, and the science and art departments; an auditorium, fine arts building, and rectory at Barry College; the two high schools; and a college and hospital in Puerto Rico.

The letter continued,

> ... *You will say when you read this far, "what is it that we can do since we are not architects, carpenters, builders, stone masons, craftsmen, men of brawn or sinew?" You can be each and all of these above-mentioned important people because you can be humble under the mighty hand of God and make an effort to provide the means of hiring the important ones. You can each make possible to the community at least one hundred dollars. Some of you can make possible many thousands of dollars according to the contacts you might have with parents, relatives, or friends, and thus show your loyalty and helpfulness.*

Additionally, she went to the parish priests and asked for their help. And while the Puerto Rican plans fell through, as has already been noted, work on all the other projects she outlined eventually moved ahead.

At Barry College, the new fine arts building and auditorium were dedicated on February 9, 1956. The science and library facilities at Siena Heights College were dedicated on May 7, 1957, but were in use before that.

The chapel at Siena Heights, at the time called Lumen Ecclesiae Chapel,[29] features artistic embellishments that were the work of noted artist Melville P. Steinfels. He had been engaged by Sister Helene O'Connor to create artwork that would embody the dedication of the chapel to St. Dominic Guzman (1170-1221) as *Lumen Ecclesiae*, or "Light of the Church," one of the titles accorded to St. Dominic. The crowning achievement of Steinfels' work in the chapel is a twenty-five-foot mosaic in the form of a flame that adorns the wall of the sanctuary.

The groundbreaking ceremony for Lumen Ecclesiae Chapel.

The tesserae of the mosaic are covered with gold leaf, giving the flame a luminous effect that conveys the fiery zeal of Dominic. Worked into the flame are scenes depicting events in the life of Dominic. A ten-foot crucifix of the Risen Christ, a sculpture created from limestone by Sister Joanne O'Connor,[30] is centered upon the mosaic. Mosaics of Mary and Joseph above the two side altars, as well as the ceramic-tiled Stations of the Cross along the walls of the chapel, are also by Steinfels.

Sister Joanne O'Connor's crucifix and Melville Steinfels' mosaic.
PHOTO CREDIT: SIENA HEIGHTS UNIVERSITY

The chapel was dedicated on the same date in May 1957 as were the science and library facilities, but the first Mass was celebrated there on

December 8, 1956. This event "was glorious," Mother Gerald wrote to the Congregation on December 10.

> *This seemed an especially appropriate feast [the Feast of the Immaculate Conception] on which to offer this new dwelling place to God, the Son of the Immaculate Mother, and now I only wish I possessed the powers of expression which would do justice to the beauty of the occasion. The chapel is magnificent, Sisters, a tribute to your spirit of generosity and sacrifice and unity. It is your offering to Almighty God along with yourselves.*

Growth in Vocations

Opening as many schools as the Congregation did in these years may have meant there were not enough sisters to staff them, but the fact remains that in the 1950s and into the 1960s the Adrian Dominicans saw a significant increase in vocations. Mother Gerald continued to exhort the sisters to bring in more and more young women. Her goal always was at least 100 a year, and she asked the sisters to pray for this number and to work hard at attracting girls to the Congregation.

Late in 1953, the General Council took the step of bringing the superiors, principals, and assistant principals of the grade schools and high schools in Michigan, Ohio, and Illinois together for a meeting on the issue. The Congregation also developed materials designed to attract prospective postulants as well as students for the preparatory school. One such booklet from the mid-1950s was *The Dominican Sisters of Adrian: World Apostolate*. It gives information about the Congregation and shows preparatory school students, postulants, novices and sisters in a variety of activities. They can be seen making profession, working in various ministries, sledding down the hill behind the novitiate, and more.

One paragraph from the text reads,

> *Youth and faith are the common bonds which draw together in the Novitiate all the various personalities, talents, backgrounds, and aims of the novices. In sacristy or infirmary, kitchen or garden, chapel or sewing room, with silence or laughter, the novice is always occupied with the business of changing a raw recruit into a trained and efficient soldier of Christ, willing and prepared for the battle for souls.*

The Bahamas

News of more expansion of the Congregation's missions came in Mother Gerald's general letter of November 7, 1956. In it, she announced that five sisters would soon be sent to Nassau, Bahamas, to teach at a normal school that would prepare both native sisters and lay women to be teachers. "It will be very interesting, I am sure," she wrote about the project. Ultimately named Aquinas College, it taught both younger students and adults in what eventually became a range of programs.

This new work came about after Bishop Paul Leonard Hagarty, OSB, the Vicar Apostolic of the Bahamas, requested Adrian Dominicans to set up a teacher training program. The Vicariate set up the school in the Hibiscus Inn, a former nightclub, and Sisters Jean Patricia McGowan, Ann Carmel Decker, Jean Kevin Aufderheide, Mary Aiden Brennan and Marie Peter Hafey-Wells arrived in Nassau in early January 1957.

Mother Gerald went with them to see them installed in their new home. It was a trip that proved costly to her health. She was already suffering from the flu and therefore not in the best condition to be traveling, and while she was in Nassau her condition worsened. The sisters persuaded her to head back to the States, where she was admitted to St. Francis Hospital in Miami Beach. Then, while she was there, one night she got out of bed, slipped on a rug, and fell, fracturing some vertebrae and extending her stay. Among her caregivers during her hospitalization was Sister Marie Brigid McDonald, a trained nurse who was on the faculty at Barry College.

En route to Nassau, left to right: Mother Gerald and Sisters Jean Patricia McGowan, Ann Carmel Decker, Jean Kevin Aufderheide, Mary Aiden Brennan, and Marie Peter Hafey-Wells.

At the end of January, Sister Benedicta Marie visited Mother Gerald at St. Francis. The Vicaress General reported to the Congregation in a January 29 letter that things were "healing nicely," that Mother Gerald could be up for several hours each day and could walk about, and that she "has resigned herself beautifully to the situation and is content to let nature take its course."

How much time she spent in the hospital is not known, but in mid-March, Mother Gerald was able to write a letter of thanks to the sisters for their prayers and notes and the Masses offered for her. She also thanked the Adrian Dominicans who were among the St. Francis nurses. "No patient in any hospital ever had more constant, tender, and devoted care than was given me by our own Sisters while I was confined to St. Francis," she wrote. "It seemed a special dispensation of Providence that placed the site of the disaster in that institution where our Sister nurses really form a part of the staff and where the glorious sunshine and warmth of Florida were vital factors in my recovery." At the end of March, she wrote to the Congregation that she was "feeling ever so much better" and could be at her desk most of the day.

At the time she wrote both of those March letters, Mother Gerald had just turned seventy-six years old. That fact, however, did not deter the delegates at that year's General Chapter from electing her yet again as Mother General.

1. Letter from Sister Benedicta Marie Ledwidge to Cardinal Edward Mooney, June 22, 1951.

2. Material on the Sister Formation movement is taken from a variety of studies, e.g., Marjorie Noterman Beane, *From Framework to Freedom. A History of the Sister Formation Conference* (New York: University Press of America, 1993); Lora Ann Quiñonez and Mary Daniel Turner, *The Transformation of American Catholic Sisters* (Philadelphia: Temple University Press, 1992); Bertrande Meyers, *Sisters for the 21st Century* (New York: Sheed and Ward, 1965), 104-123; Sister Formation communications and publications held in the archives of the Adrian Dominican Congregation.

3. Pope Pius XII, "Counsel to Teaching Sisters," First International Congress of Teaching Sisters, Vatican City, September 15, 1951. Translated from the Italian by the NCWC News Bureau in Rome.

4. Beane, *From Framework to Freedom*, 25-26.

5. Teacher Education and Professional Standards and the National Council for Accreditation of Teacher Education.

6. Beane, 60. The concluding quote was from Penet to the sisters.

7. Temporary professed sisters; those who had not taken final vows.

8. Beane, 63-64, based on informal minutes of the Everett Workshop, June 4, 1956, SFC archives.

9. Interestingly, this was not a requirement for the university's own faculty.

10. Conversation with Sister Nadine Foley.

11. It should be noted that, as Sister Formation developed, the sisters being prepared for nursing and other healthcare professions were included.

12. The Dominican Sisters of Edmonds, who did participate in the Sister Formation Conference, merged with the Adrian Dominican Sisters in 2003.

13. Francis J. Connell, "Opening Remarks," *Sisters' Religious Community Life in the United States: Proceedings of the Sisters' Section of the First National Congress of Religious of the United States* (Paulist Press, 1952), 1.

14 Mary Gerald Barry, "Welcome to Delegates at Opening Session of the Sisters' Section, National Congress of Religious of the United States," *Proceedings of the Sisters' Section*, 25.

15 "Religious and American," *Time* magazine, August 25, 1952 (online reference).

16 M. Richarda Peters, "Modern Convenience and Comfort in Their Relation to the Religious Spirit," *Proceedings of the Sisters' Section*, 86.

17 Held in the Adrian Dominican archives, dated January 31, 1956.

18 Two passages from Canon 565 are relevant to the discussion. "The year of the novitiate, under the direction of the master of novices, must have as its object the formation of the intellect and the will of the novice through the study of the rule and the constitutions, through pious meditation and continual prayer, through instructions on the vows and the virtues, and through suitable exercises the aim of which is to extirpate the very germs of vice, to master the emotions, and to acquire virtue"(1). "During the year of novitiate, novices must not be employed in preaching, the hearing of confession, or other external works of the institute, even inside the house, and they shall not devote themselves as to a task to the study of literature, of science, or of the arts. Thus, as Pius XI states, 'laying aside the study of any and every subject, the novices shall attend to this one purpose, namely, the practice of the interior life and the acquisition of the virtues'"(3). John Abbo and Jerome D. Hannan, eds., *The Sacred Canons. A Concise Presentation of the Current Disciplinary Norms of the Church, Vol I* (St. Louis: B. Herder Book Company, 1952), 581- 582.

19 Father Farrell was a friend of the Adrian Dominicans, having been taught by them in Chicago in his early years. He was an advisor to Mother Gerald on a number of things and on the issue of theological studies in this instance.

20 Among the Adrian Dominicans who pursued the three-year summer program were Sisters Carmelia O'Connor, Grace Agatha Dillon, Mary Ellen Erd, Ann Thomas Griffin, John Therese Singer, Clarita Marie Young, Evangela O'Hare, and Rose Francis Joyce.

21 The National Catholic Welfare Conference was the administrative arm of the American bishops. Presided over by a General Secretary, it directed the efforts of five original departments: Social Action, Education, Press, Legal, and Lay Organizations. To reflect its consultative nature its name was changed to the United States Catholic Conference in 1966. It was the standing secretariat of the National Conference of Catholic Bishops.

22. Some congregations that were distinctly missionary and ministered outside the United States related in Rome to these agencies rather than to the Sacred Congregation for Religious.

23. The reference is to Archbishop Joseph Ritter, originally Archbishop of Indianapolis and later Archbishop of St. Louis, the position he would have held at this time. Still later he was named Cardinal.

24. This is the term used for the bishop of the diocese.

25. For more detailed information on the negotiations between SFC and CMSW consult Beane, especially pp. 97-136.

26. General letter of October 23, 1952.

27. This group was the precursor of the International Union of Superiors General.

28. From a letter written to Sister Nancyann Turner, the Nokomis Chapter Prioress, on February 23, 1996, and reprinted in the March 1996 *Nokomis Bulletin*.

29. The name was changed to St. Dominic Chapel in 2010.

30. Sister Helene O'Connor's sister.

Chapter Six
Mother Gerald's Fifth Term: 1957-1961

One Final Election

At the General Chapter of 1957, when the delegates gave Mother Gerald 171 votes out of the 253 cast, Sister Benedicta Marie once again initiated the postulation process with the Vatican. In her letter of June 14, 1957, to Cardinal Mooney, she made the case for postulation.

> ... *In acting as it did, the Chapter showed its approval and appreciation of Mother Gerald's administration of this large Congregation which demands executive ability of the highest order. Mother's zeal in serving the cause of Christ and the Church is known not only here in our own country but in fields afar and the spirit with which the Sisters are imbued is the spirit that they have imbibed from her who ever spurs them onward in the quest for souls.*
>
> *The Congregation has enjoyed tremendous growth under Mother Gerald's direction. In the six years since the last General Chapter, 592 postulants have received the habit. No less significant is the great increase in the number of children under our charge as indicated below. This huge increase is understandable in view of the fact that we opened fifty new schools during this period.*

> *During the scholastic year just ended (1956-1957), there were 81,072 students in our grade schools —* **an increase of 32,361 since the last General Chapter.**
>
> *There were 12,516 students in our high schools —* **an increase of 5,685 since the last General Chapter.**
>
> *There were 822 full-time students in our Colleges —* **an increase of 294;** *and there were 1,832 part-time students (including summer courses and evening classes) —* **an increase of 729.**
>
> *Children in religious instruction classes outside of regular school hours numbered 32,487 —* **an increase of 17,543 since 1951.**

You yourself know, Your Eminence, Mother Gerald's missionary zeal, and this has been evidenced lately through the foundation of a Teacher's College in a very poor missionary territory — Nassau, Bahamas — where native Sisters in particular are now receiving much needed instruction. Native lay teachers also are encouraged by the Most Reverend Bishop to avail themselves of this opportunity and they, too, are present in goodly numbers in these classes.

Of the 592 postulants received during the past six years, a number came from missionary fields in which we are working and they have, for the most part, proved to be excellent subjects.

Mother Gerald's Fifth Term: 1957-1961

> *Therefore, Your Eminence, the Chapter respectfully requests that you forward to the Holy See our petition that its postulation for Mother Mary Gerald be approved and that she be permitted to continue in the office of Mother General. We humbly beg you to add your recommendation to our plea.*

Similar letters also went to Archbishop Cicognani, who was still the Apostolic Delegate, and to Cardinal Valerie Valeri, the Prefect of the Sacred Congregation for Religious.

Rome granted the delegates' request—with one stipulation. Mother Gerald could definitely serve for three years. At the end of that time, or at any time during the remaining three years of her term, the Sacred Congregation could require a new election. It did not do so.

Regina Dominican High School

The cornerstone for Regina Dominican High School was laid on November 10, 1957, in a ceremony attended by Mother Gerald[1] and a number of local church dignitaries. One of them was Monsignor William McManus, the superintendent of schools, who said in his address during the event,

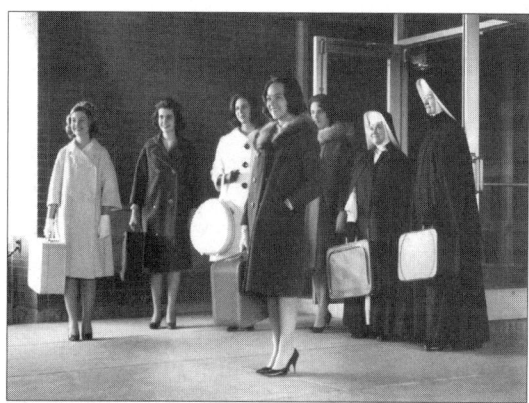

Regina Dominican students setting off on a European trip with Sisters Rose Edwina Daly (left) and Clare Ambrose Gleeson.

In 1951 our Holy Father in an address to the First International Congress of Teaching Sisters said: "Many of your schools are being described and praised to us as being very good. But not all. It is our fervent wish that all endeavor to become excellent."

The Dominican Sisters dutifully and generously interpreted the Holy Father's wish as a mandate. What the Pope wants, they said, we must do. Their response to the Holy Father's request has been a constant, tireless endeavor to achieve excellence in their many and varied educational enterprises. Their conviction is that only the very best is good enough for a pupil in a Dominican school.

Despite Bishops' and pastors' incessant pleas for more and more nuns to staff their enlarged and new Catholic schools, the Dominican Sisters have improved their teacher preparation program by giving most of their new members time to complete their basic studies before they are assigned to teaching and by giving their experienced teachers ample opportunity for advanced studies. This they have done in response to the Pope's request that teaching Sisters be masters of the subjects they expound and that their education correspond in quality and academic degrees to that demanded by the State. In this community the religious habit is no cover-up for professional mediocrity; it is rather a sign and a symbol of professional competence dedicated to the honor of God.

Mother Gerald's Fifth Term: 1957-1961

As has already been discussed, Mother Gerald certainly was stressing the importance of a good education for the members of the Congregation long before Pope Pius XII asked that teaching sisters become "masters of the subjects they expound." The fact remains, however, that Monsignor McManus thought very highly of the Adrian Dominicans and wanted to share those sentiments in his speech. Not long thereafter, on November 22, 1957, he reiterated his feelings in a letter to Mother Gerald.

> *It was a privilege to be able to participate in the ceremony for the laying of the cornerstone at Regina Dominican High School on Sunday, Nov. 10. It gave me an excellent opportunity to express some views that I have wanted to voice for a long time. There are just not enough good things to be said about the work of the Adrian Dominicans in this archdiocese.*

Sister Kevin Campbell, who had long ago firmly established her reputation as a woman who knew how to get new endeavors up and running, was appointed as the school's first principal. When it had become clear that the opening would be delayed from 1957 to 1958, she was assigned to teach at the Congregation's other Chicago high school, Aquinas, located on the other side of the city. She continued to supervise the Regina Dominican construction work as well, from a makeshift office located in the construction shack. "On a plank before a pot-bellied stove I carried on negotiations with architects, contractors, sub-contractors, tradesmen and salesmen," she wrote in a history of the school's early days. "A phone, a lunch box, a thermos, and WAITING made up my life on the site."

As the time for the school to open neared, Sister Kevin made the rounds of the area parishes to recruit students. The little construction shack became the registration site.

> As a result of all these contacts it was necessary to begin the registration of prospective students and so my week lengthened to six days and, later, to seven as we concentrated on meeting parents and daughters on Saturdays and Sundays on the site.

At one point, a mannequin modeling the new school's uniform joined her in the shack. ". . . she was so delightful that often I found myself addressing her, thinking some one was present with me," she wrote in the history.

Sister Kevin was also in charge of procuring the items needed to equip both the school and the convent. This prompted Mother Gerald to request, in an April 17, 1958, letter to the Congregation, that the sisters ask their students to have their parents donate trading stamps that could be redeemed for household items. "Your cooperation in this matter will be much appreciated," the letter continued, "and knowing how you respond to any and every suggestion ever presented in the interest of the Community, I am inclined to ask Sister Kevin to set up a stand in the middle of Soldiers' Field so that she will have room for the avalanche!"[2]

The school, which the *Chicago Sun-Times* said drew on "know-how gleaned from the operation of schools in all parts of the country" and was "an educator's dream and a student's delight,"[3] opened in September 1958. It was not necessarily welcomed by everyone on

Mother Gerald's Fifth Term: 1957-1961

Chicago's North Shore, however. According to a reminiscence written by Sister Winifred Marx, a member of the first faculty,

> *The Wilmette police seemed to be especially interested in us. They came and went through the building as they pleased. Sometimes they walked into the dining hall while . . . our night meal was being served. One evening, two of them came into the refectory and one of the policemen, who seemed to be the boss, said, "Do you people know that you are not wanted in this neighborhood?" No one replied but then we knew what we had to counteract.*

Still, however, in her history of the school's founding, Sister Kevin noted the many ways in which members of the local community came forward to help get things off the ground. For example, she wrote of one man who donated the means to clean their habits,

> *. . . we had trampled the north side to try to solve it ourselves. It is really necessary for us to use a wash board and a hand wringer on the bottom and sleeves of our habits when the weather is bad and much grime and dirt are carried into the classroom. We had almost given up hope of finding them when Mr. Peter Wickham came to our rescue. He informed us that Sears had everything, even buggy whips. We could see no need for the whips but we hailed him as our benefactor when he appeared one evening with a hand wringer and two wash boards tucked under his arms. If I were to tell you how each of our many friends came to know our needs and to help us I*

> *should far extend my time. Suffice it to say that the long list of benefactors made it evident to us that we were needed and WANTED on the North Shore . . .*

Cardinal Stritch did not live long enough to see to fruition the facility he had personally requested from Mother Gerald during that dinner at Rosarian Academy back in 1953. On March 1, 1958, he was named Pro-Prefect of the Sacred Congregation for the Propagation of the Faith, and died in Rome that May.

South to Texas

Over the last years of her life, even with her health in decline, Mother Gerald continued fairly regularly to make the rounds of the Congregation's various foundations around the country and abroad. She even made one long trip, not on behalf of the Adrian Dominican Sisters, but to assist a group of sisters from Spain.

These women, members of a congregation known as the Missionary Society of the Sacred Heart, were studying at Siena Heights College during the summer of 1958. At that same time, the pastor of St. Elizabeth's Church in Snyder, Texas, Father Edward Chrisman, was looking for sisters to staff a school he had just completed there. Mother Gerald discussed with him the possibility of the Spanish sisters taking on his school. When it was decided that they would, Mother Gerald told them that she would personally see them safely to their new home.

Sister Mary Paul (Noreen) McKeough wrote about the journey in a memorial piece on Mother Gerald published in 1962.

> *In her relationship with visiting sister-students, especially those from foreign countries, she showed the same personal, motherly interest that she took in her own subjects. Their concerns became hers. When three sisters of the Missionary Society of the Sacred Heart (Madrid, Spain) had finished their college courses at Adrian and were preparing to make their first American foundation in West Texas, in August, 1958, Mother Gerald herself with a companion accompanied them to their new home. Despite the heat and her failing health she would not be satisfied until she had personally inspected their convent and school. In an account printed in "Forward," the Society's newsletter, one of the missionaries wrote in May, 1960:*
>
> *"That action of Mother M. Gerald, taking a trip of 31 hours, at her old age, to assist three unexperienced missionaries in the start of a foundation was like a summary of her life totally spent in the service of Christ and his Church."*[4]

Meeting Contemporary Needs

Mother Gerald was visionary enough to read "the signs of the times," to borrow a Vatican II phrase used often by the Adrian Dominican Sisters today, in at least one respect when it came to educating children. She saw a need and made sure her sisters were well positioned to help meet it.

"Another matter which is receiving nation-wide attention on the part of the Church and educators is the study of the care and training of the mentally retarded [sic]," she wrote in a general letter on May 7, 1959.

> *Again, we are keeping pace since two of our sisters will attend Wayne University for courses in this special education; while two others will enroll at the St. Coletta School, Jefferson, Wisconsin, that they might avail themselves of the knowledge that can be acquired, not only through course work but through actual contact with the children enrolled in that institution. There will be a real future need for trained teachers for these children, and we should feel privileged to be included in the work.*

Over the years, several sisters earned degrees in special education and went on to work in the field. One of these was Sister Dorothy Glaister, who spent ten years at St. Coletta's as assistant principal and principal. At least two others, Sisters Ann Claudia Grant and Sabina Jabour, also ministered at St. Coletta's, although without special-education degrees.

Restructuring

By the end of 1959, the issue of how to effectively govern a religious congregation that was growing large in numbers[5] had already been discussed by the General Council for some time. At that point, a major change in the Congregation's structure was made.

A proposal concerning the matter had been introduced at the General Chapter of 1957. It involved the creation of three provinces "not for the purpose of separation but for greater spiritual unity."[6] Each would be led by a provincial with the assistance of three vice-provincials, who in turn would each have three vice-councilors. Such an arrangement would have the advantage of dividing the administrative duties. It would also relieve Mother Gerald of some of the traveling associated with the canonically required annual visitations to each house, since the provincials could take these on.

According to the General Chapter minutes, "Mother Gerald remarked that as the Congregation is growing very large no doubt something will have to be done as an aid to distribution of the burden of administration." But, she added, according to canon law, dividing into provinces would come under the scope of the Sacred Congregation for Religious, which would consider the recommendation of the General Council. Therefore, the matter was not put to a vote.

Study continued on the part of the Council, and the resulting idea for a provincial structure was taken up with the Holy See not long before Pope Pius XII died in October 1958. His death delayed the process, but on December 4, 1959, Mother Gerald broke the news to the sisters.

> *The news contained in this letter will come as a surprise to you but I am sure that you will receive it as the manifest will of God in our regard. You must all have been aware, as we have been, that, due to the extraordinary growth of the Community*

and the great number of Sisters it now contains, it has become a physical impossibility for one person to carry the burden of administration for the entire group.

. . . Now this very day we received word that, effective on the Feast of the Immaculate Conception of the Blessed Virgin Mary, December 8, 1959, the Congregation is divided into Provinces. Although the division is effective as of that date, no changes will be made in the method of administration until the opening of the scholastic year, 1960.

. . . In making this change, the greatest possible care has been taken to preserve the spirit of unity which has distinguished the Community up to this time. While, in order to secure greater ease in administration, there must be geographical divisions, there will be, please God, no division of hearts.

The new organization featured a Generalate and five provinces. The Generalate consisted of the Motherhouse campus, including Siena Heights College and St. Joseph Academy; the Adrian Dominican House of Studies; Barry College; and Aquinas College, the mission in the Bahamas. According to a document accompanying Mother Gerald's July 29, 1960, letter outlining the upcoming changes, the Generalate "shall include the Motherhouse and Novitiate in Adrian, Michigan, as well as a group of designated houses which, because of the nature of their works, serve the whole Congregation and are dependent directly upon the Prioress General." Any future "colleges and houses of general use to the whole Congregation" would also become part of the Generalate.

Mother Gerald's Fifth Term: 1957-1961

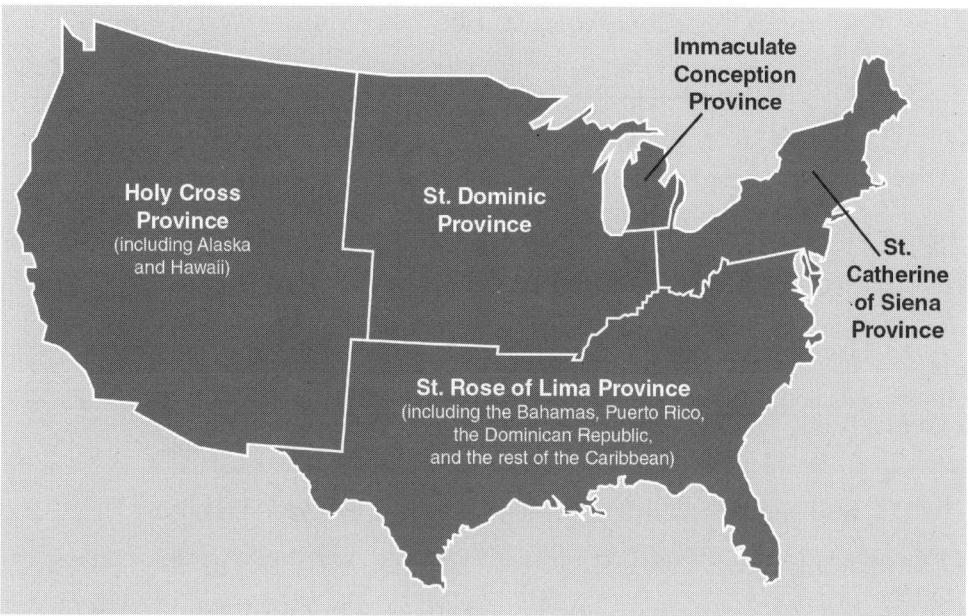

The five provinces were:

- Immaculate Conception, which included the west side of Detroit and the part of the Lower Peninsula of Michigan west of M-53, which runs between Detroit and Port Austin, located in the Thumb area of the state;

- St. Catherine of Siena, encompassing the east side of Detroit, the part of Lower Michigan east of M-53, and the states of Connecticut, Delaware, Maine, Massachusetts, New Hampshire, New Jersey, New York, Ohio, Pennsylvania, Rhode Island, and Vermont;

- St. Dominic, made up of the Upper Peninsula of Michigan as well as Illinois, Indiana, Iowa, Kansas, Minnesota, Missouri,

Nebraska, North Dakota, South Dakota, and Wisconsin;

- St. Rose of Lima, composed of Alabama, Arkansas, Florida, Georgia, Kentucky, Louisiana, Maryland, Mississippi, North Carolina, Oklahoma, South Carolina, Tennessee, Texas, Virginia, West Virginia, the District of Columbia, and the Bahamas, Puerto Rico, the Dominican Republic, and the rest of the Caribbean;

- Holy Cross Province, which included the states of Alaska, Arizona, California, Colorado, Hawaii, Idaho, Montana, Nevada, New Mexico, Oregon, Utah, Washington, and Wyoming.

The respective provincial houses were at Rosary High and Dominican High in Detroit; Mount St. Mary Academy in St. Charles, Illinois; Rosarian Academy in West Palm Beach, Florida; and Sisters Hospital in Santa Cruz, California.

Each province was governed by a provincial and four councilors. Named as the first provincials were Sisters Mary Edmund Harrison, Immaculate Conception; Mary Brigetta McDonough, St. Catherine of Siena; Mary Kevin Campbell, St. Dominic; Ann Catherine (Rita) Gleason, St. Rose of Lima; and Jean Marie Sheridan, Holy Cross. In each province, the first councilor served as the vicaress and the second councilor as the secretary-treasurer.

"I have no greater desire than to preserve unity in the midst of our glorious multiplicity, so let us all draw close, close to the Heart of Christ, and may He bless us everyone," Mother Gerald wrote in that July 29 letter which went out with all the explanatory documents. Later,

Mother Gerald's Fifth Term: 1957-1961

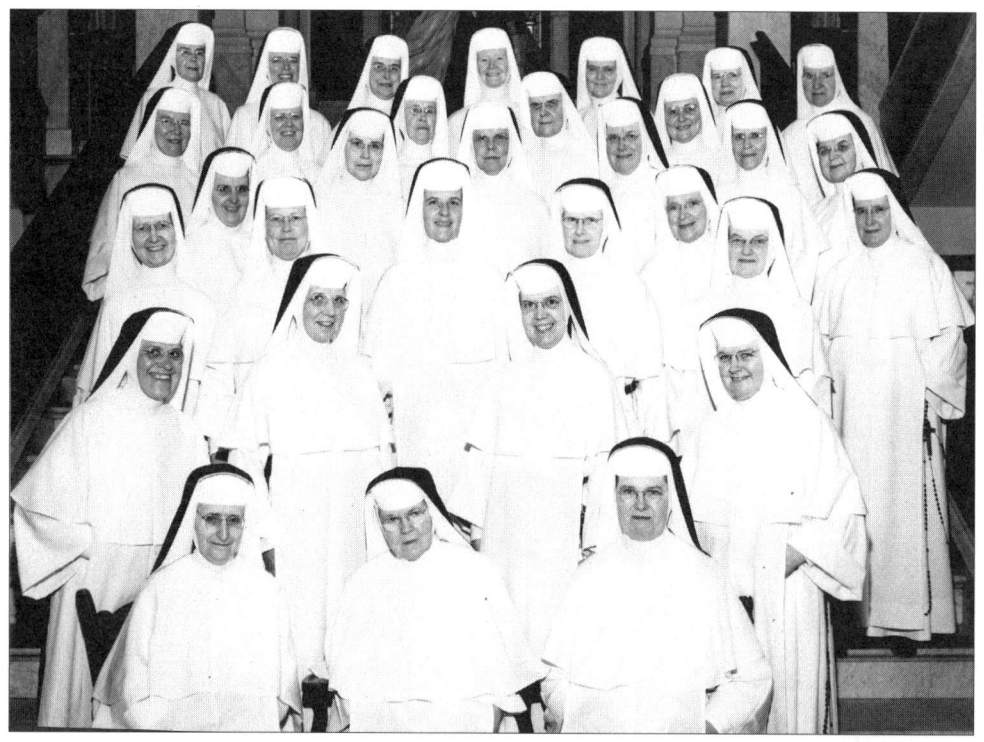

Mother Gerald (front row, center) and the Congregational leadership in August 1960.

on September 1, 1960, a week before the provinces officially went into effect on September 8, she wrote,

> *I know that with the beautiful spirit of unity and cooperation which is characteristic of our Adrian Dominican Sisters, you will comply cheerfully with all regulations and continue to pray that we may be "one in Christ" and that the close family spirit which has always prevailed among us may continue in all its strength and fervor. Never forget that ADRIAN IS YOUR HOME and that you are the beloved children of that*

To Fields Near and Far

> *home while, at the same time, you render the utmost respect and obedience to the capable and devoted members of the Community who have been chosen to assist in the administration and thus lessen the ever-growing burden at the Motherhouse.*

With that letter also went a document with some explanatory notes. Three reasons for arranging the provinces as had been done were given.

1. To equalize as far as possible the burdens of the provincials.

2. To provide for convenience and economy in making the visitations and in contacting the houses in general.

3. To equalize as far as possible the distribution of the high schools among the various provinces in order to provide for proper placement of secondary and grade school teachers.

The document also provided this numerical breakdown:[7]

Generalate and Provinces	Houses	Sisters	High Schools
Immaculate Conception Province	54	570	14
St. Catherine of Siena Province	43	425	9
St. Dominic Province	54	548	5
St. Rose of Lima Province	33	283	7
Holy Cross Province	24	189	2
Generalate (Novices: 129) (Postulants: 110)	7	157	1
TOTALS	215	2,172	38

Mother Gerald's Fifth Term: 1957-1961

Another document noted the necessary revisions of the Constitution. Essentially, the changes reflected the fact that the office of provincial superior needed to be added to several articles concerning certain issues of governance and other matters.

The Dominican Sisters of Our Lady of Remedies

In June 1960, Bishop Emilio Cinense of the Diocese of San Fernando, Pampanga, the Philippines, requested the help of Mother Gerald in beginning a new congregation. She offered to train the first candidates in Adrian and then send them back to the Philippines, with two of her own sisters, to found this new community.

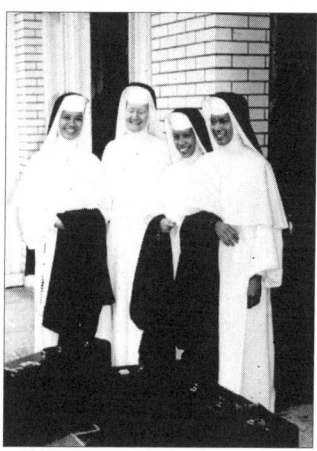

Sister Mary Philip Ryan, second from left, with Sisters Milagros Garcia (Sister Mary Regina), Digna San Vicente (Sister Thomas), and Esperanza Bonifacio (Sister Joseph).

The first three of what Mother Gerald dubbed "The Queen's Daughters"[8] arrived in Adrian in September 1961. Two more arrived in September 1962. Out of those five women, four—Esperanza Bonifacio, Milagros Garcia, Digna San Vincente, and Evangelina Garcia Fernandez—received the habit in January 1964 and began their canonical novitiate. Now known as Sisters Joseph, Mary Regina, Thomas and Dominic, respectively, the women took their vows in February 1965.

They returned to the Philippines in mid-1965. Sisters Mary Philip Ryan and Ellen Vincent McClain were the first two Adrian Dominicans assigned to help them begin the new congregation, which took the name Dominican Sisters of Our Lady of Remedies.

Sister Evangelina Fernandez

In December 1972, leadership authority was transferred from the Adrian Dominican Sisters to the Remedies sisters, with Sister Evangelina appointed Prioress by Bishop Cinense. She was later elected to the position by the sisters themselves and is recognized as the community's founding Prioress. The Congregation received canonical approval in October 1976.[9]

More New Missions

Education continued to be the priority as the 1960s progressed. At the beginning of 1961, the Congregation announced that it would establish a college for women in St. Charles, Illinois, at the request of Bishop Loras Lane of Rockford.

Lane had originally envisioned a junior college in Rockford itself, in connection with Muldoon High School. Mother Gerald and the General Council suggested instead that the school be built near Mount St. Mary Academy, on property owned by the Congregation. Additionally, their preference was for a four-year college. The final decision was helped by the donation of fifty-three acres along the Fox River by a local couple, Mr. and Mrs. Lester Norris.

Mother Gerald wrote to the Congregation on January 27, 1961, that establishing a four-year college had won the approval of the Bishop. She added that Bishop Lane agreed with the Congregation that such a college would create greater opportunities for the young women of his diocese "as well as for our own Sisters who must drink deep of the fountains of knowledge in preparation for their apostolate of Christian education."

Then on February 16, she had this to say in a general letter.

> *I have received only the most enthusiastic and favorable reactions to this [the planned college] and I know that the project will be blessed with the usual success because, again, we can count on your interest and your help. Many of the Sisters mentioned that this has been a long-time dream on the part of almost every Sister who spent any time at Mt. St. Mary's. Let us all work and pray to make this a dream come true that we might share the more in extending His kingdom on earth.*

St. Dominic College was completed in 1963 during the tenure of Mother Gerald's successor, Mother Genevieve Weber. Despite Mother Gerald's optimism, however, opening the school turned out to be an unfortunate move. There were, after all, numerous other colleges and universities, Catholic and otherwise, in the Chicago area, and many of them were struggling to build their enrollments as it was. Still, a silver lining came out of the endeavor. When the

College closed in 1970 and the property was sold to the Arthur Anderson and Company accounting firm, the investment the Adrian Dominicans had made in the school was recouped and augmented the Congregation retirement fund.

That February 16, 1961, letter to the sisters also contained the news of the final seeds of mission to be sown during Mother Gerald's lifetime.

> *We have, at the urgent pleading of the Holy See, committed ourselves to establish a foundation in Lima, Peru. The Apostolic Delegate there, our good friend Archbishop Romolo Carboni, formerly of the Secretariat of State in Rome and Apostolic Delegate to Australia, is delighted with the prospects of having the Adrian Dominicans under his jurisdiction.*

Sisters Mary Philip Ryan and Richardine Waldron were assigned to make the trip to Peru to investigate matters. When they returned from their travels, Mother Gerald wrote idealistically about the potential new mission in a May 5, 1961, general letter.

> *An assignment to South America . . . will not be a glamorous event in the life of an Adrian Dominican anymore [sic] than it has been in the lives of the other American sisters who have given themselves to the work there. It will be, in all truth, a call to sacrifice, to sacrifice self and home and those you love, but the reward of the missioner will be yours. The Maryknoll Sisters remain at their mission posts at least ten years; the others, until they are recalled which could be six, eight, or*

Mother Gerald's Fifth Term: 1957-1961

ten years. They do not come home for illness or death in the family, nor every so often for a home visit, but that is the price they willingly pay for the privilege of participating in such a soul-satisfying apostolate.

. . . There is no doubt in the minds of the Sisters [Mary Philip and Richardine] that we will be welcome in Lima, that

Left to right: Sisters María Altagracia (Teresita) Pellerano and Robert Francis (Nancy) Hanna, Mother Genevieve Weber, and Sister María Josefina (Ana) Feliz. The three sisters were the first Adrian Dominicans missioned to La Perla in Callao, Peru.

there is work for us to do, and that our Community will be blessed in the doing. We would be free to work on any level. We could have another Barry College; we could have another Colegio Santo Domingo; we could duplicate Dominican High, Hoban High, Rosary High and Regina Dominican. We could take parish schools in a nice middle class section of the city. We could teach all boys or all girls on the elementary level, or the latter alone on the secondary level. We could dare, with the Maryknollers, to mix the classes—boys and girls—an innovation there but successful thus far. We could go into the "barriados," the slum areas and there reach out to the less privileged, the spiritually, socially, economically impoverished. We could show them the charity of Christ in action through generous, unselfish service. We could do so much, Sisters. Where we shall do it depends upon the inspiration of the Holy Spirit through the power of your prayers. This is YOUR project. Through it we could really save souls for Christ.

Like St. Dominic College, however, this mission was not to be realized during Mother Gerald's lifetime. Our Lady of Guadalupe School opened in 1963 in a poor section of Callao, near Lima.

Mother Gerald's Declining Health

When Mother Gerald referred to the "ever-growing burden" of administration in that September 1, 1960, letter about the division of the community into provinces, it was a burden certainly not helped by her failing health. She was seventy-nine years old and had suffered from various physical issues for some time.

There was her fall and injured vertebrae at the hospital in Florida in 1957, the fall and resultant broken ribs at the Regina Dominican cornerstone dedication in November of that year, a hospitalization in the spring of 1959 for what she wrote was either "sciatica, an injured disc, or just plain arthritis,"[10] a broken wrist in March 1960, and quite possibly other ailments she did not mention in her letters of those years.

She was in a wheelchair on February 1, 1961, when she was at Loyola University to accept her third honorary doctorate. Later that month, she was also in the wheelchair when she and the Congregation were both honored by the Adrian Chamber of Commerce for their impact on the local community over almost eight decades.[11] "She is recovering from an injury suffered in a recent fall," noted the *Adrian Daily Telegram*, as the local newspaper was then known, to explain Mother Gerald's being photographed in the wheelchair for the paper's February 24, 1961, coverage of the award presentation.

When interviewed in October 2010, Sister Rosemary Ferguson said she thinks in hindsight that Mother Gerald should not have been re-elected Prioress in 1957. "But it was a sentimental vote, and we were not made aware of her declining health," she said.

The Mother Gerald of those last years is the one that many sisters in the Congregation today knew when they entered: frail, often wheelchair-bound, unable to conduct the community's business in the way she had done ever since becoming Vicaress General three decades earlier. But while her health had clearly been deteriorating for quite some time, when the end came, it did so with a suddenness that still surprised those closest to her.

A Leader's Death

Sister Richardine Waldron, who served as Mother Gerald's personal secretary from 1951 until the General Chapter of 1957, when she was elected Secretary General of the Congregation, wrote an account of Mother Gerald's final hours in a letter to members of the Barry family in Ireland. She had just returned from a visit to the Emerald Isle during which she had visited with the Barrys, and was bringing their greetings back to Mother Gerald. This is what she found:

> *I arrived in Adrian late Sunday night, Nov. 19, so was unable to see Mother until the next morning. She had been nauseated through the night so did not receive Communion but when Sister Benedicta Marie told her that the travelers had returned she said to send them in. I went in first and was somewhat surprised to note that Mother had failed considerably since I left Adrian. It was evident that she was very weak and her eyes were closed. I greeted her and asked if she remembered me, to which she only uttered a weak "Umm." I then told her that I brought lots of love from the two Fathers Joe[12] and from everyone in Ireland. She again uttered "Umm" but this time with much more feeling. I could say no more for her condition alarmed me.*

. . . Later in the morning the doctor arrived and he, too, was startled in the sudden change in her condition.

Late that afternoon, Mother Gerald's health swiftly grew even worse, and it quickly became clear that she did not have long to live. For the next four hours or so, she lay in her bed attended by priests and visited by her beloved Adrian Dominican Sisters. Sister Benedicta Marie Ledwidge, Mother Gerald's faithful assistant for her entire tenure as Mother General, described those final hours in a letter to the Congregation sent on December 3.

Every professed Sister on the Adrian campus had the privilege of being with Mother during those last precious hours and you all know how she loved to have her Sisters around her. Kneeling in the room and the adjoining corridor, they joined the succession of rosaries which was interrupted only by the singing of the Salve at frequent intervals and the absolutions given over and over again by our devoted priests. It was truly a Dominican death scene. An hour or so before the end, Father Gaynor, Mother Edmund, Mother Brigetta, and Sister Mary Philip[13] arrived. At the same time we knew that most of the Sisters in the Community were united in prayer with us for the news that her hours on earth would be few had been sent as far and wide as possible.

At 10:15 p.m., November 20, 1961, the end came. It was "the eve of the Presentation of our Blessed Lady—a beautifully symbolic time," Sister Benedicta Marie wrote. The letter continued,

. . . her soul returned gently and sweetly to the God Whom she

> *had served so wholeheartedly. It would be difficult to describe the utter peace of her dying. In the five hours during which she lingered on the brink of eternity, there was not the least sign of anxiety or struggle and those of us beside her could scarcely tell when she drew her last breath.*

"Her passing was almost imperceptible, so easy was it," Sister Richardine wrote to the Barry family. ". . . There was no struggle, no pain, nothing but genuine peace surrounded her during her last moments and all agreed that everything went as Mother would have it."

Mother Mary Gerald Barry was eighty years old when she died. She had led the Adrian Dominican Sisters for twenty-eight years and been the guiding force behind schools, hospitals, and other missions across the United States and internationally. Under her leadership, the Congregation had more than doubled in members and educated thousands upon thousands of children. And she had helped shape the future of Catholic women religious around the world.

On Thanksgiving morning, November 23, two days before her funeral, Archbishop John Dearden of Detroit celebrated a Mass for her in Adrian at Lumen Ecclesiae Chapel. His homily included these words:

> *God gave her length of years; almost a half century as a professed religious. He gave her fruitful opportunities to do good for the Community and for the Church. She used them well and from beginning to end she was the humble, dedicated, devoted servant of the Divine Master with a personal, direct,*

immediate interest in the welfare of each of the sisters of her Community. The growth that she was to bear witness to over these years and to which she undoubtedly contributed was significant. This Community has grown so impressively in numbers during the years that she served as superior and yet, far more important in her judgment and far more important in the eyes of God is the fact that with this growth there has been joined always a full and complete dedication to the ideals of religious life that are represented in the Rule of this Community. This came first, and because it came first her work was conspicuously blessed. After so long a span of service we cannot deny her the right to enter into the reward that God has promised for the faithful servant.

In a testament to her impact on the Church, her funeral on November 25 was attended by five archbishops, seven bishops, some sixty monsignori, and two hundred priests. Her brother Monsignor William Barry was the presider, with her nephew Laurence, a Jesuit priest, serving as the deacon and her grandnephew Father William Barry as the subdeacon. The Very Rev. Vincent Hughes, OP, preached,[14] as did Archbishop Edward Hoban of Cleveland, who

Monsignor William Barry presiding at Mother Gerald's funeral.

said he believed himself to be "the oldest friend of the Community in the Hierarchy at present." He had known the Adrian Dominican Sisters, he noted, since the days of Mother Camilla Madden and through the time of Mother Augustine Walsh,

> ... and Mother Gerald now, who has gone to her reward, has summed up all their virtues, all their kindliness, all their wisdom, and has advanced this Community to this marvelous degree of perfection in numbers, in quality, in ability, and in all the virtues that make up a wonderful sister in the eyes of God and His Blessed Mother.

Messages of sympathy also poured in to the Congregation from members of the hierarchy around the world, as well as from dozens of members of other religious communities, from Adrian Mayor Walter Bohn, and from the governor of Michigan, John Swainson.

The words of Sister Mary Paul (Noreen) McKeough, excerpted from the Winter 1962 *Dominican Educational Bulletin,* provide a fitting epitaph for a woman who gave her all to her God and to her Congregation.

> *Mother Gerald resists type-casting. She was no more a schoolwoman in the narrow sense of the term than she was a builder, or a financier, or an administrator. She was a specialist only in the sense that she directed all the powers of her compelling character to Christian education, that education which, as Chesterton said, "in older and somewhat plainer language would have been called 'the saving of the soul.'"*

Mother Gerald's Fifth Term: 1957-1961

Even those who disagreed with her on details of educational policy or practice could never reasonably doubt her simplicity of motivation and singleness of purpose. Tirelessly she reminded the sisters of their duty to instruct their pupils unto justice. Her letters to the community through the years are punctuated with admonitions to prepare lessons well, to share knowledge, to live in sisterly charity.

. . . From the point of view of her religious family, at least, Mother Gerald's work as an educator, a teacher of teachers, might be said to derive from two principles: preparing and sharing.

The funeral procession.

And these two activities, flowing into and enriching each other, become one manifestation of the great Dominican ideal: to study seriously and then transmit or "surrender" the fruits of such study to the hungry and needy of the world.

. . . The sisters know that her outstanding reputation as a leader, and especially as an educator, rests simply on her genuine charity. Like all human beings, she made errors in judgment; she sometimes made hasty decisions later to be regretted; in her younger days she was quicktempered. But

transcending all these is the real keynote of her character and the clue to her astonishing achievements: her simple, magnificent love of God.

Mother Gerald Barry, Mother General, 1933-1961

1. The fall she took at the ceremony has already been noted on p. 21.
2. About a year later, when it came time to furnish the dormitory at St. Joseph Academy which was then under construction, she made an identical request.
3. September 15, 1958, issue.
4. *Dominican Education Bulletin*, Vol. III, No. 1, Winter 1962.
5. By this time, the community numbered about 2,100 members, and more growth was ahead over the next several years.
6. Minutes of the Chapter.
7. These figures are noted in the document as being of August 18, 1960.
8. According to a 1997 history of this group of sisters written by Sister Mary Philip Ryan, Mother Gerald gave the young women this name because she was impressed by their "gracious manners."
9. Over time, the Remedies sisters decided that they wished to become a pontifical congregation, rather than diocesan, and requested a merger with the Adrian Dominicans. The merger officially took place in October 2011, with the Filipina sisters becoming the Our Lady of Remedies Mission Chapter of the Adrian Dominican Sisters.
10. General letter of May 7, 1959.
11. "For 79 years the Dominicans have influenced the cultural, educational, scientific, religious and economic life of the community—and all for the good.... Through the students who have come to Adrian, and through the Sisters of the order, the good name of Adrian has been coupled with the good work of the Dominicans around the world," wrote the *Adrian Daily Telegram* in a February 18, 1961, editorial.
12. This is a reference to Mother Gerald's brother Joseph and a nephew who was named Joseph. Both were priests, and for at least some time served the same parish near the Barry family home.

[13] Father George Gaynor, the Congregation's chaplain; Mother Mary Edmund Harrison, Provincial of the Immaculate Conception Province; Mother Mary Brigetta McDonough, Provincial of the St. Catherine of Siena Province; and Sister Mary Philip Ryan.

[14] An excerpt from his homily can be found on p. 5.

Afterword

Mother Gerald died in November 1961. Not only was it the end of her long tenure as Mother General of the Adrian Dominican Sisters, it was the end of an era. Pope John XXIII had ascended to the seat of St. Peter and was about to announce the convening of an ecumenical council, the first since Vatican Council I which had ended in 1870. Mother Gerald's illness during the last years of her life had prevented her from seeing the signs of change evident even in her own sisters. The Council, which came to be known as Vatican Council II, was a call for *aggiornamento*, an opening of the Church to the modern world. It was to have a profound impact on the Church and, to a certain extent, on the world.

Religious orders and congregations were called upon to renew themselves. Congregations of women were directed to have general chapters of renewal within three years, to consult all of the members of their congregations in preparation, and to revise their constitutions and statutes to meet the needs of the renewal. For the first time in their religious lives, all sisters had the opportunity to speak of their concerns and their hopes for the future.

What would Mother Gerald have thought of all that took place as processes for renewal were undertaken—in governance, in ministries, in prayer forms, in lifestyles, in dress, in mobility, and in much more? Would she have led in implementing the changes that took place, or would she have resisted and tried to hold on to the values that had formed her strong adherence to a hierarchical form of control?

Mother Gerald was a woman of her time and that factor cannot be discounted. She had a fierce loyalty to the Church and to its representatives. At the same time, however, she had a strong conviction about her own authority and its exercise on behalf of her sisters and their work for "the salvation of souls." Yet she could step outside the prevailing rules for the sisters when she had a vision of her own to be accomplished.

One small indicator of her possible openness to change is found in a letter she wrote to her sisters after she returned from a trip to Rome in 1950. Father Timothy Sparks, OP, a Dominican priest stationed in Rome as the assistant to the Master of the Order, took her for a visit to the University of Rome. She wrote,

> *The women's division was of particular interest to me, and the Dean is a religious attired in secular garb. Her associates are of the same community and they certainly gave the appearance of cultured and gracious women.*

While the processes of renewal of congregations of women religious took place after the death of Mother Gerald, her sisters were ready for them. The level of trust that she had in them inspired the creativity and innovation with which they set about the task of renewal. Her spirit lives on in the freedom that was her legacy to the sisters whom she loved.

Afterword

Nonetheless the transition was difficult. It fell to the lot of Mother Genevieve Weber, successor to Mother Gerald, to prepare the way for a new and as yet unclear vision of the future.

Appendix One

Mother Gerald and Priests

In the Irish family of the early twentieth century there was no greater gift of God than to be blessed with vocations to the priesthood and to religious life. In that respect the Barry family was amply endowed. Among the thirteen children of Michael and Catherine Barry who lived to adulthood, three were to be ordained to the

The Barry siblings: (front row, left to right) James, William, Patrick, Sister Gerald, Joseph, (back row, left to right) Michael, Frank, Richard, Lawrence, Susan, Gerald, Mary, John.

priesthood—one later to be ordained a bishop—and one to become a Dominican sister.

The latter, Mother Gerald, held her priest brothers in familial love and in the reverence accorded to the priestly office that they held. That reverence extended to the many priests and bishops whom she encountered in various ways during her long tenure as Mother General of the Adrian Dominican Sisters.

Father Michael Fleming

One of the early chaplains to St. Joseph Academy was an Irish born priest, Father Michael J. Fleming. He served the Academy and the sisters from 1912 until 1916. He was the chaplain when Catherine Barry entered the Congregation in 1912 and she had fond memories of him. In the early years of her first term as Mother General she found time to carry out a desire of Father Fleming that she remembered from his time in Adrian— to be buried in the Congregation cemetery among the sisters whom he had served.

When he left Adrian because of serious illness, he spent his last days in St. Joseph Sanitarium in Mount Clemens, Michigan. His relatives in the Port Huron, Michigan, area arranged for his funeral and interment in Port Huron.

On March 17, 1936, certainly at a time when the new Mother General had many Congregational matters to occupy her attention, she did not forget Father Fleming. She wrote the following to his relatives.

> *Nearly every day during the nice weather, numbers of the sisters walk to the cemetery and offer their suffrages for all who rest in that hallowed soil. Father Fleming himself had expressed the wish that this privilege might be his but through some oversight he was, as you know, buried elsewhere. Now I am pleading to you and the other relatives, in my own name and that of the community, to permit his sacred remains to be transferred to our little "God's Acre" where we may give him the honor he deserved. I am sure you will look with favor on this plea, knowing that it comes from hearts filled with affection and esteem for this member of your own fine family.*

Initially, the family respectfully refused Mother Gerald's request. A letter signed by E.E. Fleming of Eau Claire, Wisconsin, cited their understanding that Father Fleming had requested burial next to his brother and sister in Port Huron. Furthermore, he said, it would be more convenient for his relatives in that area to visit his gravesite.

Mother Gerald persisted, however, although it was not until 1945 that she was able to bring the remains of Father Fleming to the cemetery in Adrian. By that time the family members saw the merit of her request, as well as acknowledged the approval that she had obtained from then Archbishop Edward Mooney of Detroit. Today the remains of Father Fleming rest near the altar in the Congregation cemetery along with other members of the clergy revered by the Adrian Dominican Sisters.

To Fields Near and Far

In 1919 another Irish born priest, Father Anthony Philbin, became the chaplain to the Dominican Sisters in Adrian and continued in that capacity until 1933 at the time Mother Gerald assumed the position of Mother General. She had, of course, known him throughout his years of service to the sisters. Just at this time of transition for her, however, Father Philbin received word of his transfer as pastor to the nearby Catholic parish in Blissfield, Michigan. But his ties to the Adrian Dominican Sisters remained strong and supportive. The common Irish heritage that he shared with Mother Gerald is reflected in correspondence he exchanged with her while on a trip to Ireland in 1936. He wrote from the Cunard White Star liner *Laconia* of his shipboard experience, lauding the service, the food and the Irish atmosphere on board.

Father Anthony Philbin

> *We have all kinds of Irish melodies, "My Wild Irish Rose" and Galore, and as for step dancing you could not see so much in Ireland.*

Mother Gerald wrote to him while he was in Cloonfinish, Swinford, County Mayo, the part of Ireland from which he had come.

> *I hope that the pleasant going over was only a foretaste of Heaven you have had since landing. I learned today that St. Boniface was the man who actually turned the Celts from*

paganism to Christianity, and I am afraid I can't take that.[1]
*This erroneous doctrine must have crept in through the
teutonic texts, and there again I am annoyed.*

*I suppose you cannot have much taste or patience now with
American politics, but there is quite a deal of excitement over
the presidential candidates, especially since Father Coughlin
has openly endorsed Congressmen Lemke and O'Brien of
Boston for President and Vice-President.*

*Have you seen Father Joe [her brother] and mine yet? Tell
them I am asking for them and thinking about them many a
time. I hope every field is fair and every stone shining for you,
and that all the dear and familiar faces are there to greet you.
I hope too that all those who have gone to take the angels places
will gather many a blessing for you. Pray for me while you
are at the Altar in Ireland, and know that I shall cherish those
prayers.*

The care and concern for Father Philbin followed him through a succession of assignments—to Blissfield, Burnside, and Northfield, Michigan. During those years he was afflicted with a progressive illness. He underwent an operation at St. Mary's Hospital in Rochester, Minnesota, during which time Mother Gerald corresponded with a Sister Thomas at that facility in order to monitor his condition. She had recommended his going there and, knowing his funds were limited, had told him that she knew where there was a "little pile" that she could get for him. Later he spent time at St. Joseph Mercy Hospital in

Ann Arbor, Michigan. Throughout, Mother Gerald maintained contact with him and followed his progress always with homely advice on how to care for himself. Eventually, she was instrumental in sending him to her sisters at St. Ann on-the-Lake Academy[2] in West Palm Beach, Florida, where she thought the weather would have a beneficial effect on his health. But his health deteriorated and he was admitted to St. Mary's Hospital there and did not recover. He died on February 11, 1941.

His remains were returned to Adrian where a funeral Mass was celebrated and where he was interred in the Congregation cemetery as he had requested. He is buried next to the altar as was his predecessor Father Fleming.

As Mother Gerald began her term as Mother General, the Congregation had been provided customarily with a priest from the Diocese of Detroit as chaplain. Over the years a number of priests served in that capacity and became devoted friends of Mother Gerald and of the sisters in general. Friars of the Dominican Order also became friends of the Congregation and served to impart the history and traditions of the Order to the sisters in initial and ongoing formation. A spacious rectory had been completed on the Motherhouse campus in 1908 to house the priests who served the Congregation. In addition, a beautifully appointed dining room in Madden Hall was reserved for their meals, prepared by the legendary Sister Annunciata Redumsky and served by novices.

In 1933 Mother Gerald received word that a new chaplain had been appointed for St. Joseph College and Academy. He was Father

Appendix One

Monsignor James Cahalan

James Cahalan, a distinguished priest who had served parishes in Trenton, Grosse Isle, Hillsdale, Marshall, and Ann Arbor, Michigan, and the Cathedral Church in Detroit. Coming to Adrian, Father Cahalan was entering into a period of retirement at age fifty-three due to failing health. He was to remain in Adrian as chaplain for nineteen years until his death in 1952. During that time he served the sisters, the students at both the College and the Academy, and the postulants and novices, as confessor, teacher, and counselor.

In 1936 Father Cahalan was recognized for his exemplary service as priest of the Diocese of Detroit by being elevated by Pope Pius XI to the rank of domestic prelate with the title of Monsignor.

Yearly, Monsignor Cahalan spent some of the winter months at St. Ann on-the-Lake/Rosarian Academy. Always solicitous of the priests who served the sisters in Adrian, Mother Gerald made the southern climate available to them. A section of the West Palm Beach building was renovated with separate bedrooms and bathrooms and a private dining room to accommodate the priests.

During his winters there Monsignor Cahalan and Mother Gerald carried on correspondence that kept her aware of the visitors who took advantage of her invitations. The Monsignor acted as a host to the succession of priests and bishops who availed themselves of her hospitality. Two letters exchanged in March 1937 are typical. Monsignor Cahalan wrote on March 2,

> "All alone by the seaside they have left me." Fr. Daly O.P.,[3] the last of them took his departure today. You will have seen Fr. Walsh[4] before reading this. We had a very enjoyable time together. I am planning on leaving via Washington Monday March 15th and arrive in Adrian via Toledo Friday morning 19th. . . . When you see, or more important consult, the Rev. P.J.J.,[5] tell him that Fr. Walsh and I have selected the new Bishop, but are not allowed to disclose his identity until public announcement by Rome, probably the middle of next July. All you can say is that he will be "a great leader," and this of course will fill the bill to his satisfaction.[6] It was a year ago this week that the good Bishop Gallagher came to Florida. His spirit still hovers around St. Ann's. . . . I thank you for your kind letter and check.
>
> With good wishes to yourself and all the Sisters as well as inquiring friends I am
>
> Sincerely, J. Cahalan

Monsignor Maurice Walsh

Appendix One

While Monsignor Cahalan's comment about selecting the new bishop of Detroit might seem to be facetious, apparently it was not. Mother Gerald wrote to him on March 4 about Father P.J.J., saying,

> *Yesterday I had my first interview with Father P.J.J. He stopped in while taking his constitutional walk, prescribed by Dr. Marshall. In fact, he is taking every precaution to safeguard his health, so that he will be in trim, I imagine, for the momentous thing that he is expecting with the new leadership, though I must say that he was very secretive about his hopes and ideas. There was no way of confiding to him the intimate relations which you and Father Walsh have entered into with the Delegate nor was I inclined to tell him about the part you played in advising the same about the new Bishop, he was that conservative himself.*

Extensive correspondence between Monsignor Cahalan and Mother Gerald indicates that he spent January through March of each year in West Palm Beach. His letters to her indicate that he waited to receive instructions from her about departing and returning to Adrian. She customarily arranged his transportation to and from Florida. In a letter to him on January 14, 1946, she wrote,

> *We had "The Bells of St. Mary's"[7] last week and I am sorry that you and Father Dorsey[8] missed it for I know it would have given you a good laugh. You know it has not yet been released in many of the big show houses and so we were very, very fortunate. Sister Thomasine[9] might be lucky enough to get it*

> *again in the summer time and then you will surely have to see it. It is quite typical.*

Monsignor Cahalan died on November 15, 1952, in Adrian. Funeral services were conducted in Holy Rosary Chapel attended by two hundred or more members of the clergy with the Most Reverend Allen J. Babcock, auxiliary bishop of Detroit, presiding. Monsignor G. Warren Peek, pastor of St. Mary Church in Ann Arbor, gave the homily. In it he said of Monsignor Cahalan,

> *. . . He was a pious man who performed the duties of his priestly life extraordinarily well. He had no opportunity to build massive buildings as testimonials to his zeal. He built unseen monuments in the souls of those whom he helped.*

Monsignor Cahalan was buried in the Congregation cemetery.

In 1939 an assistant chaplain, Father Clarence A. Dorsey, was appointed for St. Joseph Academy and Siena Heights College. He was to become beloved by students and sisters alike. But, like others who came to minister to the Adrian Dominican Sisters, Father Dorsey was not well. He suffered from a severe asthmatic condition with complications. Mother Gerald responded to his needs by making accommodations available to him both in the south and in the north. Over the years he spent extended periods of time at Rosarian Academy in West Palm Beach; at Colegio Santo Domingo in the Dominican Republic; and in Puerto Rico. He was also sent by

Father Clarence Dorsey

Appendix One

her to Munising and Escanaba in the Upper Peninsula of Michigan and for a time to the Mayo Clinic in Rochester, Minnesota. In all of these places Father Dorsey wrote to her expressing gratitude to her and to the sisters in those various locations.

On September 1, 1949, eight days before his death, Father Dorsey was in the hospital in Escanaba. He was being visited that day by his priest brother, Father Leo Dorsey, and his sister and brother-in-law. Sister Eugenia Dwyer, superioress at the catechetical center operated by St. Patrick Church in Escanaba, brought him some mail including a letter from Mother Gerald. Sister Eugenia wrote,

> *Father was very interested in his mail (a good sign, says the doctor) but the letter which gave him the most pleasure was the one we brought from Mother Gerald. He could hardly wait for the Sister-nurse to open it for him. Father Leo kept saying, "What does Mother Gerald say?" but Father paid no attention to any of us. If Mother could only have seen the pleasure her letter gave him!*

At that time Father Dorsey showed signs of improvement and Mother Gerald wrote to him again on September 5. She said,

> *When they release you we will be happy to have you in Adrian if the doctor approves of the climate. You know, Father, we will be happy to have you any place we are in any climate that the Lord allows us.*

Father Dorsey died on September 9. At the time he had been pastor

To Fields Near and Far

of St. Anne's Church in Detroit Beach, Michigan, for a year and three months.

Among other priests of the Archdiocese of Detroit who served as chaplain to the Adrian Dominican Sisters during Mother Gerald's time were Father George Gaynor, Father William McGoldrick, and Father James H. Frawley.

Father Gaynor was appointed assistant chaplain to Monsignor Cahalan in 1948. Upon Monsignor Cahalan's death in 1952, Father Gaynor was named chaplain, a position he held until 1958. He was a

Left to right: Sister Benedicta Marie Ledwidge; Father Francis Dominic Nealy, OP; Monsignor Carroll Deady; Bishop Alexander Zaleski; Father Cyril Burke, OP; Mother Gerald; and Father George Gaynor.

gregarious man of expansive personality who reached out to everyone he met and became a local celebrity in the Adrian community. He was a great traveler and often enjoyed the hospitality of the Congregation in West Palm Beach; Miami; the Dominican Republic; Las Vegas; Santa Cruz, and Oakland, California. But he vacationed in other places around the country that were not ministries of the Adrian Dominicans. He made a point of visiting the missions of the Congregation when he was anywhere near them and reported back to Mother Gerald about the work of the sisters in these places.

Father McGoldrick was appointed chaplain in 1958. His was a short tenure in Adrian for, in 1961, he was appointed co-pastor of the newly established St. Edmund Parish in Warren, Michigan. While in Adrian Father McGoldrick served the needs of the sisters, St. Joseph Academy, Siena Heights College, and the Girls Training School which was also located in Adrian. Despite the brevity of his chaplaincy Father McGoldrick retained a lasting friendship with Mother Gerald and the Adrian Dominican Sisters. Mother Gerald made the usual arrangements for him to spend vacations at Rosarian Academy, even after he left Adrian. At the time of his departure Mother Gerald wrote to him in part,

> *We are confident that through contact with you as their host, many professional men, not blessed with our holy faith, especially those from secular universities, have received an inspiring impression of the Church and of the priesthood.*
>
> *We render you special thanks, also, for the time and effort*

you have unselfishly given to securing material aid for Siena Heights and we want you to know that we have taken real pride in having you as our representative in the work of the Michigan Colleges Foundation[10] among the business and industrial leaders of the state.

Father Andrew P. McEntee, although never a chaplain in Adrian, had served as chaplain of Dominican High School in Detroit and became a good friend and support for Mother Gerald. It was he who accompanied her on her initial flight to the Dominican Republic. He returned with Monsignor William Barry to negotiate legal matters in obtaining the site for the Colegio and spent additional months there overseeing the building of the facility.

Father Andrew McEntee with Mother Gerald.

Dominican Priests

A letter dated July 21, 1932, was sent to Mother Augustine Walsh by the Dominican Provincial of the Province of St. Joseph, T.S. McDermott, OP. He wrote,

Father T.S. McDermott, OP

Your letter has just been received and I am definitely appointing Father V.R. Hughes as professor in your college. I am instructing him to communicate with you immediately as you can

inform him regarding his classes, the opening of the college and other matters which can be amicably arranged. Be assured, dear Mother, that I am most happy to renew contact with your community.

In a footnote to this cordial letter Father McDermott added that Father Hughes was currently teaching at Mount St. Dominic's in Caldwell, New Jersey. In light of subsequent events it is important to note that Father Hughes was appointed as "professor" in the College, but not as chaplain. "Chaplains" continued to be appointed by the bishop of the Detroit diocese (or, beginning in 1937, archdiocese).

The letter appointing Father Vincent Reginald Hughes was the beginning of a long association of the Dominican friars with the Adrian Dominican Sisters. Father Hughes came to Adrian in the fall of 1932, only five months before the death of Mother Augustine. The mutual regard that developed between him and Mother Gerald is chronicled in letters that they exchanged over the years culminating in her death in November 1961. It was continued through her successor, Mother Genevieve Weber, until his death on October 30, 1965.

The tenure of Father Hughes as professor of theology at St. Joseph College in Adrian lasted only six years, from 1932 to 1938. He was then assigned to the Dominican House of Studies in River Forest, Illinois, where he was to teach the novices who were preparing for the priesthood. Throughout the remainder of his life, however, he remained close to the Adrian Dominican Sisters. He returned to Adrian to teach in summer sessions and also taught at Mount St. Mary's in St. Charles, Illinois, where some sisters studied in the summers. He attended virtually all reception and profession ceremonies and was called upon to speak on special Congregational occasions. Like others he enjoyed vacations in West Palm Beach, Miami, Puerto Rico, and the Dominican Republic. One year he was invited to give the commencement address at both Barry College in Miami and at Siena Heights in Adrian. Since he had accepted the invitation to Barry first, he had to turn down Siena Heights, much to his regret.

After he had left Adrian and served for a time in River Forest, Father Hughes had a varied career in his own province as Prior of St. Peter Martyr in Winona, Minnesota, and as Director of the Archdiocesan Confraternity of the Holy Name Society in Minneapolis. He also continued his teaching in a series of Midwestern Catholic colleges. But always, when it was possible, he found his way back to Adrian, his veritable "second home."

On August 30, 1957, Mother Gerald wrote to him after he had spent the summer session teaching at Siena Heights,

> *We are all very sad about your leaving Adrian and would be almost inconsolable were it not for the fact that your going is "according to His will." Your friendship and goodness will always be among our most cherished possessions and among our greatest blessings in the future will be your visits to Adrian. The oftener you come the more convinced we will be that you regard the Motherhouse as we would have you regard it—as your home.*

Over the years Father Hughes would appeal to Mother Gerald when he was in need of something. Once it was a ciborium which she readily provided and also an altar cloth. On another occasion he requested the assistance of Sister Helene O'Connor in designing the main altar for the friars' St. Dominic Church in Denver. While Sister Helene had sent him preliminary designs and instructions, he very respectfully suggested that it would be a help both to him and to her if she could spend even a day at their church. Mother Gerald responded readily and sent Sister Helene, a noted liturgical artist, along with a companion, to provide the assistance that Father Hughes had requested.

Father V.R. Hughes, OP

At the General Chapter of the Dominican friars in 1960 Father Hughes was accorded the highest academic recognition given by the Order—the Master of Sacred Theology. This degree, unique to the Dominican Order, is a "master's degree" in the most ancient sense, comparable to an honorary doctorate conferred only upon Dominicans who are already scholars of theology. To qualify the honoree must have been a full-time professor for ten years and have published books and articles of international scholarly repute. The friar must first be nominated by his own province and then approved by the intellectual commission of the Generalate in Rome. The Master of the Order and his Council make the final decision. At the ceremony of conferral the recipient is given a ring and a four-finned biretta trimmed with bishop's purple.[11] Father Hughes was pleased that Mother Gerald and Sister Bertha Homminga attended the ceremony in which he was awarded this distinguished degree.

Mother Augustine Walsh, predecessor of Mother Gerald, first became acquainted with Father Vincent's Dominican brother Father Edward Hughes. To him she extended support for his work with the Rosary Mission Society, the name given to the American Dominican Missions of the St. Joseph Province of Dominican friars to which both brothers belonged at the time. She provided a monthly donation for his work with missionaries at home in the United States and for their work at the time in China. She also sent him checks of one hundred dollars from time to time for the Gregorian Masses[12] offered on the occasion of a sister's death.

Father Edward Hughes, OP

After Mother Augustine's death on January 6, 1933, Father Edward Hughes wrote to Sister Gerald, who at that time was Vicaress of the Congregation. His brother had just been appointed to his position in Adrian. He wrote in part,

> *It is gratifying to learn of my brother's position at St. Joseph's College and Motherhouse. He speaks in highest terms of the work there, the cooperation given him and of the matchless kindness of the Sisters.*

> *Sometime, and soon I hope, I plan to visit Adrian to enjoy not only his company but to meet you and the Sisters and to be refreshened [sic] in spirit by contact with such a vigorous expression of the Dominican vocation.*
>
> *Your splendid offering for the missions is proof indeed of the very real existence of the virtue of magnanimity which was such a high mark in the character of our Holy Father, St. Dominic.*

While he was never assigned to Adrian this was the beginning of a long association of Father Edward Hughes with Mother Gerald comparable to that of his brother.

He assisted the Director of the Holy Name Society, directed the Third Order of the Dominicans, and was editor of its periodical *The Torch*. He was devoted to promoting the canonization of Blessed Martin de Porres. Mother Gerald provided monetary gifts and the prayerful support of the sisters of the Congregation for all of his endeavors. Because the canonization process for Blessed Martin de Porres required evidence of miraculous intervention on the part of the proposed candidate, Father Edward wrote on December 12, 1935,

> *I wish your dear, spiritual charges would report their favors — even if they don't wish to name them explicitly. We know that many are receiving them just from the large numbers that are being sent in here from all parts of the country. Our Roman authorities have asked us to investigate two of the favors*

> *reported in* The Torch—*one of them from Detroit. They have the marks of something more than ordinary.*

Mother Gerald offered him the hospitality of the Congregation's places in Florida and the West and on one occasion was instrumental in securing an automobile for his work. She offered the facilities in Adrian for regional meetings of the Third Order which Father Edward graciously accepted.

In 1939 a new province of Dominican friars formed, splitting off from the eastern St. Joseph Province. The new entity, Province of St. Albert the Great, had its headquarters in River Forest, Illinois. Both of the Hughes brothers chose to become members of the new province. In 1948 Father Edward was elected Provincial of the Province and subsequently re-elected to a second term that ended in 1956. During his tenure he brought about an extensive building program and established new missions in Nigeria and Bolivia. As it had with his brother, the Order conferred the Master of Sacred Theology on him. When he left the office of provincial he was appointed pastor of St. Pius Church in Chicago and superior of the resident fathers.

In December 1960, Father Edward received word of his new assignment to St. Dominic Church in New Orleans. Upon hearing the news, Mother Gerald wrote,

> *The news contained in your letter of the third surprised me not a little. I hardly know what to say other than "God's will be done," and I know it will be done generously and wholeheartedly by you no matter what this change may cost*

you personally. Perhaps Blessed Martin needs just this sacrifice to make sure his cause and he would know to whom to turn for help. Naturally, we are sad to have you leave the environs of Michigan, and you can hardly blame us for being so selfish when you realize what the Fathers Hughes have learned to mean to the Adrian Dominicans. You are, in the truest sense of the word, our brothers and we would rather keep you close to home if that were possible. . . . We shall never, never forget your goodness to us, Father, and we hope you will always remember Adrian as your home and come here often.

Correspondence between Father Edward and Mother Gerald is contained in numerous files. Letters from her to him congratulate him on honors accorded to him; offer sympathy over the death of family members; express concern for his health at various times and offer Congregational facilities for his care and recovery; take note of his various assignments; and keep him apprised of his brother's health. The letters from him are generally expressions of gratitude for the many ways she had assisted him in his work. Mother Gerald rejoiced with him when, in May 1962, Blessed Martin de Porres was canonized in Rome.

He continued to maintain his contact with Mother Gerald and with her successor Mother Genevieve. When he died on March 18, 1966, he was still at St. Dominic Church.

When Father Vincent Hughes was transferred from Adrian to the House of Studies in River Forest in 1938, the Provincial, Father

McDermott, assigned Father J.C. (Joseph Clement) Della Penta to replace him. Mother Gerald wrote in reply to inquire if Father Della Penta had a Doctor of Philosophy degree. Expressing her readiness to welcome the new faculty member, she added, ". . . if Father Della Penta is wanting in this respect, may I ask you to consider the present need for the College." While he did not have the doctorate, Father McDermott wrote of him,

> He has an M.A. in Philosophy. He also taught in our Studium of St. Albert's at Oakland, California. He is well qualified to teach Philosophy as he is a very bright young man. He also has credits for his Doctorate at C.U., and is likewise a Lector of Sacred Theology. In looking over the list of our Fathers with Doctorates in Philosophy I find that I cannot assign one to Adrian this year.

There was further correspondence but in the end Father Della Penta arrived in Adrian and proved to be an excellent teacher. When in 1939 Father McDermott wrote that he was assigning Father Della Penta to The Catholic University of America to pursue the doctorate in philosophy, Mother Gerald wrote, speaking of the need for a priest with a doctorate,

> . . . although we still stand in need of this magical title, we do not care to surrender Father Della Penta. He is a worthy match for any of the titled ones and we highly commend him as priest, teacher, and Dominican. Of course, I would not want to deny him the opportunity to study if you still have such a thing

in mind for him, but, if not, we shall all welcome him back to Adrian.

A Dominican priest who was never assigned to Adrian was Father Walter Farrell, noted particularly for his publication of *The Companion to the Summa*. Father Farrell was educated by the Adrian Dominicans in his elementary school days in Chicago, and retained a long and affectionate relationship with the sisters. Mother Gerald often consulted him on issues related to theology. It was he who advised her when she was considering sending her sisters for theological studies.

Father Walter Farrell, OP

Father Edward C. LaMore, OP

On September 9, 1940, Mother Gerald received word of the appointment of Father Edward C. LaMore, OP, to the faculty of Siena Heights College. She hastened by telegram to welcome Father LaMore to Adrian and requested that he be present by September 14 for the beginning of classes on September 16. Father LaMore indicated that he could not meet that date but would arrive the morning of the sixteenth. So began his tenure as a much admired and appreciated addition to the faculty of Siena Heights. Upon his arrival Mother Gerald cautioned him about observing appropriate relationships with the

Father Edward LaMore, OP

young women students at the College. She made reference to some unfortunate incident that had taken place at Siena Heights prior to his coming but there are no particulars on file.

During his tenure of eight years at Siena Heights College Father LaMore became an integral part of the community of sisters and students on the campus that encompassed both St. Joseph Academy and the College. In the rectory on the campus he lived in the company of Monsignor Cahalan and Father Dorsey. Always at the disposal of the sisters and students, Father LaMore did not limit his ministry to the classroom. He offered daily Mass for the College students, heard confessions on a regular basis, presided at Benediction of the Blessed Sacrament when it was allowed, counseled students, and was generally available to them. He instituted a chapter of the Third Order of St. Dominic among the students. He also represented the College at events both in the city of Adrian and in other places when asked.

As a teacher of courses in philosophy Father LaMore had a great influence on the young women students at Siena Heights. He was often heard saying to them, "Don't ever let anyone tell you that you can't learn something because you are a woman." He instituted an annual award for the senior student who excelled in the field of philosophy. It became one of the most coveted honors bestowed by the College.

Because the young postulants and novices of the Congregation needed to take the courses required for degrees, he taught philosophy classes in the novitiate as well. These students, however, had little or no time for study and this situation became a great source of frustration to him as a teacher. As time went on he began to express his concerns to the novice mistress, Sister Mary Philip Ryan, and to Mother Gerald. In one of his later years in Adrian he failed an entire class of novices as an expression of his dissatisfaction with the situation. No doubt he thought that this action might bring about needed changes for study by the novices but it did not have the desired effect. A novice, graduate of Siena Heights and of Father LaMore's classes in philosophy, was appointed to teach the logic class to the novices.

During his years in Adrian Father LaMore, as others before him, enjoyed the hospitality of the Congregation's missions in Florida, Puerto Rico, and the Dominican Republic. He spent the summer of 1947 teaching at Barry College, an opportunity he thoroughly enjoyed. At the end of that summer session Mother Gerald arranged for him to go to the Dominican Republic. The excitement he felt in preparing for that visit is evident in a letter he wrote to her on July 22, 1947, shortly after she had visited Barry.

> *I rushed out to thank you for the check, just as you were leaving, but the crowd of your adoring daughters kept me from approaching near enough. . . . I have already arranged the trip to Santo Domingo. I am taking a movie camera with me, so I can bring back some color-film of the Colegio. I thought, too, it might be nice to take some pictures of the Sisters there (moving pictures), for their folks in Detroit. I think it might give great joy and consolation to their parents who haven't seen them in so long, if they could see some real live pictures of their daughters, talking and laughing.*

Later he wrote a long and glowing account of his visit there. He would have been happy to remain in that land of Dominican history. He wrote to Mother Gerald on August 19, 1947:

> *I hate to tell you this, but I have decided to stay here at Trujillo.*[13] *It is such a wonderful place I can't bring myself to leave. The good Archbishop and the Nuncio have both been after me to remain here and teach in the University, i.e., if I can get a position there. I told them I had nothing to say about it, but if my superior in New York should decide to assign me here I would be glad to remain. Perhaps, you could help arrange it for me.*

In the same letter he described special recognition given him at the presidential inauguration that had just taken place. He was honored to serve as the Archbishop's senior chaplain along with a Jesuit priest from Puerto Rico. They sat with the Archbishop on "that ancient throne in the sanctuary," just opposite the throne of President Rafael Trujillo, who was being inaugurated to a new term. They were joined in the sanctuary by members of the diplomatic corps and other notables. When the ceremony was over the Archbishop asked him to lead him to the presidential throne[14] so that he, the Archbishop, might extend his felicitations. Father LaMore too was introduced to the President as a Dominican professor from the Motherhouse of the Adrian Dominicans. The next day he attended the inaugural of the new University and again was privileged to be included with the diplomatic corps and other invited guests.

Appendix One

It is clear that these occasions were highlights of his career. At the conclusion of his letter he wrote,

> *Believe it or not, but this is the very first vacation I have had since ordination. Other summers I have always gone directly home and helped out in my home parish. While it was good to be near my mother, it was never a real vacation. Thanks to you for this wonderful opportunity to see something I have wanted to see for a long time. If I never come south of the Mason and Dixon line again, I have seen enough to give me pleasant memories for years to come.*

Father LaMore returned to Siena Heights for the following school year which would be his last at the College. There is no evidence that Mother Gerald followed up on his suggestion that she might intercede for him in procuring an assignment to the Dominican Republic. In late summer of 1948 he received a new assignment from his Provincial, one that was surprising and, at the same time, unwelcome.

His departure from Adrian was shrouded in confusion and prompted Mother Gerald to write in long hand a detailed account of the situation as she perceived it. During his last year at Siena, she noted, he had seemed uncommonly moody to her and had been heard criticizing the Congregation in his classes. After having been away from the Motherhouse during the summer break, she wrote, he returned one evening with two other priests and proceeded to pack up for his departure. He did not contact her, nor any other of the sisters. It was her principle never to enter the priests' residence, but, according to her custom, she went into the dining room where the priests were having breakfast and greeted them, but found Father LaMore less than friendly. After two days he and the other priests departed without saying good-bye.

In trying to assess the situation, Mother Gerald thought that he expected her to object to his Provincial about his being changed from Adrian. If this were true, it would only add to his disappointment about not being assigned to the Dominican Republic. It is quite clear that Father LaMore had found a home with the Dominican sisters in Adrian and in the Dominican Republic and was disappointed that it was coming to an end. Mother Gerald on the other hand thought that his new appointment was a distinguished one and that he would be honored to have it.

Later, in a letter dated October 18, 1948, he wrote to her describing his new responsibilities and added,

> *On the day of my departure from Siena, I was so overcome emotionally, I fear my expressions of gratitude were most inadequate. I have always found it difficult to express my feelings anyway, but I really did appreciate sincerely the kindness you and the Sisters showed me, and I shall always treasure the memory of my final moments at the Academy.*[15]

The new assignment was to an office at the Catholic International Press in New York City where he was to work to bring a new Dominican international university into being. The burden of this venture was his alone and, after working for its realization for a time, he admitted in a letter to Mother Gerald that he was never cut out to be an administrator. He developed a curriculum and initiated a search for faculty members, but the university never came to fruition. In the meantime he began to experience the onset of a serious form of arthritis.

By January 27, 1954, he had returned to teaching, this time at Mount Mercy College in Pittsburgh. In a letter to Sister Benedicta Marie, he indicated that his teaching was interrupted from time to time by weeks of treatment at Mercy Hospital. The crippling type of arthritis with which he was afflicted was growing worse.

In August of that year Mother Gerald, learning that Father LaMore's illness was advancing, wrote to him about St. Joseph Hospital in Hot Springs, Arkansas. She had sent several sisters there who had received help for conditions similar to his. She described their experiences there and then said,

> *Would you, then, write at once for accommodations and go there at the earliest opportunity? And will you accept the enclosed check as a help toward the initial expenses? Don't be at all concerned about the cost of the treatments or any other bills which might be incurred during your time there. We would be more than happy to take care of them, Father, and you need only have them directed to me.*

After obtaining permission from his Provincial, Father LaMore went to Hot Springs where he was to remain for four years until his death in 1958. He had occasional signs of improvement and was able to offer classes to the nurses from time to time, but he experienced no lasting relief. At Christmas time in 1957 he went to spend the holidays with the community of Dominican friars in Memphis, Tennessee, but then returned to Hot Springs. His greatest joy over his years there was the occasional visits from his sister Henrietta to whom he was devoted. During all his time there he and Mother Gerald carried on continuous communication with assurances from her that she would take care of his expenses.

Father LaMore died on August 11, 1958, in Hot Springs. His funeral Mass was celebrated in St. Vincent Church in New York City and he was buried in New York State. In one of his last letters to Mother Gerald he wrote,

> *In more ways than I can describe this illness has been a blessing in disguise and a great privilege. It has deepened my understanding and appreciation of spiritual values, as no other experience in my priestly life. I feel I am a better priest and religious because of it.*

At the time of Father LaMore's departure from Adrian, in a letter of August 19, 1948, Mother Gerald learned from Father McDermott that he was appointing Father L.B. O'Connell[16] to replace Father LaMore. This was to begin a new phase in the experience of the Adrian Dominican Sisters with the Dominicans of the Province of St. Joseph. It proved to be problematic.

In hand written notes Mother Gerald listed some of the difficulties that were being encountered with Father O'Connell. From her perspective he was unhappy in his new assignment. She commented that he was uninterested in his classes and was complaining that he was overworked. The sisters who served him in the dining room and those who met him at the College and elsewhere found him unmannerly, even rude. She sensed a strained attitude that was affecting the entire community and she was disappointed and discouraged.

None of these observations find their way into her correspondence with Father O'Connell's superiors, however. On the contrary she expressed to Father McDermott concern for Father O'Connell's health. She proposed the usual possible solutions in offering to give him the hospitality of the Congregation's missions in Florida for rest and restoration if that might meet with the approval of Father McDermott. He, however, sent Father Philip Mulhern, Regent of Studies, to assess the situation in Adrian after which Mother Gerald received a rather surprising letter in response. Father McDermott wrote,

> *After speaking to Father Mulhern and Father O'Connell, may I inform you that it is my intention to remove Father Sadlier[17] and Father O'Connell from your motherhouse, Adrian, Michigan, next June. The priests who were assigned as professors to Adrian, are part time chaplains and do not receive the respect and consideration due to priests. This has been the complaint of other fathers who were assigned to Adrian. The main reason for my bringing Father Jurgelaitis[18] back to the states from your college in Santo Domingo was due to the treatment he received while there.*

> *Father O'Connell, you write, is not well. Father himself states that he is well, and certainly he looks well. He is a young priest but nevertheless dislikes the way he has been treated. You have stated publicly that you have sisters who could take the courses Father Sadlier and Father O'Connell are teaching. If this be true I shall be happy to remove both these fathers immediately. (October 28, 1949)*

This was the beginning of a period of controversy over the role of the Dominican friars who served the Adrian Dominican Sisters. From the viewpoint of the friars, they were appointed as professors for Siena Heights College, a position that did not include chaplaincy duties. Such services in their view were the sole responsibility of the priests appointed by the archdiocese. This was a distinction that could be honored during the academic year at the College, although Father LaMore had never hesitated to say daily Mass in the College chapel, hear confessions on a regular basis, preside at Benediction of the Blessed Sacrament, and offer counseling for students and others when required.

The situation during the summer sessions was quite different, however. As many as nine hundred or more sisters were customarily present on the campus for summer courses. To accommodate their needs there were five chapels—Holy Rosary, a chapel in Archangelus Hall, one in the infirmary, another in the novitiate, and a temporary one set up in the Academy building, Dominicana Hall. After Lumen Ecclesiae Chapel opened in 1957, it supplanted some of the previous locations.

Appendix One

It was an assumption on the part of the sisters that the Dominican friars would be available at least for daily Mass in these chapels since there were only two diocesan chaplains on the campus. Canon law required that the sisters attend daily Mass as well as go to weekly confession. The Passionist fathers from Detroit served as confessors.

An exchange of letters in 1950 illustrates the problem. Father Ambrose Paschal Regan was appointed to teach at Siena Heights and received a letter dated May 16 from Sister Benedicta Marie, who in addition to serving as the Congregation's Vicaress was at that time Dean of the College. She indicated that he was scheduled to teach Ethics and the History of Philosophy and then added,

Father Arthur Stewart, one of the Passionist fathers.

> *We have none of the ordinary extra-curricular activities during the summer, but you would be expected to say Mass daily and distribute Holy Communion to the sisters in one of the five chapels on the campus, as we shall have a large number of sisters of our own as well as from other communities attending the session.*

Father Regan replied on June 7 expressing his delight with his summer appointment to Siena Heights and included the instructions he had received from Father McDermott.

> *I am to be professor of Philosophy at Siena Heights for six weeks. He especially forbids chaplain's duties of any kind,*

> Mass, Communion, Benediction, etc. If confirmation of the above is necessary, I beg that you communicate with Father Provincial in New York City as soon as possible.

Sister Benedicta Marie contacted Father McDermott by telegram and received the following in a letter dated June 20, 1950:

> To my mind, the telegram is impertinent and disrespectful. When Mother Gerald communicated with me regarding two Fathers to teach at your Summer school, nothing was stated in her letter regarding the duties of a chaplain.
>
> Your Motherhouse is notorious for the impositions the Sisters place on professors and the unreasonable demands you make. I wish to know immediately if you cannot dispense with the services of the two professors assigned to Adrian, as well as the services of Father Sadlier, next year. I also intend to withdraw Father Cyril Burke from Barry College, Miami Beach, since you can so readily secure chaplains and Sisters as professors for your community.
>
> May I inform you that your Community at Adrian is the only community of Religious Sisters—Dominicans or otherwise—that has caused our Province so much trouble in your treatment of our professors.

It is difficult to understand the kind of indictment of the Congregation contained in this letter from Father McDermott.

Appendix One

Sister Benedicta Marie was well known as a woman of unparalleled integrity, dignity, and discretion. In her defense it would be difficult for her to understand that a priest, ordained to offer Mass on a daily basis, might not offer that service to the large number of sisters on the Motherhouse campus during the summer sessions at the College. As to the treatment of the priests while in Adrian, most would attest to the extraordinary deference they received. All of their personal needs were entrusted to a team of sisters who entered the rectory during meal times when they were away. Beds were made, laundry collected and later returned, drinks and snacks were provided on a daily basis. During the noontime beds were turned down so that the priests might take an afternoon nap. Every Dominican priest left Adrian with a new habit made by the Congregation's premier seamstress, Sister Mary Rita Riedel.

Father McDermott apparently did not make good on his determination to remove the priests he had assigned to Siena Heights and Barry. The priests themselves seemed to have volunteered to assist with chaplain duties as needed. One of the accommodations was to establish a rotation among the several chapels so that one priest did not have to serve the larger numbers of sisters on a regular basis. Of the five chapels to be served, Lumen Ecclesiae was the largest one. But the issue did not go away.

Father McDermott served as Provincial of St. Joseph Province from 1930 to 1955. He then went to Rome to preside over the election of a new Master of the Order.

His successor, Father W.D. Marrin, was still addressing the issue of priestly duties as late as December 1961 when he wrote the following to Sister Benedicta Marie:

> *The Father assigned is to undertake, principally, teaching duties. Chaplain duties were not understood to be part of his formal assignment. Nevertheless, such Fathers who have been resident at Adrian have undertaken to assist, in terms of Mass, Communions, etc., in meeting the needs of the college students. I have no wish that this custom, arising from the generosity of the Fathers, be discontinued. Since the Chaplain assigned by the Archdiocese is, as I understand the situation, also the proper Chaplain of the College, he will wish to fulfill this duty periodically in terms of divine services. On those occasions the Dominican Father involved will, I am sure, gladly assist in one or the other spheres of the Chaplain's many obligations. However, I do not think it would be wise to have the Dominican Father represented as committed to any or all Chaplain duties anywhere or at any time.*

The list of Dominican priests who taught over the years at Siena Heights College in summer sessions is long. As the 1960s progressed, however, the winds of change were affecting many aspects of traditional religious life for both the women and men religious. It became no longer necessary for the Dominicans of St. Joseph Province to supply teachers of philosophy and theology for Siena Heights College. For a short time priests of St. Albert Province were able to fill the need. But now, sisters of the Congregation were obtaining degrees for teaching theology and philosophy. Catholic colleges in general were taking a new look at their curricula and in many instances were reducing requirements for courses in these areas. New theologies were emerging and the concentration on the teaching of St. Thomas Aquinas, in which the Dominican fathers were expert, was declining. All of these things were in the air when Mother Gerald died in 1961, just as the ferment that would lead to the convening of Vatican Council II was beginning.

Archbishop Amleto Giovanni Cicognani

Archbishop, later Cardinal, Amleto Giovanni Cicognani was ordained a priest in Italy in 1905 and rapidly rose to recognition in the Roman Curia, or diplomatic corps, of the Vatican. After holding a number of positions he was appointed Apostolic Delegate[19] to the United States in 1933. He was to hold that position for twenty-five years. While the United States did not maintain full diplomatic relations with the Vatican at the time, the position he held had two functions: to relate on behalf of the Vatican State to the United States government as situations required, and to serve as the means through which the bishops of the United States related to Rome. Among the latter responsibilities was the

Archbishop Amleto Cicognani

recommendation of new bishops for dioceses in the United States. At the headquarters of the Apostolic Delegation he was assisted by a staff that ordinarily included three secretaries and a canon lawyer. The latter position was customarily filled by a Dominican. For a time Edward Celestin Daly, OP, served in that capacity. He was later named bishop of Des Moines, Iowa. Among others who served as secretary to the Apostolic Delegate were Leo Binz and Joseph Mark McShea. These two were later ordained bishops—Binz, appointed to the Archdiocese of Dubuque, Iowa, and later to that of St. Paul, Minnesota, and McShea, to that of Allentown, Pennsylvania.

Mother Gerald was well known by many of the bishops of the United States through the placement of her sisters in their dioceses. Some, such as Bishop Edward Hoban of Rockford, Illinois, later of Cleveland, had been friends of the Congregation for many years and had become her close personal friends. Her own brother, Bishop Patrick Barry of Florida, was also a conduit through which she came to know many of the American bishops. Because of these kinds of contacts she came to know Archbishop Cicognani.

Mother Gerald learned that Archbishop Cicognani suffered from the excessively cold winters of Washington, DC. In 1937 he was afflicted with a particularly virulent case of pneumonia. With her usual expediency she offered accommodations for him and his staff in West Palm Beach for the winter months. The Archbishop accepted and began a thirteen-year practice of spending a few weeks from mid January to mid February at St. Ann on-the-Lake (later Rosarian)

Academy. He customarily brought with him two secretaries in order that he could carry on the business of his office while there. He was also often accompanied by Bishop Hoban with whom he had a special relationship.

Rosarian Academy was housed in one large building serving the classrooms, dormitories, and dining rooms for the students.[20] The second floor of the building was renovated to provide accommodations for the visiting clergy. One nicely appointed bedroom with adjoining bathroom was designated the "Delegate's Room." Another room was called the "Bishop's Room." These rooms were on the same floor as the Academy chapel.

The correspondence between Mother Gerald and Archbishop Cicognani, retained in the Adrian Dominican archives, is extensive. Their early letters were written during World War II. Mother Gerald often expressed concern for the suffering people of Europe and enclosed a substantial check for the Archbishop to send to the Pope along with another that the Delegate might use at his own discretion. Over the years almost every letter included such enclosures. Mother Gerald also made a substantial contribution toward the building of the official Washington headquarters of the Apostolic Delegation. When it was finished the Archbishop wrote her to thank her for furnishing one of the suites in the building.

Many Adrian Dominican Sisters attended summer sessions at The Catholic University of America over the years. Each summer it was the custom of the Archbishop to invite them to his official residence for an afternoon visit. They were given a tour of the facility followed by light refreshments. It was one way in which the Delegate attempted to show his gratitude for the hospitality and care given him by the sisters in West Palm Beach.

Mother Gerald repeatedly invited Archbishop Cicognani to visit Adrian. Because of the many demands upon his time, both secular and ecclesial, it was difficult for him to accept the invitation. Eventually he came, however, urging that there be no publicity attending his visit. Mother Gerald wrote to the sisters to let them know that his visit to Adrian must be held in the strictest confidence. The Archbishop was concerned that if his visit to Adrian became known he would be inundated with invitations to visit other motherhouses and he would be unable to accept them. He wrote in part to Mother Gerald on July 10, 1937,

> *I am writing particularly at this time to tell you that I am quite sure plans can be arranged for the visit I promised at Adrian. I expect to arrive at the Convent with Bishop Hoban and one of my secretaries in time for supper on July 30th. I must be in Detroit the evening of August 2nd; but I hope to have the intervening days for a quiet rest at Adrian. I know you will respect my wish to have my plans kept confidential.*

Mother Gerald secured permission to include her brother Bishop Barry among the guests when the Delegate came for his visit. When she wrote to request this favor from him she added,

Appendix One

> *I am delighted that our good friend, Bishop Hoban, will accompany you for he has always been one of our most beloved guests, and we have never had enough of him.*

Through her acquaintance with Archbishop Cicognani, Mother Gerald was kept aware of some of the Pope's concerns about the United States and other nations as well. In one letter the Archbishop mentioned that he was enclosing a copy of a circular letter that the "Sacred consistorial Congregation addressed to all the local Ordinaries of this Country." Dated August 24, 1936, it pertained to "the work among the Colored [sic] in the United States." Shortly afterward Mother Gerald sent sisters to open a school for the "colored" in Fort Pierce, Florida. Segregation still held sway.

Mother Gerald was influenced in her theology of the priesthood by a sacramental understanding of priests as "other Christs." This teaching stemmed from the belief that through the conferring of the sacrament of Holy Orders by the bishop in the ordination ceremony the character of the ordinand was substantially changed. There was an indelible mark imprinted upon the soul of the man that could never be changed. Accordingly, Mother Gerald herself, and her sisters whom she schooled in appropriate behavior toward the priests they encountered, accorded them extraordinary deference.

At the same time she did not welcome unsolicited advice from members of the clergy. She had a strong sense of her own authority in determining the affairs of her Congregation. She had her own preferred advisors who were sometimes bishops and priests who accorded her the same reverence that she extended to them. She was also adroit in recognizing those who could assist her in advancing the well being of the Congregation.

At her death the tributes extended in her memory are witness to the extraordinary eminence in which she was held by bishops and priests at home and abroad.

Appendix One

1. She would see this as an affront to St. Patrick.

2. This boarding school situated on the inland waterway in West Palm Beach became Rosarian Academy in 1939.

3. The reference is to Father Celestin Daly, OP, who served the Apostolic Delegate from the Vatican to the United States as canon lawyer. The association of the Apostolic Delegate and his staff with St. Ann-on-the-Lake is discussed further beginning on page 275.

4. Father Maurice Walsh, brother of Mother Augustine.

5. This seems to be a reference to Father Peter J. Jordan, one of the priests at St. Mary of Good Counsel Parish in Adrian.

6. Bishop Gallagher had died in January of that year. On May 31, the Diocese of Detroit was made an archdiocese and, that same day, the Vatican announced the appointment of Archbishop Mooney as the new ordinary. It is possible that Mooney is the "new Bishop" to whom this letter refers.

7. The popular film released that year starring Bing Crosby.

8. This reference is to Father Clarence Dorsey, who is further discussed later in this chapter.

9. This is a reference to Sister Thomasine McDonnell, who selected the films to be shown to the St. Joseph Academy students.

10. The Michigan Colleges Foundation is a group of colleges and universities located around the state. It works to promote Michigan's independent liberal arts institutions and to involve businesses, industry, and foundations on their behalf.

11. Material taken from http://en.wikipedia.org/wiki/Master_of_Sacred_Theology.

12. Pope St. Gregory the Great (Pontiff from 590-604) once offered thirty consecutive Masses for a deceased monk to assure his release from Purgatory. The custom of offering such "Gregorian Masses" was honored in the Congregation at the death of a sister. The practice has been discontinued in the Congregation, although it is still an honored observance in some places.

13. At this time the capital city was called Ciudad Trujillo, after the President of the time.

[14] Archbishop Richard Pittini was virtually blind by this time.

[15] This is a strange allusion, since Father LaMore was always a professor at the College.

[16] The reference is to Father Louis Bertrand O'Connell.

[17] Father Charles Sadlier was for a time named the resident chaplain for Maria Hall. Otherwise he spent time in Adrian resting from illness. He may have taught a class at Siena Heights on an interim basis.

[18] This is a reference to Father Anthony Jurgelaitis.

[19] At this point in time the United States and the Vatican did not maintain full diplomatic relations. Cicognani was not an ambassador but a representative, called an Apostolic Delegate, of the Vatican to the United States. Myron Taylor was his counterpart at the Vatican. At the present time the situation has changed and full diplomatic relations between the United States and the Vatican are maintained. The current Vatican diplomat is called an Apostolic Nuncio with the rank of Ambassador.

[20] See Foley, *Seeds Scattered and Grown*, 93 and ff.

Appendix Two

A Circle of Devoted Support

In the history of the Adrian Dominican Sisters from 1924 until 1961, three names are firmly intertwined: Mother Gerald Barry, Sister Benedicta Marie Ledwidge, and Sister Bertha Homminga. The three were appointed in 1924 by Mother Augustine Walsh to direct matters concerning the fledgling St. Joseph College and worked together for the next thirty-seven years until Mother Gerald's death. In doing so, they shaped both the Congregation and Siena Heights College into the institutions they are today.

Sister Benedicta Marie Ledwidge

Sister Benedicta Marie was born Sarah Clare Ledwidge on July 5, 1888, near Pinckney, Michigan, in a town called Anderson that no longer exists. Born with a twin sister who died in infancy, she was one of five children of William and Mary Ledwidge.

Sister Benedicta Marie Ledwidge

Clare, as she was known, apparently knew very early in life that she wanted to be a sister. She spent several years as a teacher first, after earning her Life Certificate from Michigan State Normal College, now known as Eastern Michigan University.[1] In March 1915 she entered the postulate of the Sisters of St. Joseph in Kalamazoo, Michigan. After three months, the length of the postulancy in that congregation at the time, she made profession and was given the religious name Sister William in honor of her father.

With her teaching experience and the fact that she was already certified as a teacher, she was appointed to teach the boys in the sisters' boarding school. But ill health forced her to leave the congregation and return home less than a year later.

Within a few years she had recovered and, having not abandoned her dream of religious life, asked to enter the Adrian Dominican Sisters. Clare had come to know them through visiting her younger sister Germaine and their cousin, Elaine McClear,[2] when the latter two were students at St. Joseph Academy. She entered the Congregation in July 1920 at the age of thirty-two, became a novice and received the name Sister Benedicta Marie in January 1921, and was professed in August 1923.

Between the time Sister Benedicta Marie entered and 1925, she taught at St. Matthew in Chicago, St. Alphonsus in Dearborn, Michigan, and St. Joseph Academy. At the latter, she was put in charge of the junior and senior students. According to her Congregation biography,

> *Her students, many of them Adrian Dominicans now, remember her as an excellent teacher, soft-spoken, gentle and compassionate, sharp, penetrating but always willing to give the student the benefit of the doubt. The minute she began to speak, there was instant silence, even when the group was*

> *large and they were in the "old auditorium." They knew that she always said something interesting, something genuine. They believed in her. She never gave them a written task for punishment, lest it would stand in the way of a love for writing and good literature.*

Then illness, this time a respiratory condition that it was feared would become tuberculosis, struck again. For two years beginning in 1925 she was confined to the Congregation's "white cottage"[3] and then to St. Clement Infirmary once it was built.

She used those two years well. In addition to being a highly skilled teacher, she was an excellent writer, and she put the latter talent to good use during her illness. Writing under two pen names, Aileen Roche (Roche was her mother's maiden name) and Mary Elizabeth O'Rourke, she composed numerous poems and short stories, many of which were published. One of her stories, "Minus the Velvet Glove," which had been printed in *The Michigan Catholic*, won first prize in 1928 in the Stepping Stones Short Story contest conducted by Catholic newspapers nationwide. Another story won fifth place in the same contest.

As the contest was being judged, a story in *The Michigan Catholic*[4] mentioned that "Minus the Velvet Glove" was likely to be a winner. It quoted her (without identifying her by name, but indicating that the pen name was that of a nun) as saying, "Writing can never be more than an avocation for me as I have chosen teaching for my life work, but I hope during leisure moments to do my little bit toward providing wholesome reading and thus help to raise the literary standards of the day."

When she finally recovered from her illness in 1927, she returned to teaching at St. Joseph Academy. Then in 1932, she was sent to Visitation High School in Detroit. Her feelings about her chosen field are evident from a letter she sent during that time to Sister Gerald, who was Vicaress General at that point: "We have had a very restful and delightful vacation but I shall not be sorry to go to school again tomorrow. I have such an incorrigible love of teaching and I do like my work here very much."

But when a General Chapter convened in July 1933 to elect a new Mother General, Mother Augustine having died that January, Sister Benedicta Marie was called into Congregational service. Sister Gerald was elected Mother General and Sister Benedicta Marie was elected Vicaress General, a post she would hold for the next thirty-four years.

Mother Gerald was often gone from Adrian, usually on visitations to the Congregation's many missions around the country or on other Congregational business. It therefore fell to Sister Benedicta Marie to be in charge of the community's day-to-day matters for much of the time. She often found herself in the position of giving counsel to sisters seeking help in times of Mother Gerald's absence from Adrian. Her letters to Mother Gerald frequently contained advice about how to handle a particular situation.

When Mother Gerald was away, Sister Benedicta Marie always kept her informed through almost daily letters and, when necessary, telegrams, and generally consulted her before any action was taken. But it is clear from the archival documents that Mother Gerald trusted Sister Benedicta Marie's judgment completely when it came to handling matters in her absence. For example, a handwritten note she sent from Roy, New Mexico, on June 28, 1942, instructed Sister Benedicta Marie not to forward any mail unless it was very urgent, and continued, "You can take care of everything and what you do is O.K."

And just as Mother Augustine had relied on Sister Gerald, as her Vicaress, to occasionally deal with critical problems, so too did Mother Gerald rely on Sister Benedicta Marie. She proved more than capable of the challenge, as is indicated by the way she handled a serious conflict in 1954 between the priest at St. Ann's in Gilbert, Arizona, and the sisters missioned to the catechetical center there.

Mother Gerald was away, visiting the Dominican Republic and other locales, when the trouble erupted. After having made life difficult for the sisters in several ways, the priest had sent the superior, Sister Pauline Mary LaVoy, an extraordinarily critical letter. Making matters worse, he had done so while she was recuperating from surgery in a Phoenix hospital. Mother Gerald instructed Sister Benedicta Marie in a telegram to go there and deal with the situation, getting the bishop involved if necessary.

Apparently Sister Benedicta Marie handled the matter with a blend of firmness and compassion that would not have surprised anyone who knew her. She wrote to Mother Gerald on February 6, 1954, after her return, that she had gone to see the bishop first and then headed for

Gilbert to meet with the priest.

> While in G. I interviewed the shepherd of the flock and the interview was interesting to say the least. I found it necessary to define quite carefully the limits of his jurisdiction so that in the future no one would be guilty of 'rank insubordination'. We parted on friendly terms after he had given both Sister Pauline M. and me his blessing and of his own accord told her he was sorry about the letter. The poor lad is young, inexperienced and needs our prayers.

Despite her position in the Congregation, Sister Benedicta Marie was possessed of both humility and humor. Sister Corinne O'Connor wrote in a reminiscence about her:

> Her kindness and humility was evident in her everyday living. She expected no special consideration because of her office as Vicar in the Congregation and waited on herself, if she came to the kitchen for a little lunch in mid-morning and afternoon.

Her wry sense of humor often came through not only in her dealings with other sisters but in her letters to Mother Gerald. One such example is in this passage from January 20, 1934.

> There has been very little mail as I imagine most of the Sisters know that you are in the South. Somebody wrote something about wanting to arrest us because somebody didn't pay a bill somewhere sometime (Please pardon me if this is not quite clear—I have been living in the realms of mystery so long that

I have grown a bit mysterious myself)[5] but I wrote and told him that we always preferred to have you with us whenever we were arrested because we did not like to deprive you of any little pleasure that the rest of us had and would he please not bring the handcuffs until after the eleventh of February.

At the same time as she had the tremendous responsibilities involved in being Vicaress General, especially one for a Mother General who was constantly on the go, she shouldered many other burdens for the Congregation as well. From 1934 to 1951, she served as the Dean of Siena Heights College,[6] then, beginning in 1951, she spent six years as the Executive Vice President. And, from 1957 to 1965, she was the institution's President.[7]

During her years as an administrator at the College, she was recognized as an expert on matters of teacher education and her input was often sought on the topic. In December 1948, Lee M. Thurston, Superintendent of the Michigan Department of Public Instruction, asked her to serve on a committee to help deal with the problem of not having enough adequately trained elementary teachers. She not only accepted, but Siena Heights College hosted a conference on the matter in February 1949. The meeting was attended by local school superintendents, administrators and faculty from Siena Heights and Adrian College, and the President of the Michigan Association of School Administrators.

Another example of her influence came in 1964 when her input was sought as a "leading educator" by the people putting together the Hall of Education at that year's World's Fair in New York. She was asked to provide observations on a series of questions, and her answers show a sharp educational mind at work that was up-to-date on contemporary issues. Among the questions, and a sampling of her answers, were:

What major advances in technique and methodology have there been in education?

- Awareness of the teacher as a "director of self-realization and potentiality."
- Awareness of teaching as an opportunity to "contribute to the cultural, social and civic needs of our American democratic society."
- Awareness of man [sic] as "a composite creature of spirit and matter who seeks by his very nature to participate fully in the infinite life of God and the finite life of society."
- Awareness of "imparting a world perspective" by teaching children foreign languages early in life.
- Awareness of "our greatest national need: achieving a unified democratic nation out of the diverse ethnic groups of our varied national origins."

What are the weaknesses in education?

- A lack of awareness "of the understanding that we live in a transition between a jet age and a space age."
- A lack of awareness of need to involve parents.

- A lack of awareness of failure to teach basic skills.
- A lack of awareness of knowledge of individual differences in students.

What are the needs in schools?

- More and better teachers for gifted students and mentally disabled students.
- More emphasis on reading.
- Stronger fine arts programs.
- Consolidation of smaller schools.
- Programs for underachieving students.

What should the "School of Tomorrow" stress?

- Training in "the intellectual virtues," not stressing vocational training over intellectual proficiency.
- Revamp social studies programs to include "the latest research in sociology, economics, world history and anthropology."
- Introduce comparative religion studies.

Her educational leadership was honored in other ways as well. In 1961, the Adrian Chamber of Commerce gave her a citation for, as Siena Heights President, leading an institution that advanced the local community. And in 1964, the Michigan Colleges Foundation honored her with a citation in recognition of outstanding achievements and services on behalf of Michigan colleges.

To Fields Near and Far

Throughout all her years in the College's leadership, she had a profound effect on faculty and students alike. After her death in 1968, the *Sienae* (Siena's alumnae association newsletter) ran a tribute to her that included these words:

> *A small woman, but exceedingly keen and with seemingly unlimited, driving energy, she was a veritable genius behind the executive's desk. She exerted, in fact, a greater influence in the development of Siena Heights College than her seven years in the presidency might indicate.*
>
> *In reality she was dean of the college from 1934 to 1957 and removed most of the load from Mother Mary Gerald, who already was busy with other responsibilities. In fact, even when she was dean of the college she carried much of the executive responsibility.*
>
> *. . . Who of us can truly say with any certainty when Sister Benedicta Marie's influence began in her? Who of us can truly say when that influence will end? Or where? Who of us, then, is not truly grateful for having shared a part of life with her?*[8]

This is another passage from Sister Corinne O'Connor's reminiscence:

> *A born educator, she revered her profession. She came from a family of teachers, and she held teaching as one of the noblest professions. The student was her primary consideration: her character, her welfare, her success, her future were worthy of*

study and concern. A quiet excellence pervaded the realm of her classroom and college office. When she was President of Siena, teachers, recognizing the excellence of the courses taught at the college, enrolled in large numbers for day and evening classes. 'Professionalism' was the hallmark of the products of Siena while she was its administrator. She held the faculty in high regard and showed a sincere respect in her speech and actions for the talents of her faculty.

After Mother Gerald's death in November 1961, Sister Benedicta Marie's role as Vicaress General required that she step into the Mother General's role until a General Chapter could be convened. She led the Congregation until Mother Genevieve Weber was elected in 1962.

At that same General Chapter, Sister Benedicta Marie was once again elected Vicaress General of the Congregation. She continued in that capacity, and as President of Siena Heights College, despite being confined to St. Clement Infirmary a short time after the election due to her failing health. Later that year she moved to Maria Health Care Center and lived there until her death.

The College honored her in 1966 by naming its newest building Ledwidge Hall. In response she sent a letter addressed to Mother Genevieve; to Sister Petronilla Francoeur, who had succeeded her as the College's President; and to the College's trustees. It is a letter that displays her characteristic humility, even as she is clearly pleased by the honor.

> *You can hardly imagine how surprised I was at this announcement. Never had the thought of such a thing entered my mind. I have been a religious for more than forty years and have made an honest effort to attain the ideal of "All for God, nothing for self." Yet, I am human and never succeeded in conquering myself to the fullest extent. So from my own heart, I thank you for this beautiful remembrance, but I thank you even more for the sake of my family, and especially for my beloved parents who struggled so hard to give their children the things they themselves never had.*[9]

Sister Benedicta Marie died of arteriosclerosis and heart disease on April 1, 1968, at the age of seventy-nine. Father Bernard Dominick, the Congregation's chaplain, said in her funeral homily,

> *. . . she was wholeheartedly intent on living the spirit of the rule she embraced. She was joyfully committed to the promises that she made to God. And she gave to all those who knew her a sterling example.*
>
> *Each of you has in your own hearts and memories many pleasant experiences from your knowledge and contact with her. She was a religious of spirit and enthusiasm; she was a religious of loyalty and devotion to duty. She had an exuberance for life. She possessed a love for people and especially her fellow Sisters. She had a thirst for the modern expression of the Gospel message. And her zeal promoted a very sincere commitment to the Church and all the dimensions of the apostolate.*

. . . Although Sister Benedicta Marie was many things to many people in the service she gave to the Community, she was above all a woman of Vision. She was deeply convinced that the very reason for the existence of the Church is to bring the light of Christ, brightly visible, to all men [sic].

. . . She wanted earnestly to be a religious of today's Church. So she determined to be a religious who is thoroughly imbued with the documents of Vatican II. When she could she must have read, thought, prayed, argued, and re-read them many times. She wanted so much to know the mind of the Church today. She was anxious to open her mind to the inspiration of the Holy Spirit. She was persuaded that there was no place in the Church or the Community for saintly, silent stones. If you make no contribution, only sit silently, you are shirking responsibility. Once she said to me that it is better to speak, even poorly, than not to speak at all.

Sister Bertha Homminga

In the history of both the Congregation and Siena Heights College, no one was more legendary for her memory and organizational skills than Sister Bertha Homminga: Directress of Studies, Registrar of the College for forty-seven years beginning in 1922, the Congregation's Secretary General for twenty-seven years, and Registrar of St. Joseph Academy for many years as well.

Sister Bertha's prowess in her area of expertise was remarkable. Sister Mary Philip Ryan spoke about it in Sister Bertha's funeral homily, on March 2, 1977.

Sister Bertha Homminga

> *It has been said that she had a computer mind. Many of you can recall the piercing look from those deep dark eyes penetrating right through anyone who might be playing with the idea of changing a major or dropping a course without asking her; some even fancied they could hear a clink in her mind registering their grades and sequence of studies as she spotted them in the hall.*
>
> *Her memory did seem to be illuminated, and certainly her mind was an extraordinary gift from God. Educators in various universities and colleges recognized her ability and held her in esteem. She was so highly respected in the [Education Department] of Michigan that her signature alone was enough on any application for a teacher certificate. And this was in the 1930s, 40s, and 50s when new regulations were making constant and exacting demands on educational institutions.*
>
> *On one occasion, Dr. Carroll Deady, then superintendent of Detroit Archdiocesan schools, was presiding at a meeting of college presidents and registrars, listening to their miseries, when he interrupted them to say: "It's too bad that you don't have a Sister Bertha."*
>
> *When the Detroit Archdiocesan school office was in a state*

Appendix Two

> *of confusion over teacher certification, the cry went up, "Let's borrow Sister Bertha from Adrian."*
>
> *Indeed her services were borrowed often. She spent long hours with registrars from other colleges and congregations who came from many places to learn her procedures in cutting through the complications.*

Sister Bertha was born Gertrude Homminga[10] on December 20, 1893, in Milwaukee. She was raised by an aunt from the age of three and at age nine was adopted by her. Apparently, this arrangement was worked out because the family was already very large and at the time her mother was expecting another baby.

She attended school in Lake Leelanau, Michigan, her mother Margaret's home town, until sixth grade. She then went to St. Joseph Academy until her last year of high school, which she spent at Central Catholic in Grand Rapids. One of her sisters entered the Grand Rapids Dominicans, while another joined the Sisters of St. Joseph.

She entered the Adrian Dominican Congregation in October 1914 and made her profession in September 1916. As a postulant, she taught at St. Joseph Academy for a year and then was one of the first three faculty members at Aquinas High School in Chicago, where she spent another year. For the 1916-1917 academic year, she studied at The Catholic University of America in Washington, DC.

Her work as Registrar began in 1920, when Mother Camilla Madden gave her a three-by-five-inch file box and instructed her to find all the missing records for St. Joseph Academy students and to keep the records for the current students. Since the Academy was twenty-four years old at the time, the former task was no small challenge. Later, Mother Augustine Walsh gave her a larger file box and asked her to organize the grades and credits of the sisters in their continued studies. Finally, Mother Gerald directed her to set up a personal file for each sister and develop the Congregation's study program.

In keeping with what Sister Mary Philip Ryan said in her homily, an oral history from Sister Marie Wiedner, kept in the Siena Heights archives, includes this about the period in 1954 during which she worked in Sister Bertha's office:

> *I admired Sister Bertha tremendously; she was so dedicated and conscientious. She would take files home with her at night and pore over them so she knew every student's major and minor. She had a reputation for being able to look at you and tell you what your major was and what kind of grades you were receiving.*

Siena Heights paid tribute to her with an honorary doctorate of education in 1969. The citation read in part,

> *From the pioneering days until 1968 this courageous Sister has served the needs of the people of God as teacher, registrar, and religious leader with dedicated effort and deep interest. She consistently kept her eyes open for the significant small tasks that had to be done because she believed the major*

accomplishments to be merely an accumulation of these small tasks. Truly, it may be said of her, "With joy she served, and with pride she gave in true humility." It seems fitting that we honor on this occasion one who not only has the attributes of humility, perseverance, perceptiveness, and dedication but one who has worked with an unceasing eagerness and determination for the education of youth and adults.

For much of the time she was the College's Registrar, she also held Congregational leadership posts. In 1930, she was elected Secretary General,[11] a post she held until 1957 when she apparently stepped down because she had cataracts that required surgery. Then, in 1962, she was elected to the General Council and served in that capacity until 1968, when she resigned after suffering a stroke. She died on February 27, 1977.

Together with Mother Gerald and Sister Benedicta Marie, Sister Bertha was instrumental in raising standards for the education of the sisters and, as a result, in raising the educational level of the children the sisters taught. And just as Sister Benedicta Marie was unhesitant in giving advice and counsel to Mother Gerald on Congregational business, so too was Sister Bertha unafraid to stand her ground. From Sister Mary Philip Ryan's homily,

She said that her association with Mother Gerald and Sister Benedicta Marie began unofficially in the 1920s in their common interest for teacher preparation and higher standards in our schools; and that they became closely bound after 1933

when in response to their election they set out to work together in the expansion period of our Congregation. These three women, each one so different, were of one heart and mind in serving the Church in the special needs of the time. Theirs was a service of trust. They were three women keeping a sacred commitment.

Mother Gerald and Sister Benedicta Marie discovered in Sister Bertha a deepdown wellspring of wisdom and integrity. They knew that she could not say what she did not feel or believe. Mother Gerald used to say that a hundred people could be in the room nodding "yes" to an idea, and, if Sister Bertha could not agree, she preferred to incur censure than to nod "yes" when she was thinking "no." She could not be easily swayed by the opinion of the moment. Mother Gerald also admitted that rather than take action at such a time she waited until she could hear Sister Bertha's argument—and she always got it in stout, unadorned Anglo-Saxon prose.

In these later years, Sister Bertha would chuckle when she remembered that indeed Mother Gerald yielded to her many a time when they were appointing sisters to their missions—if not immediately, she said, granting that it would be too much for a woman like Mother Gerald to give in so soon, but the next day or the next, she knew by the twinkle in the eye of Mother Gerald that she was going to say, "Bertha, you are right."

Appendix Two

Sister Mary Philip Ryan

Teacher, novice mistress, superior and principal, author, historian, and a vital part of two major Congregational endeavors in the Dominican Republic and the Philippines—all these things describe Sister Mary Philip Ryan.

Margaret Mary Ryan was born May 9, 1901, in Chicago to Irish immigrant parents. Her father, Philip, a steelworker, and her mother, Mary Ellen, met in Cleveland and later moved to Chicago for a better job at a steel mill there. In all, they had seven children: Thomas Patrick, James Edward, Julia Cecelia, Ellen Mary, Mary Etta, Margaret Mary, and Philip Pius.

Sisters Rudolf (Dorothea) Beuttenmuller (left) and Mary Philip Ryan, with Humberto Ruíz Castillo, architect of Colegio Santo Domingo, and the Archbishop of Santo Domingo, Richard Pittini, at the groundbreaking for the Colegio.

After graduating from Aquinas High School in Chicago, she worked for a very short time as a receptionist in a doctor's office and then entered the postulate in Adrian on February 2, 1920. She made first profession on August 17, 1922.

Over the next several years, she taught in Detroit; Assumption, Ohio; and Royal Oak, Michigan. She also earned her bachelor's degree from St. John University in Toledo, Ohio, majoring in English and minoring in Latin and history, and later earned a master's in English, with a Latin minor, from the University of Detroit.

After Mother Gerald was elected Mother General for the first time in 1933, she appointed Sister Mary Philip to succeed her as novice mistress. Sister Mary Philip held that post for the next twelve years. Years later, she wrote that she had felt "anything but qualified" for the job, and told Sister Joanne Screes, in an interview transcribed for the Congregation archives, that she felt pressured, even if indirectly, by Mother Gerald to make the novices perfect.

"Mother Gerald got after me for faults of the novices," she said in the interview. "And you know, I didn't realize it at the time, but my anger at her would go toward the novices. ...I've atoned for that. Those young women were really wonderful."

During this time, she also was called upon to work many nights on the correspondence of Mother Gerald and others, and lack of sleep likely affected her daytime disposition as well. Additionally, on Mother Gerald's instructions, she began talking with the older sisters and writing down their recollections. This was the basis of what eventually became the first volume of the Congregation's history, *Amid the Alien Corn*.

Mother Gerald also "commissioned" her to write a biography of Mother Gerald's brother Bishop Patrick Barry. The result, the unpublished work *A Long Hot Day*, earned Sister Mary Philip a Hopwood Prize in the essay category from the University of Michigan in 1944.

Appendix Two

After shaping the religious lives of hundreds of young women over the course of her twelve years at the novitiate, Sister Mary Philip received a new assignment from Mother Gerald in 1945. She and Sisters Thomas Ann (Eileen) Burke and Rudolf (Dorothea) Beuttenmuller were sent to the Dominican Republic to open the Congregation's first overseas mission, Colegio Santo Domingo. It was a task that involved having the school literally built from the ground up and meant countless challenges, both in construction matters and in navigating the country's tricky political waters.

Sister Mary Philip led the Colegio for eleven years and for much of that time also served as a professor of English at the University of Santo Domingo. Then, in the summer of 1956, she returned to Adrian to edit Mother Gerald's letters and work on the first draft of *Amid the Alien Corn*. That fall, she took care of all the official paperwork needed for that year's Colegio faculty to get to the Dominican Republic, fully expecting to return there. Instead, however, she was appointed principal and superior at Rosary High School, still under construction in Detroit.

When her six-year term as superior at Rosary High was completed—a term during which, in November 1961, her beloved Mother Gerald died—she was assigned to teach English at Siena Heights College and spent two years there. She was able to complete most of *Amid the Alien Corn* over the summers, in 1964 and 1965.

Then Mother Gerald's successor, Mother Genevieve, sent her on a new overseas adventure: to the Philippines to help form a new congregation of women religious. The Dominican Sisters of Our Lady of Remedies got their start in June 1960, when Emilio Cinense, the Bishop of the Diocese of San Fernando, Philippines, asked Mother Gerald to help form a new congregation in his diocese. She countered by offering to have a group of candidates trained in Adrian and then to send two sisters to the Philippines to work with this fledgling congregation. Sister Mary Philip was one of those two, along with Sister Ellen Vincent McClain.[12]

After several years in the Philippines, during which time she finished the text of *Amid the Alien Corn*, Sister Mary Philip returned to Adrian and spent the last years of her life there, most of them as the Congregation historian. In that capacity, she was instrumental in capturing not only the Congregation's overall history but also the individual stories of its sisters.

When she died on October 22, 2002, she was 101 years old and in the eightieth year of her religious profession. It was a time frame that saw the Congregation go from its often difficult early years, into a period of tremendous growth, and through the sea change brought about after Vatican Council II.

Sister Margaret Helen Lynch

Sister Margaret Helen Lynch was Mother Gerald's secretary from 1935 to 1943 and again from 1951 to 1952. She was the Congregation's Bursar/Treasurer[13] in the intervening years.

Born Margaret Mary Lynch on August 7, 1905, in Joliet, Illinois, she spent her last year of high school with the Adrian Dominicans at Mount St. Mary Academy. Although she was attracted to religious life, after graduation she went to work for the Woodruff Securities Company. In June 1924, two months before her nineteenth birthday, she entered the postulate and quickly was sent to St. Ambrose School in Detroit to teach music.

Sister Margaret Helen Lynch

She spent a total of a year and a half at St. Ambrose, but in her second year she found herself teaching not only music but tenth grade, and "I broke down physically," she later said. "Mother Gerald, who was then novice mistress, was going to Rosarian in Florida and took me with her. I went back to my parents' home at the end of that summer and stayed there for four years."

The turning point came when Sister Gerald called her at home to ask if she would drive her to St. Columbanus in Chicago. During the trip, Sister Gerald asked her when she was coming back to the Congregation, a question which prompted her to decide to return.

She did so on March 25, 1930, spent her novitiate year in Adrian, and made first profession on August 11, 1931. After spending time teaching at St. Mary School in Adrian and St. Paul in Grosse Pointe, Michigan, she did summer study at St. John College in Toledo. She earned her bachelor's degree from St. Joseph College in Adrian in 1935 with a major in English and minors in history and French.

Her first experience in working for Mother Gerald came while she was studying in Adrian and helping Mother Gerald with her correspondence in the evenings. She stayed on as Mother Gerald's secretary after her graduation.

After Sister Margaret Helen's death in 2000, Sister Nadine Foley, in her funeral homily, summed up her contributions to the Congregation in this way:

> *These were positions [secretary and bursar general] in those days that carried a high degree of responsibility and a certain prestige within the Congregation. Sister Margaret Helen was conscious of both. She was extremely capable in organization and brought that talent to the development of the archives. She handled much sensitive material and understood the boundaries of confidentiality. She staunchly maintained her position in Mother's outer office to provide the greatest possible privacy and protection for Mother Gerald who was very much the center of her life.*
>
> *. . . As we think of the computer, the printer, the internet, the FAX machine, the security people we have, the conveniences we enjoy, we have to think back to all those, like Sister Margaret Helen, who worked for the Congregation without all of these conveniences, and whose diligence here and elsewhere around the Congregation all contributed to who and what we are today. And we give thanks.*

> *. . . Many of us here know that Sister Margaret Helen was secretary to Mother Gerald and Bursar General of the Congregation. But she was more than that. She was an adviser, a consultant, one who recommended courses of action in administrative and legal affairs and a trusted confidante. Through her interest in current events she could recognize movements that had a significance for the Congregation and propose new directions.*

In 1952, Sister Margaret Helen was sent to Europe to continue her education, which she did at the University of Fribourg, Switzerland; Maria Assunta University in Rome; Oxford; and the University of Madrid. She earned a licentiate in 1954 and a doctorate in 1955, both in history, from the University of Madrid. During her time in Spain, she became acquainted with a number of communities of sisters, and it was she who arranged for members of the Missionary Society of the Sacred Heart to attend Siena Heights College prior to opening their mission in Texas.

Upon her return, she joined the Siena Heights faculty in 1956-57 and then taught at Barry College. When the Congregation was divided into provinces, which took effect in 1960, she served for five years as a provincial councilor and as secretary-treasurer for St. Catherine Province.

Next, she taught history at St. Dominic College, the Congregation's new college in St. Charles, Illinois, before going back to Siena Heights and then to Barry again.

In 1969, at the age of sixty-four, she went to Dominican Santa Cruz Hospital as medical librarian and then as the assistant personnel director. She spent nine years there before returning to Adrian to work as the archivist for about nine months. From 1979 to 1982 she served as secretary at Our Lady of Lourdes Parish in Melbourne, Florida, and then as pastoral minister at St. Jude Parish in St. Petersburg, Florida.

In 1982, she came back to Adrian again and served first as a driver for the sisters and then as the Motherhouse secretary before retiring completely in 1990. She died September 10, 2000.

Sister Mary Richardine Waldron

For a time, the service of Sister Mary Richardine Waldron as a secretary to Mother Gerald overlapped with that of Sister Margaret Helen Lynch. Sister Richardine worked with Mother Gerald from 1951 until being elected Secretary-General of the Congregation in 1957.

She was born Mary Agnes Waldron on September 10, 1911, in Chicago, of Irish immigrant parents. Like Sister Margaret Helen, she did not join the Congregation until relatively later in life, spending seven years working as a secretary until she decided to follow her sister, Sister Jane de Chantal, into the Adrian Dominicans. She entered the Congregation in August 1936 and made profession a year later.

Sister Mary Richardine Waldron

Appendix Two

While a student at Siena Heights College, she helped out in various offices as a secretary, and after she earned her bachelor's degree in 1940 she became secretary to Sister Benedicta Marie in the latter's capacity as Dean of the College. She served in that role until becoming personal secretary to Mother Gerald.

According to the biography of her kept in the Congregation archives,

> *As a secretary she was found to be efficient, prudent, and in possession of the important qualities needed for this kind of service.*
>
> *From the outset, Mother Gerald recognized the intrinsic worth of this young sister. It was frequently necessary to tell her only the substance of a reply to give to some piece of correspondence. Sister's job was to write the letter without benefit of direct dictation. Mother Gerald used to say that she never failed to be amazed at the unique facility Sister Richardine had of capturing not only the phraseology of her speech, but the ability to clothe it with the very spirit which she herself would have given.*
>
> *It was not surprising, therefore, that Sister Richardine was the choice of the Sisters at the General Chapter when they elected her in 1957 as Secretary-General of the Congregation. She discharged this office with the same efficiency, prudence, and discretion which had marked her every work previously.*

In early 1961, she and Sister Mary Philip Ryan were sent to Peru to investigate the possibility of opening a mission there. There was a hepatitis epidemic there at the time, and she apparently contracted the disease. By 1962, her health started to fail. She went to a series of doctors, but nothing could be done. She came to St. Clement Infirmary in February 1963 and stayed there until August 1964. At that point, she went to St. Bridget Convent in Loves Park, Illinois, at the invitation of the pastor. She was there until the fall of 1965 when, her health growing worse, she returned to Adrian. She died on August 11, 1966, at the age of just fifty-five.

Father Bernard Dominick, the Motherhouse chaplain, preached the homily at her August 16 funeral. It included these words:

> *Her acceptance of the cross that God sent was admirable. And because she was such a willing victim of immolation, it seems to us, who had only the privilege of standing by, to be almost mysterious. Because she did not fight God or His great plan, she had the grace and blessing of great peace. And in the memory of her great trial, this will be a source of considerable consolation to us.*
>
> *Sister Mary Richardine was an outstanding and gifted religious. We will all have many wonderful memories of her. Each of us can recount and recall many attractive qualities of her beautiful soul. Her greatest asset was her developing maturity. She had that quality that I choose to call, spiritual insight, by which she knew how to order her life according to*

the principle of first things first. She was, above all, true to the God Whom she served so faithfully; she was soberly devoted to her religious life; she was loyal and helpful to her friends. In a word, we may say, that she was true to herself.

. . . All of us are richer today for having known her. Our best tribute to her would be to model our lives on hers. We do not have to do extraordinary things. Like her, we simply have to do the ordinary in a most remarkable and extraordinary way.

None of these five women was ever an elected major superior. For them, there was only one person to whom they dedicated their fidelity in loving service: Mother Gerald. In that way, they shared in the vision of the remarkable woman they felt privileged to follow.

1. She later studied over two summers at DePaul and Loyola, earned her Bachelor of Philosophy degree from St. Joseph College and her MA from the University of Detroit, and did further "professional study" at the University of Notre Dame. In 1939, Michigan State Normal College awarded her an honorary master's of education degree.

2. Elaine McClear became the Congregation's Sister Ann Terence.

3. This was a house that had been moved to the Academy grounds in 1906 from the nearby St. Joseph School, where it had served as a residence for boarders. It became the Congregation's first infirmary.

4. The exact date of the issue in which the story appeared is undeterminable from either the Congregational or *The Michigan Catholic* archives, but it was in late 1927.

5. She had only recently returned to Adrian after spending several months in Hot Springs, Arkansas, as a companion to a sister being treated there. This might be a reference to still needing to get back up to speed on Congregational matters.

6. Characteristic of her dry wit, to say nothing of the fact that she had College as well as Congregation business to attend to, she ended a September 1, 1942, letter to Mother Gerald with this sentence: "There is a prospective day student out in the corridor and I must go and set my trap for her."

7. Typically at that time, when a religious congregation operated an institute of higher learning, the Prioress served as the college president. Mother Gerald was President of Siena Heights College from her election as Mother General in 1933 until 1957. She was also President of Barry College from the time it opened in 1940 until her death in 1961.

8. May 21, 1968, issue.

9. Letter dated November 23, 1966.

10. At some point, her brothers dropped one "m" from the family name, but she retained the original Dutch spelling.

11. In 1974, the post of Secretary General became appointed rather than elected. In 1980, the title of this position became Secretary of the Congregation.

12. In 2011, this group merged with the Adrian Dominicans, becoming the Our Lady of Remedies Mission Chapter.

Appendix Two

[13] In the early years of the Congregation, the position of Secretary/Bursar was held by one person. Margaret Helen Lynch was the first person to hold the post of Bursar/Treasurer. After her, the person in that position was known first as the Bursar General, then as the Treasurer General, and now as the Treasurer of the Congregation.

Index

A

Adelson, Sister Mary Hyacinth, 126
Adrian Dominican House of Studies, The, 42, 52, 141, 214
Amid the Alien Corn, 302, 303, 304
Aquinas College, 197, 214
Aquinas High School, 207, 297, 301
Archangelus Hall, 42, 55, 270
Aufderheide, Sister Jean Kevin, 198

B

Barry College, 22, 48, 78, 84, 85, 86, 90, 177, 194, 198, 214, 224, 254, 263, 272, 307
Barry, Bishop Patrick, 8, 50, 65, 78, 79, 82, 85, 86, 276, 278, 302
Barry, Gerald (nephew), 50, 56, 82
Barry, Monsignor William, 8, 57, 79, 80, 81, 82, 98, 110, 229, 252
Barry, Mother Gerald, 5, 11, 18, 23, 26, 30, 37, 40, 42, 51, 52, 55, 57, 58, 61, 64, 65, 66, 73, 77, 79, 81, 86, 89, 90, 92, 94, 108, 109, 110, 117, 118, 121, 124, 125, 128, 129, 134, 136, 137, 138, 141, 147, 150, 152, 153, 154, 163, 167, 168, 171, 180, 183, 184, 185, 186, 187, 189, 190, 192, 196, 198, 199, 203, 205, 207, 210, 213, 224, 225, 236, 241, 244, 245, 248, 251, 257, 258, 261, 263, 265, 268, 269, 276, 278, 279, 283, 286, 287, 298, 299, 300, 302, 305
Barry, Mother Gerald, death of, 226
Bartlett, Selma, 135, 136
Bartley, Sister Helen Patrick, 152
Baske, Sister Mary Pauline, 54, 70
Baxter, Sister Petra, 126, 144
Benincasa Dining Hall, 42, 55
Bentz, Sister Marie, 15
Beuttenmuller, Sister Rudolf (Dorothea), 109, 116, 301, 303
Binder, Sister Mary Henrice, 98
Birch, Sister Rose de Lima, 54, 70
Bishop, Father Howard, 122, 123, 124
Bjerring, Sister Marie Dominic, 75, 76
Bonifacio, Sister Joseph (Esperanza), 219
Bowler, Sister Jean Margaret, 152
Bradley, Colonel Edward, 50
Brennan, Sister Mary Aiden, 198
Britz, Sister Rose Clare, 126
Burke, Father Cyril, 20, 272
Burke, Sister Thomas Ann (Eileen), 109, 116, 144, 303
Burns, Sister Jeanne, 69
Burns, Sister Thomas Annette, 32

C

Cahalan, Monsignor James, 118, 245, 246, 247, 248, 250, 262
Campbell, Sister Kevin, 123, 124, 125, 181, 189, 207, 208, 209, 216
Casa Francesca, 98, 99

Catholic University of America, The, 52, 141, 142, 151, 167, 176, 178, 260, 277, 297
Cawley, Sister Cyril Joseph, 171
Cicognani, Archbishop Amleto, 51, 109, 118, 150, 205, 275, 276, 277, 278, 279
Cinense, Bishop Emilio, 219, 220, 304
Colegio Santo Domingo, 109, 112, 224, 248, 252, 263, 303
Collins, Sister Mary Alice, 50
Condon, Sister Elizabeth, 19
Conference of Major Superiors of Women, The, 169, 171, 180, 188
Conway, Monsignor J.D., 172, 173
Coressel, Sister Marie Lucy, 152
Corrigan, Archbishop Michael, 66
Creighton, Sister Louis James, 144
Culhane, Sister Raymonda, 65
Culleton, Monsignor James, 90, 91, 92, 94
Curley, Archbishop Michael, 24

D

Daly, Bishop Edward, 141, 142, 143, 276
Daly, Sister Rose Edwina, 205
Darga, Sister Mary Reynold, 54, 70
Davis, Bishop James, 125, 126, 127
Deady, Dr. Carroll, 40, 296
Dearden, Archbishop John, 228
Decker, Sister Ann Carmel, 198
Della Penta, Father Joseph Clement, 260
Dillon, Sister Grace Agatha, 201
Dominican High School, 78, 86, 110, 216, 224, 252

Dominican Republic, 45, 109, 110, 125, 143, 153, 171, 177, 216, 248, 252, 265, 287, 301, 303
Dominican Santa Cruz Hospital, 136, 138, 308
Dominican Sisters of Our Lady of Remedies, 219, 220, 304
Dominick, Father Bernard, 294, 310
Dorsey, Father Clarence, 247, 248, 249, 262
Dorsey, Mother Mary Blanche, 61
Doyle, Sister Helen Clare, 152
Duggan, Sister Georganne, 94, 96, 97, 115
Dwyer, Sister Eugenia, 249

E

Ebbitt, Sister Immaculata, 123, 124
Emery, Sister Mary Xavier, 178
Erd, Sister Mary Ellen, 201
Everett Workshop, 159, 160, 162

F

Farrell, Father Walter, 179, 261
Farrell, Margaret Brady, 57, 82
Feliz, Sister María Josefina (Ana), 223
Ferguson, Sister Dolores Marie, 22, 23
Ferguson, Sister Rose Eileen, 98
Ferguson, Sister Rosemary, 14, 15, 18, 20, 22, 27, 48, 225
Fernandez, Sister Dominic (Evangelina), 219, 220
Fidecicchi, Monsignor Augusto, 62, 63

Fleming, Father Michael, 240, 241, 244
Flores, Sister Donald Marie, 126
Flowers, Sister Ann Felice, 126
Fojtik, Sister Mary Nicholas, 126, 144
Foley, Sister Nadine, 24, 37, 70, 115, 200, 282, 306
Folliard, Sister Dorothy, 178
Francoeur, Sister Petronilla, 293
Frawley, Father James, 250

G

Gallagher, Bishop Michael, 25, 45, 58, 59, 61, 62, 63, 246
Gallagher, Sister Michael Patrice, 144
Galvin, Monsignor John, 91
Garcia, Sister Mary Regina (Milagros), 219
Gauthier, Sister Rose Norine, 120
Gaynor, Father George, 227, 250
General Chapter, 5, 6, 30, 73, 112, 117, 143, 147, 149, 199, 203, 204, 213, 226, 286, 293, 309
General Council, 6, 55, 63, 74, 82, 90, 109, 110, 128, 129, 136, 137, 196, 212, 213, 220, 299
Glaister, Sister Dorothy, 212
Gleason, Sister Ann Catherine (Rita), 216
Gleeson, Sister Clare Ambrose, 205
Glenmary Sisters, 78, 121, 123, 124, 125, 143
Goan, Mother Mary de Lourdes, 66
Golden, Sister Frances Eugene, 18

Gorman, Bishop Thomas, 128, 129, 134, 135
Graham, Sister Mary Celeste, 16, 54, 70
Grant, Sister Ann Claudia, 212
Gray, Sister Mary Aurelia, 54
Greene, Sister Gonzaga, 82, 83, 84, 85, 114
Griffin, Sister Ann Thomas, 201

H

Hafey-Wells, Sister Marie Peter, 198
Hagarty, Bishop Paul Leonard, 198
Haidysz, Sister Felicia, 133, 134
Hanly Hospital (Sisters Hospital), 92
Hanna, Sister Robert Francis (Nancy), 223
Harrison, Sister Carolyn, 131, 132, 133, 134, 144
Harrison, Sister Mary Edmund, 216, 227, 234
Hayes, Archbishop Patrick, 58, 61
Hoban Dominican High School, 52, 191, 224
Hoban, Bishop Edward, 51, 99, 100, 191, 229, 276, 277, 278, 279
Hoffman, Sister Martha James, 142
Homminga, Sister Bertha, 64, 68, 111, 256, 283, 295, 296, 297, 298, 299, 300
Horback, Sister Ann Lorraine, 144
Hughes, Father Edward, 256, 257, 258, 259
Hughes, Father Vincent Reginald, 5, 6, 229, 252, 253, 254, 255, 256, 259

I

Innisfail, 103, 104

J

Jabour, Sister Sabina, 212
Joachim, Sister Ann Joachim, 44, 68, 69
Joyce, Sister Rose Francis, 201

K

Keenan, Sister Thomas Marie, 54
Kelley, Sister Mary Noel, 126
Kelly, Father Liam, 48, 49
Kelly, Sister Attracta, 9, 10, 48, 49
Kenowski, Sister Agnes Michael, 140
Kinney, Sister Cyril Edwin, 127, 178
Kirk, Sister Jean Mildred, 142
Klinkhamer, Sister Marie Carolyn, 178
Kruse, Sister Joseph Therese, 16

L

Lalonde, Sister Regina Marie, 22, 45, 126
LaMore, Father Edward, 261, 262, 263, 264, 265, 266, 267, 268, 270
Lane, Bishop Loras, 220, 221
LaVoy, Sister Pauline Mary, 287
LeBlanc, Sister Rose Dominic, 94, 96, 97
Lederer, Sister Joseph Loretta (Elaine), 144
Ledwidge, Sister Benedicta Marie, 20, 22, 23, 64, 65, 90, 108, 110, 111, 118, 128, 141, 149, 154, 170, 171, 180, 183, 185, 199, 200, 203, 226, 227, 267, 271, 272, 273, 274, 283, 284, 286, 287, 288, 292, 293, 294, 295, 299, 300, 309
Lenaway, Sister Mary Albert, 178
Liturgical Meditations, The, 107, 108
Loftus, Sister Rose Concepta, 127
Loyola University, 31, 152, 225
Lumen Ecclesiae Chapel, 194, 228, 270, 273
Lundy, Sister Marie Daniel, 131, 134, 144
Lynch, Sister Margaret Helen, 108, 111, 171, 172, 174, 175, 177, 304, 305, 306, 307, 308, 313
Lynch, Sister Winifred, 20, 21, 22, 23

M

Madden, Mother Camilla, 58, 59, 60, 63, 115, 150, 151, 153, 230, 297
Mainville, Sister Denise, 178
Marrin, Father W.D., 274
Martin, Sister Colette, 126
Marvin, Sister Rosaleen, 99
Marx, Sister Winifred, 209
McAllister, Sister Jean Irene, 20
McClain, Sister Ellen Vincent, 107, 220, 304
McClear, Sister Ann Terence, 284, 312
McDermott, Father T.S., 252, 253, 260, 268, 269, 271, 272, 273
McDonald, Sister Marie Brigid, 198
McDonald, Sister Marie Catherine, 142
McDonald, Sister Marie Regina, 76
McDonnell, Sister Helen Agnes, 54, 70
McDonnell, Sister Thomasine, 92, 247

Index

McDonough, Sister Mary Brigetta, 216, 227, 234
McEntee, Father Andrew, 110, 252
McGeever, Sister Maura Padraig, 95, 96, 97
McGoldrick, Father William, 250, 251
McGoldrick, Sister Marie Jane, 76
McGowan, Sister Jean Patricia, 103, 198
McGowan, Sister Marie, 46, 47
McKeough, Sister Mary Paul (Noreen), 46, 47, 69, 163, 164, 178, 211, 230
McManus, Bishop James, 127
McManus, Monsignor William, 205, 207
McNicholas, Archbishop John, 53, 75, 121, 124
Meagher, Father Raymond, 75
Meyers, Sister Bertrande, 154, 155, 177
Miller, Mother Mary Frances, 64
Mooney, Cardinal Edward, 25, 55, 99, 129, 141, 149, 185, 191, 203, 241
Moran, Father Peter, 129, 130, 131, 133, 134
Mount St. Mary Academy, 50, 51, 216, 220, 253, 305
Muldoon High School, 51, 220
Mullins, Sister Patrick Jerome (Mary), 107, 178
Murphy, Father Joseph, 125
Murray, Sister Philomena, 46, 69

N

National Committee for Sisters, The, 166, 187, 188
Neville, Sister Laurine, 19
Noetzel, Sister Leonita, 120
Nolan, Father Louis, 61, 62, 64, 65, 66, 67
Notre Dame, University of, 27, 29, 31, 152, 166, 169

O

O'Connell, Father L.B., 268, 269, 270
O'Connell, Sister Rose Celeste, 104, 105, 106
O'Connor, Sister Carmelia, 152, 180, 201
O'Connor, Sister Corinne, 10, 18, 31, 42, 102, 103, 288, 292
O'Connor, Sister Helene, 45, 47, 56, 178, 195, 202, 255
O'Connor, Sister Joanne, 195
O'Connor, Sister John Joseph (Anne), 122, 125
O'Hare, Sister Evangela, 52, 201
On the Strings of Time, 101
O'Neill, Sister Ursula, 54

P

Pellerano, Sister María Altagracia (Teresita), 223
Penet, Sister Mary Emil, 157, 158, 159, 184
Peru, 45, 222, 310
Pety, Sister Aquiline, 127
Phelan, Mother Emmanuel, 59, 60
Philbin, Father Anthony, 242, 243
Philippines, 219, 220, 301, 303, 304
phonetic reading method, 118

319

Pittini, Archbishop Richard, 109, 110, 264
pontifical status, 58
Posedly, Sister Andrew Marie, 77
postulation, 117, 147, 148, 203, 205
Prendergast, Sister Agnes Cecile, 52, 163, 164
preparatory school, 102
Providence College, 179
provinces, list of, 215
Puerto Rico, 108, 109, 125, 127, 143, 216

Q

Quinlan, Sister Cyril Therese, 94, 96, 97

R

Radtke, Sister Paul Mary, 142
Ransing, Father Bernard, 181, 183, 184, 186
Redumsky, Sister Annunciata, 244
Regan, Father Ambrose Paschal, 271
Regina Dominican High School, 21, 191, 193, 205, 207, 224, 225
Regina Mundi Pontifical Institute, 190
restructuring into provinces, 212
Reuter, Sister Agnita, 52, 144
Riedel, Sister Mary Rita, 273
Roche, Sister Agnes Raphael, 77
Rosarian Academy, 22, 49, 50, 52, 191, 210, 216, 248, 251, 277, 305
Rosary High School, 191, 192, 216, 224, 303

Rose de Lima Hospital (St. Rose Dominican Hospital), 134, 135, 136
Ryan, Sister Mary Philip, 35, 71, 101, 109, 116, 193, 219, 220, 222, 223, 227, 233, 234, 263, 296, 298, 299, 301, 302, 303, 304, 310

S

Sacred Congregation for Religious, 62, 165, 166, 169, 174, 181, 182, 184, 185, 186, 187, 188, 189, 205, 213
Sacred Heart Hall, 56
Sadlier, Father Charles, 269, 270, 272
San Vincente, Sister Thomas (Digna), 219
Santo Domingo, University of, 30, 303
Scanlon, Sister Marie Kevin, 142
Scher, Bishop Philip, 87, 88, 89, 92, 128
Schmagner, Sister Mary, 119
Schrembs, Bishop Joseph, 62, 63, 64
Screes, Sister Joanne, 302
Seeds Scattered and Grown, 35, 68, 70, 282
Seissiger, Sister Marie Augustine, 95, 96, 97, 133, 134
Shea, Father Henry Matthew, 77
Sheridan, Sister Jean Marie, 216
Shields, Sister Ann Patrick, 94, 96, 97
Siena Heights College, 42, 48, 55, 100, 103, 109, 124, 177, 193, 194, 210, 214, 248, 251, 252, 254, 261, 262, 263, 265, 270, 271, 274, 283, 289, 291, 292, 293, 295, 298, 303, 307, 309

Singer, Sister John Therese, 152, 201
Sister Formation Conference, 155, 159, 163, 164, 171, 184, 187, 188
Sister Formation movement, 150, 153, 159, 170
Sisters Hospital, 17, 86, 95, 128, 136, 137, 216
Smith, Sister Daniel Therese, 133, 134
Smith, Sister Marie Joyce, 133, 134
St. Ann on-the-Lake (Rosarian Academy), 49, 50, 244, 245, 276
St. Dominic College, 220, 221, 224, 307
St. John Provincial Seminary, 141, 143
St. John's Parish, 54
St. Joseph Academy, 18, 42, 104, 105, 214, 240, 244, 248, 251, 262, 284, 286, 295, 297, 298
St. Joseph College (Siena Heights), 42, 55, 151, 244, 253, 256, 283, 305
St. Rose Dominican Hospital, 128
St. Theresa Home for the Aged, 53
Steele, Sister Angeline, 111, 181
Steinfels, Melville P., 195
Stiglitz, Sister Ruth Ann, 144
Stimson, Sister Miriam Michael, 178
Stritch, Cardinal Samuel, 77, 186, 191, 192, 210
Studio Angelico, 57

T

Thompson, John, 80, 81
Trujillo, Rafael, 111, 264
Turner, Sister Nancyann, 202

V

Valeri, Cardinal Valerie, 205
Vath, Sister Loyola, 127

W

Wagner, Sister Pius, 38
Waldron, Sister Jane de Chantal, 308
Waldron, Sister Richardine, 222, 223, 226, 228, 308, 309, 310
Walsh, Father Maurice, 246
Walsh, Mother Augustine, 5, 6, 24, 37, 38, 43, 51, 58, 63, 76, 150, 153, 230, 252, 253, 256, 283, 286, 287, 298
Walsh, Sister Mary Jean, 126
Wasco, Sister Marie Angelita, 133, 134
Webber, Carole Dawson, 103, 104, 106
Weber, Mother Genevieve, 99, 221, 223, 237, 253, 259, 293, 303
Weber, Sister Magdalen Marie, 111
Wiedner, Sister Marie, 69, 298
Wolff, Sister Madeleva, 155, 167, 180, 184

Y

Young, Sister Clarita Marie, 201

Z

Zahn, Sister Arthur Marie, 144
Zynda, Sister Judy, 191